HOW BASEBALL HAPPENED

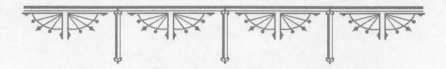

How Baseball Happened

Outrageous Lies Exposed!
The True Story Revealed

THOMAS W. GILBERT

With an introduction by
JOHN THORN

GODINE · BOSTON

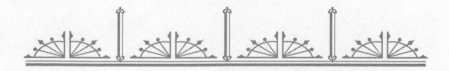

First published in 2020 by
GODINE
Boston, Massachusetts
godine.com

Copyright 2020 © by Thomas W. Gilbert

LIBRARY OF CONGRESS CATALOGING-IN-PUBLICATION DATA

Names: Gilbert, Thomas W., author.
Title: How baseball happened : Outrageous lies exposed! the true story revealed / Thomas W. Gilbert ; with an introduction by John Thorn.
Description: Boston, MA : David R. Godine, Publisher, 2020. | Includes bibliographical references and index.
Identifiers: LCCN 2020019007
ISBN 9781567926774 (hardcover)
ISBN 9781567926880 (ebook)
Subjects: LCSH: Baseball—United States—History—19th century. | Baseball—Economic aspects—United States.
Classification: LCC GV863.A1 G5754 2020 | DDC 796.3570973—dc23
LC record available at https://lccn.loc.gov/2020019007

ISBN 9781567927238 (paperback)

Cover design by Alex Camlin

Second Printing in Paperback, 2023
Printed in the United States of America

CONTENTS

INTRODUCTION
– 7 –

EARLY BASEBALL TIMELINE
– 11 –

CHAPTER ONE
The Wrongness of Baseball History
– 15 –

CHAPTER TWO
Wasps in the Attic
– 43 –

CHAPTER THREE
Escape from the City
– 81 –

CHAPTER FOUR
What Makes a River
– 117 –

CHAPTER FIVE
It Happened in Brooklyn
– 151 –

CHAPTER SIX

A Ballplayer's Tale

– 183 –

CHAPTER SEVEN

Philadelphia Stories

– 219 –

CHAPTER EIGHT

Amateur Hour

– 281 –

CHAPTER NINE

Traveling Team

– 313 –

AFTERWORD

– 353 –

ACKNOWLEDGMENTS

– 357 –

BIBLIOGRAPHY

– 359 –

INDEX

– 367 –

INTRODUCTION

To those who care about the past, great institutions may be of most interest when they begin. Why? Because in their sparse fields and green shoots may be seen essential attributes less visible when the endeavor is in full flower. How did photographs come to be, or movies or automobiles or computers? All origin stories fascinate.

In baseball, which is the matter at hand, why nine innings, nine men, and 90 feet? Why a bat and ball and, later, a glove? Why are the bases set in a circle? Indeed, *why baseball*—as a game, then a sport, then an emblem for the nation in which it was formed if not truly born?

To the fan of today the answers seem so obvious as to require no explanation, yet to historians of the game they have been, until quite recently, enduring mysteries. In the 1840s and 1850s, the reasons for the rise of baseball would have been first, the novelty and excitement of play, an unseemly activity for grown men; second, the opportunity for urbanites to exercise amid fresh air in a sylvan setting; and third, the assertion of a binding national identity, independent of John Bull and his national game of cricket. As America entered the 1860s and was nearly torn asunder, other reasons emerged as to how baseball happened, and why.

About ten years ago, when I was completing my own book on the early game, I was asked at a cocktail party, "What, after all your years of research, remains the great unanswered question in baseball?"

With no forethought and yet not skipping a beat, I offered,

"What is it that is so satisfying about a game of catch?"

In my eighth decade I am a bit closer to an answer, I suspect. The simple idea of "to and fro" suffices to explain all that was once complex.

I still follow baseball every day, watching more than a hundred games each season. Baseball may be the one thing that I have cared about unceasingly since I was five. In my earlier work I went forward, advancing analytic notions of how the game might be improved, or at least measured more realistically. I began to wonder about what might really be going on, hidden from sight yet discernible from the game's statistical residue. More recently I have looked back, to a time a century and more before my birth, to provide a firmer grasp of baseball's serpentine story and the lies and legends that have attached to it. The pleasure I take in baseball games today is enriched by a knowledge of distant games and long-dead players no less vivid for their seeming invisibility.

I attended my first games at the Polo Grounds and Ebbets Field, and my worship of baseball heroes—first on cardboard, then on television, and at last at the ballpark—began with Duke Snider and Jackie Robinson. Today my favorites—a grownup may not be permitted heroes, right?—are the players and innovators whose stories are fascinating because what they did, they did first: Doc Adams, George Wright, Al Reach, King Kelly . . . oh, I could go on.

Why baseball? One may approach the question philosophically, socially, culturally, and of course historically. Tom Gilbert looks "not in box scores, in game accounts, or in baseball rules changes—and certainly not in baseball's own ridiculous creation tales—but instead in larger cultural, economic, and social trends and in the whole lives and times of the men who played, promoted, and wrote about the game." In his splendidly created necropolis he summons the ghosts of Jim Creighton and Joe Start and other ancient worthies to cavort once more.

When journalists become historians—a path often taken—they retain the useful guidelines of their former craft: *who, what, where, when,* and *how.* In their invaluable works, Robert Henderson and David Block addressed the origins of bat-and-ball games (the where and when) around the world. My own *Baseball in the Garden of Eden* moved from Europe and Africa to America and addressed the *what,* i.e., the facts surrounding the game's beginnings rather than what self-anointed fathers of the game wished us to believe. Gilbert addresses *how* baseball happened and, delightfully, its anagram of *who.*

For him—and for me; I have been convinced—the game may have been "invented" elsewhere but, like a certain tree, it grew in Brooklyn. *People* made this game grow, amid a swirl of larger cultural, economic, and social trends, and he tells their stories brilliantly.

What had begun as a field sport in the 1830s, a sort of out-door gymnastics precipitated by an embrace of muscularity and a fear of cyclically recurring cholera, became an enterprise and cultural phenomenon. The need for playing grounds prompted New York baseballists to leave Manhattan for the Elysian Fields of Hoboken, New Jersey. The open land of Brooklyn, a separate city from New York, beckoned, too. Grassy fields were enclosed and flooded, to become rinks for skating, a craze predating the onset of baseball.

By the 1860s shrewd promoters took advantage of the spring thaw to create baseball fields for paid admission. Money came in, simultaneously corrupting and condemning the amateur game and stimulating the professional one that followed. En-trepreneurs, journalists, and gamblers made a buck off it, and many spectators placed their wagers at the game or took part in betting pools. But the outcome that could not have been fore-seen was the emergence of a fan base, attached to a particular locality and club simply for the reflected glory of belonging, apart from any pecuniary interest. People would pay simply to watch young men vie for honors.

How Baseball Happened is a brilliant new approach to our game and its author tells a hundred stories you haven't heard before. It is my honor to invite you to enter into his world.

How is baseball history to be written henceforth? Like this.

JOHN THORN
Official Historian,
Major League Baseball

EARLY BASEBALL TIMELINE

1821   John Stevens launches ferry service between Hoboken and New York City

1832   Cholera epidemic, first of many epidemics, 1832–1878

1833   First penny newspapers

1834   Camden and Amboy Railroad links New York City and Philadelphia

1845   Knickerbocker club founders pull out of New York Club, relocate to Hoboken

1848   Benjamin Baker's play *A Glance at New York* popularizes the Bowery B'hoy

1849   Astor Theatre Riot, 30 killed

1851   Nativists break up German American picnic at Hoboken

1854   Excelsior club formed in Brooklyn

1854   Baseball club formed in Hamilton, Ontario, Canada

1856   Clubs formed in Chicago, Albany (N.Y.), and Buffalo

1857   Clubs formed in Philadelphia, Springfield (Mass.), New Orleans, and Detroit

1858   Baseball's first governing body, the NABBP

1858   Clubs formed in Boston, San Francisco, Connecticut, Baltimore, Maine, Cincinnati, Rochester, and Syracuse

1858   First paid admission to a baseball game, Game 1 of Brooklyn vs. New York City series

1859   Clubs formed in Washington D.C., Georgia, and St. Louis

1860   Excelsiors of Brooklyn make playing tour of Upstate New

York, Baltimore, and Philadelphia

1862 Brooklyn's Union Grounds ballpark opens as a business

1863 Harvard Class of 1866 club founded

1865 End of volunteer firefighting in New York City and Brooklyn

1867 Washington Nationals tour Midwest

1867 NABBP puts exclusion of African Americans in writing

1868 Cuban Fordham alumnus Esteban Bellan plays for Unions of Morrisania

1869 Pay for play legalized; Cincinnati Red Stockings tour the country and go undefeated

1869 First games between African American clubs and (white) NABBP clubs

1870 Atlantics of Brooklyn stop the Red Stockings' undefeated streak at 84

1871 Opening season of National Association, the first professional league

1871 Octavius Catto assassinated on Election Day in Philadelphia

1876 The modern National League is formed

HOW BASEBALL HAPPENED

Before the Civil War there were no ballparks. Played mostly by part-time athletes in and around New York City, baseball was primarily something people did, not something they watched.

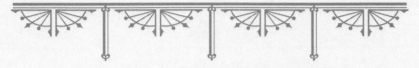

CHAPTER ONE
The Wrongness of Baseball History

HERE IS MORE THAN ONE WAY to get history wrong. Sometimes the truth is forgotten. Sometimes it is misunderstood. Sometimes it is erased and replaced with lies. When it comes to telling the story of where it came from, baseball has accomplished all three.

Professional and amateur sports take up a staggering amount of space in America. In 2019 we spent $73.5 billion on sports as entertainment and $50 billion on sports that we play—more than we spent on the space program, the National Institutes of Health, and Mexican food put together. To the rest of the world we are the sports-mad country where the four seasons of the year are baseball, football, basketball, and ice hockey—where ordinary people run and work out into their 40s and 50s; where old age and golf are inseparable; and where someone coined the word "athleisure."

Until shortly before the Civil War, however, America was known for the exact opposite. We had no sports leagues. There were no widely popular adult team sports except cricket, which was dominated by immigrants from Great Britain, (then about 6 percent of the U.S. population). English celebrity tourists like

Charles Dickens and Frances Trollope commented on their American cousins' dreary devotion to making money and their indifference to physical fitness and sports. There were exceptions like boxing and horseracing, but they were about money, too. Americans participated in those by betting on them.

Then baseball happened. Long played in New York City as a folk game, baseball began to catch on nationwide in the 1850s, first as recreation, second as entertainment. A year or two after the end of the Civil War, the game was played and watched from coast to coast. Baseball the sport was completely and gloriously new. It was American-made. It was not primarily an occasion for betting. Sports fans were another baseball first. They began to appear, unexpected and uninvited, by the hundreds and then by the thousands at baseball games in Brooklyn. They came to root for clubs that represented their neighborhood or their city, not to gamble.

Fans and spectators are not the same thing. A burning building attracts spectators; the essence of fan interest is following an athlete or a team over time, with nothing at stake except emotional commitment. The baseball fans of the late 1850s were America's first sports fans in that sense. They were a phenomenon so new that for years there was no word for them (the term fan was coined at least a half-century later). At a loss to explain why a non-bettor would care who won a baseball game, journalists mistook these early fans for a strange new breed of gambler.

We fans might not have been invited to the baseball party, but we crashed it and changed everything. Fans brought big money into baseball by buying tickets and newspapers—by caring—well before baseball turned professional. Ultimately we deserve the credit or the blame for creating the baseball business. In this and in everything else, baseball blazed the path that other American sports followed.

As central as baseball is to the American experience, you might expect that basic questions like where baseball came from, who first played it, and why would have been settled by now. But they aren't. One reason why is that for as long as it has existed as an organized sport, baseball has been telling weird lies about where it came from. For almost a century fans have packed the kids into the car and driven to Cooperstown, New York, thinking that they are visiting the quaint rural village where Abner Doubleday invented baseball. But they are in the wrong place. Baseball was born 200 miles away in noisy, in-your-face New York City.

To be fair, the folks at the Baseball Hall of Fame no longer pretend to believe that Abner Doubleday thought up baseball in Cooperstown or anywhere else, but the majority of Americans who are not trained historians remain confused by the layers of bullshit burying baseball's true origins. The so-called Abner Doubleday myth was just plain made up 112 years ago, for reasons that nobody today understands. Before that, professional baseball had a different origin story, but that story wasn't true, either. And even before that, when baseball was played only by amateurs, the people who ran, wrote about, and promoted the game told their own untruths about how baseball began. Most of us have heard these stories from childhood. Not everyone still believes them, but they continue to warp our view of baseball's beginnings.

IF YOU WANT to know how baseball really happened, you have to pay a visit to the Amateur Era, the period before 1871, the year when the first professional baseball league started. The reason it is called amateur is not because the baseball players of the time weren't serious about baseball; it is because until the very end of that period, they were not supposed to be playing the game as a profession. Thanks to the brutally competitive world they inhabit, today's professional baseball players tend to be fairly one-dimensional human beings. The players of the Amateur Era had rich lives off the field. They built businesses, practiced medicine or law, and fought in the Civil War. You won't read much about them in most baseball history books. The major leagues tend to suck up all of the historical oxygen and professional baseball has never had much interest in other kinds of baseball. But it was not the professionals who took an obscure local pastime and made it into a fully formed modern sport. That was done by amateurs. Baseball toward the end of the Amateur Era—the late 1860s—was not organized in the same way as today's major and minor leagues, but it was a modern sport that would be instantly recognizable as baseball by a fan of today. Daily newspapers covered it. There were box scores and ballparks. The top players were national celebrities. Late Amateur Era dynasties like Brooklyn's Atlantics, Washington's Nationals, and Philadelphia's Athletics crisscrossed the country, fighting for championships and thrilling large paying crowds.

These clubs all called themselves amateur, but they paid some of their players, even before professionalism was legalized in 1869. Historians are understandably confused by this. Many Amateur Era players have been called cheaters or hypocrites. But the truth is not that simple. The Amateur Era was a period of rapid change. The line between amateurism and professionalism was subtle and changeable. The issues at stake in drawing it were as much cultural and social—sometimes even racial—as economic. As a result, the words amateur and professional had different meanings in 1848, 1858, and 1868, but they never meant nothing. In 2019 Major League Baseball celebrated the 150th anniversary of the 1869 Cincinnati Red Stockings club, which is widely credited with being the first professional club, and which major league baseball considers its forebear. The closer you look, however, the less sense this makes. The Red Stockings may have been first in some things, but they were not the first club to sell tickets, to pay their players, or to pay their players openly. In this case, following the money gets us nowhere.

THE AMATEUR ERA began in New York City in the early decades of the 19th century, when ordinary adult men started to play baseball in a serious way. We don't know exactly when this was or who they were. The game they played was one of several bat-and-ball games that were played in different parts of America. Some of them were called baseball, others something else. All of them had pitching, batting, fielding, and baserunning. The fundamental on-field characteristics that made New York baseball different from every other bat-and-ball game on Earth were the "three out, all out" inning structure, the distinction between reaching base and scoring runs (in cricket and rounders they are the same), and the concept of foul territory. The New York game is the only one with all three.

From now on, when I use the word "baseball" in this book, I am talking about the New York version of the game and its descendants. People in the rest of the country originally called baseball "the New York game" or, after the establishment in 1858 of a governing body called the National Association of Base Ball Players, "the National Association game" (baseball was usually spelled "base ball" in the 19th century). Reports of games between amateur men's clubs appear sporadically in New York City newspapers in the 1840s. In the 1850s a new kind of baseball club appeared and began to spread in Manhattan, Brooklyn, and the greater New York metropolitan area. The sport went national on the eve of the Civil War. In the 1860s the New York game was so dominant that everyone called it, simply, baseball. The National Association of Professional Base Ball Players, America's first national sports league, turned its first stile in 1871.

EVEN BEGINNINGS HAVE beginnings. We know next to nothing about baseball's more distant ancestry. A good guess is that it was first played as a children's or folk game on the southern end of the island of Manhattan—probably only in certain neighborhoods—and spread to the rest of New York State, western New England, and other places where New Yorkers did business, settled, or, in the case of New York's 50,000 or so Loyalists (including my own misguided ancestors), were driven into exile in southern Canada after the American Revolution. This certainly helps explain why in the 1850s and 1860s people in those places so readily formed baseball clubs, and how quickly some of those clubs became competitive with those in the baseball hotbeds of New York and Brooklyn.

But the earliest history of the Amateur Era is murky. The bogus origin stories that baseball has been telling for 150 years have only made it murkier. To the dedicated debunker, baseball history is a target-rich environment. Even some of the better known debunkings have been debunked. Take the so-called Abner Doubleday myth. The Doubleday origin tale is only interesting in the way that lies sometimes are, for what they say about the people who tell them and about the truths that they are trying to obscure. It is no myth. Myths grow organically out of human experience into a narrative that expresses a cultural or religious truth. If the Doubleday story expresses any truth, it is that the truth can be bought, or at least rented, by power. The story was made up by a commission of seven baseball lifers in three-piece suits, picked for that purpose by Albert Spalding, the rich owner of the Chicago Cubs and de facto CEO of major league baseball. None of them really thought that Abner Doubleday had created baseball.

BULLSHIT

Abner Doubleday led a life of action and accomplishment, which makes it doubly odd that he has gone down in history for something he did not do. Doubleday served his country by spending most of his life in the army, where he was above replacement level as a commander. He fought in many of the key battles of the Mexican War and the Civil War, distinguished himself at the battle of Gettysburg, and rose to the rank of Major General, but not everyone was a fan; hls tactical cautiousness earned him the nickname "48 Hours." His prospects for further promotion were spoiled by a wartime feud with General George Meade, who disliked Doubleday's strong opposition to slavery. After the war, Doubleday, who was educated as an engineer, obtained a charter to build San Francisco's first cable car system, but sold it on to Andrew Hallidie, who is remembered today as the Alexander Cartwright of San Francisco public transit.

Doubleday never claimed to be baseball's father. In 1905, 12 years after Doubleday's death, baseball and sporting goods magnate Albert Spalding was sick of hearing Henry Chadwick say that America's national pastime descended from an English children's game called rounders. Spalding put together a commission of non-experts to refute Chadwick's theory. In 1908 the commission announced its findings, that "Baseball is of American origin, and has no traceable connection whatever with 'Rounders,' or any other foreign game;" and that "the first scheme for playing it, according to the best evidence obtainable to date, was devised by Abner Doubleday at Cooperstown, N.Y. in 1839."[1]

In his 2005 work *On Bullshit*,[2] Princeton philosophy professor Harry G. Frankfurt defines bullshit not as mere lying—sometimes bullshit is true—but as the product of a post-truth state of mind. "It is," he writes, "[a] lack of connection to a concern with truth—this indifference to how things really are—that I regard as the essence of bullshit." Baseball's Abner Doubleday origin story persisted for decades even though it couldn't have withstood the most superficial fact-checking. Other than the fact that his great-great-grandnephew bought part of the New York Mets in 1980, Abner Doubleday has no real connection to baseball. Even worse, commission chairman A.G. Mills, Dou-

---

1. Chadwick, Henry ed. *Spalding's Official Baseball Guide 1907*. New York: American Sports Publishing Co., 1908, p. 35
2. Frankfurt, Harry G. *On Bullshit*. Princeton, New Jersey: Princeton University Press, 2005

bleday's close friend for thirty years, knew better than anyone that Doubleday did not invent baseball. Henry Chadwick refused to take the Mills Commission report seriously. He called it "a joke between Albert and myself," but it was not a joke. It was bullshit.

THE STORY OF the Doubleday story begins in 1903, when major league club owner and sporting goods magnate Albert Spalding, who published *Spalding's Official Baseball Guide*, professional baseball's official annual, found himself in a public debate over baseball's origins with one of his own employees, the *Guide's* 79-year-old and increasingly crotchety editor Henry Chadwick. Chadwick, who had come to Brooklyn from England as a boy, argued that baseball had grown out of an English children's game called rounders. He may have been trolling his old friend and employer, but these were fighting words at a time when the United States was emerging from Great Britain's shadow as a world power, not to mention that baseball had always made a point of marketing itself as purely American.

Spalding responded by creating the infamous Mills Commission, which concluded on less than zero evidence that Abner Doubleday invented baseball in 1839. (In a way, Spalding, who preserved the New York Knickerbockers' scorebooks and club records, and whose widow donated them to the New York Public Library, had a hand in both of baseball's bogus creation myths.) The worst part of the so-called Doubleday myth is not that it was wrong, but that it was intended to block serious inquiry into where baseball really came from. For a while it succeeded. In living memory, to publicly dissent from the Doubleday myth was to displease the professional baseball establishment—something sportswriters who want a career don't do—or, even worse, to appear unpatriotic. Now that the Doubleday myth has been tossed onto history's scrapheap, the Mills Commission episode is a black mark on Spalding's reputation. History has taken sides, and it has chosen Henry Chadwick.

Could it be, however, that history and Henry Chadwick were both wrong? Any defense of Albert Spalding must begin with a guilty plea to fraud for creating the Doubleday myth. With that crime disposed of, however, a good argument can be made that Spalding was right about almost everything else. The same issue of *Spalding's Guide* that published the Mills Commission's findings also printed long letters from Chadwick and Spalding detailing their opposing views on where baseball came from. Chadwick's argument that baseball is descended from rounders is weak. He defines baseball's essence as the "use of a ball, a bat, and of bases, in the playing of a game of ball," and points out that rounders and baseball have these in common. He asserts without proof that English rounders is older than American baseball. As historian David Block points out in his seminal 2005 work *Baseball Before We Knew It*,[3] Chadwick ignores the key fact that there is no record of rounders being played in America earlier than the various versions of baseball. This casts serious doubt on the theory that baseball evolved directly from rounders.

Chadwick's historical reasoning is simple-minded. His idea of the defining characteristics of baseball is too vague. Focusing myopically on arbitrarily selected parts of the rules and structure of the games, he fails to consider social context—for example, the immense difference between a children's game and an adult sport—or the possibility that the two games could be related in some way other than direct lineage. As Block writes, "Because [Chadwick] was introduced to rounders early in life, before knowing that baseball even existed, he naturally assumed that

---

3. Block, David. *Baseball Before We Knew It*. Lincoln, Nebraska: University of Nebraska Press, 2005

rounders was the older of the two sports. He then made the logical leap of inferring that baseball descended from the older game."[4]

Spalding correctly points out that the world is full of bat-and-ball games with baserunning that arose independently. He knew this from first-hand experience. During the major league offseason of 1888–89, he took two baseball teams on a world tour in order to play exhibition games and promote the sport. "During my baseball trip," Spalding writes, "we were frequently reminded of the resemblance between baseball and some local game in nearly every country we visited. Invariably, upon investigation, we failed to see the resemblance. . . ."[5] In January 1889, for example, Spalding's baseball tourists played an exhibition game in Columbo, Sri Lanka, where they would have encountered a local baseball-like game called *elle*. Still popular today, *elle* features pitching, batting, and baserunning. It might look like a duck and walk like a duck, but good luck getting it to quack. *Elle* is much older than baseball and verifiably indigenous. Spalding adds that "whenever a baseball exhibition was given before an English audience, whether in New Zealand, Australia, Ceylon, Egypt or England, it was not infrequent to hear an expression something like this: 'Why, this American game of baseball is nothing more than our old English game of Rounders that we used to play with the girls when we were boys, you know!'" Like Columbus thinking that the manatees he saw in the Caribbean were mermaids, English observers thought that baseball was a kind of rounders simply because it was the closest thing to it in their frame of reference.

When he landed in England at the end of his world tour and

---

4. Block, David. *Baseball Before We Knew It*. Lincoln, Nebraska: University of Nebraska Press, 2005, p. 23
5. Chadwick, Henry ed. *Spalding's Official Baseball Guide 1907* New York: American Sports Publishing Co., 1908, p. 37 ff.

actually witnessed rounders for himself, Spalding saw a game that resembled cricket far more than it did baseball. Rounders had no diamond, no foul territory, no strike zone, and no three-out innings; it was played with a flat bat and stakes instead of bases. Cricket has all of these characteristics; baseball has none. "Whatever similarity may be found between ancient Rounders and early baseball," Spalding argues, "does not in itself constitute evidence that the latter game derived its origin from the former, and therefore should be treated simply as a coincidence and not as an established fact. The fact that not even one scrap of evidence has been produced showing that the game of Rounders was ever played in the United States, or that it was even known by name, clearly substantiates my position in declaring that baseball was not derived from Rounders but is of American origin."

Spalding saves his most interesting argument for last. "The tea episode in Boston Harbor, and our later fracas with England in 1812, had not been sufficiently forgotten in 1840 for anyone to be deluded into the idea that our national prejudices would permit us to look with favor, much less adopt any sport or game of an English flavor." In other words, if the members of the Knickerbockers, Gothams, and Eagles had thought that there was anything remotely English about baseball, they would have looked elsewhere for a national sport. This is undeniably true; they had taken a hard pass on cricket for exactly this reason. However, Spalding overreaches when he says that similarities between baseball and rounders "should be treated simply as a coincidence." Baseball the game may be a distant cousin of cricket, rounders, and other English and American bat-and-ball games. But that in itself does not make it foreign. The United States Constitution is no less American because it draws on English political and legal traditions. Like the Constitution, the sport of baseball may have English roots, but that does not change the fact that it was something new and a rejection of an English model. In both cases that was the point.

IT IS TEMPTING, especially for a writer, to take Henry Chadwick's side in the baseball-came-from-rounders debate. Chadwick was a man of letters who lovingly guided baseball's early development as a sport. There is no questioning Chadwick's integrity and good faith. Albert Spalding is wide open to the charge that his argument that baseball is completely American was colored by personal business interests, prejudice, or Jingoism. But good faith and good character are not historical arguments. As we will see, on the fundamental point in question

Some say the first baseball game was played in Cooperstown, New York in 1839; others say it was in Hoboken, New Jersey in 1846. Both are wrong. Both cities held bogus 100th anniversary celebrations. This 1946 photo shows MLB Commissioner Happy Chandler cutting a baseball-shaped birthday cake, along with NL President Ford Frick and—appropriately enough—three comedians: Gracie Allen, George Burns, and Al Schacht.

Albert Spalding was right and Chadwick was wrong. The sport of baseball is, in every way that matters, American.

The Doubleday story replaced a different standard account of baseball's origins: that the game was invented by a New York City bank clerk named Alexander Cartwright and his friends in the Knickerbocker baseball club. In the late 20th century, when the Doubleday tale started taking on water, Cartwright and the Knickerbockers made a comeback. Cartwright makes a more plausible father of baseball than Abner Doubleday. But what is plausible is not necessarily true. Like Abner Doubleday, Alexander Cartwright was a real person. Unlike Doubleday, he played baseball. Cartwright belonged to the Knickerbocker club in the 1840s, but he did not invent baseball, write the first rules, or, other than serving a couple of terms as club vice president, play a significant role in the history of the Knickerbockers. Cartwright also left New York, never to return, in the California Gold Rush of 1848. He ended up in Hawaii, where he is remembered as an early chief of the Honolulu volunteer fire department and an active Freemason—typical interests for an Amateur Era baseball player—but not for any involvement in baseball. Alexander Cartwright did not and could not have had anything to do with baseball after the 1848 season because he wasn't in New York. In 1848 all of the baseball clubs that we know about today were playing within a 25-mile radius of New York City Hall.

MONEY BALLS

Only 27, Albert Spalding retired from baseball because of acute wealth. He was a winning pitcher, but he was too busy making money selling sports equipment to play baseball. His company is still around today; it makes the official NBA basketball and lots of other balls. Spalding rocked the national baseball scene in 1867, when he was only 17.

Pitching at a Chicago tournament for his little-known hometown club, the Rockford Forest Citys, Spalding upset the touring Washington Nationals and their powerful lineup of eastern stars, 29–23. Spalding later pitched for Harry Wright's Boston Red Stockings in the National Association, baseball's first professional league, and for Chicago in 1876, the first season of the National League. His pro record over seven seasons was 252–65 with a 2.14 ERA. His career professional WAR was 53.6, higher than that of Sandy Koufax or Whitey Ford.

As millionaire cofounder of the National League and owner of the club now called the Chicago Cubs, Spalding was the strategist behind the major league baseball cartel's victory over baseball's first union movement in the ugly Players League War of 1890. In 1911 he published *America's National Game*, a history of early baseball, much of which he had personally witnessed. From the 1870s to the 1940s he published Spalding's Official Baseball Guide, which for many years was edited by Henry Chadwick. Spalding was sure that baseball would eventually take over the world as it had the United States. He was involved in both 19th-century foreign baseball tours, in 1874 and 1888–89. The 1888–89 tour circled the globe, stopping at Australia, Sri Lanka, Egypt, Italy, the U.K., and Ireland. In 1921 Spalding's widow donated his priceless collection (sadly, not entirely priceless; several items from the collection have been stolen and sold) of early baseball material, including the New York Knickerbockers' original scorebooks, to the New York Public Library. Later in life, Albert Spalding developed an interest in an oddball quasi-religion called Theosophy. Abner Doubleday, Spalding's hand-picked candidate for the inventor of baseball, was also a Theosophist, which explains a lot.

BASEBALL WAS IN a primitive state in Alexander Cartwright's day. Unlike modern baseball clubs, clubs like the Knickerbockers were groups of friends who played most of their games among themselves. This simple fact explains why virtually none of the early clubs—not even clubs made up of white racial liberals and Abolitionists—was racially integrated. In mid-19th-century America, there were almost no communities, northern or southern, where whites and African Americans lived together voluntarily. As a result, racial segregation did not have to be enforced or even discussed. Baseball clubs were segregated and so were churches, schools, and neighborhoods. When the subject of integrating baseball first came up in the late 1860s, the issue was admitting entirely African American clubs into all-white organized baseball, not allowing individual African American players to join white clubs.

The early baseball clubs were islands with their own rules and cultures. Going back to the beginning of the 19th century, a rare interclub match sometimes attracted enough public interest to be noted in the papers, but for decades no one took the hint that people might enjoy watching one club play another or that interclub and intercity rivalries could be exploited to promote baseball—or to make money. Early Amateur Era pitchers tossed a lively ball, packed with rubber, softly underhand to the batter, who hit it as far as he could. To save their fingers, the gloveless fielders could catch a fly ball for an out on one bounce. There was no strike zone. Games were played to 21 runs, not nine innings; and the number of players in the field depended on how many showed up. More important, no one watched or followed the game other than friends of the players and, for the occasional interesting interclub match, gamblers. The idea that Cartwright invented the diamond, wrote the first rules, and spread the game beyond New York is a fairy tale created by his own relatives promoting him as the father of baseball and by sportswriters patching a threadbare, hand-me-down origin narrative. In the 1850s, while baseball was evolving, spreading, and hurtling toward modernity, Alexander Cartwright was 5,000 miles away, pruning his hibiscus bushes.

WHEN WE TALK about how baseball happened, it helps to re-member that the word baseball has many meanings. It can mean what it meant 200 years ago—a loosely defined family of folk *games*. It can mean what it means today, a mature *sport* with rules, statistics, and media coverage. It can also mean a range of things in between. Whatever definition you choose, no one in-vented baseball, just as no one invented other cultural phenom-ena like rock and roll, bachelor parties, or brunch. In 1962, co-median Bob Newhart had fun with the absurdity of the single inventor idea in a sketch in which he imagines Abner Doubleday phoning a game manufacturer to pitch his new concept. ("Why four balls for a walk, Mr. Doubleday? What? No one ever asked you that before?")[6] Still, the idea that baseball had one or more founding fathers goes all the way back to pre–Civil War New York City. It is a historiographical zombie, beaten and bloodied but im-possible to kill. There is a long list of men who have been called "Father of Baseball." Some of them have it written on their graves.

The idea that baseball had a definite starting point defies common sense as well as the available evidence. Consider the game played in Hoboken, New Jersey, on June 19, 1846 between the Knickerbockers and an opponent called the New York Nine, an event that is often called the first baseball game. If you ac-cept the conventional narrative, this was the first time that the Knickerbockers tried out their new game against an outside opponent. The scoresheet from that game survived in the New York Public Library until an unknown thief with a weak grasp of baseball history (or a firm grasp of the collectibles market) walked off with it in the 1970s. We know from copies that the mysterious New York Nine, a team ostensibly made up of nov-ices, routed the Knickerbockers, 23–1. You don't need a baseball

---

6. https://www.youtube.com/watch?v=5anAHCvl0v0

A Game of Ball.—A match at the good old game of Base Ball, was played last week at Hoboken, between the New York and Brooklyn Ball Clubs, eight on a side. The day was cold and windy, but the exhilarating sport made the players forget the weather. A large number of spectators were on the ground, and among them several ladies. After showing fine play on both sides, the New Yorkers were declared winners.

The New York Knickerbockers are widely credited with inventing baseball and playing the first baseball "match" (i.e., interclub game) in 1846. This item from the Boston *Daily Bee* newspaper tells us that players from Brooklyn and New York played a three-game series one year earlier than that. It also makes it very clear that baseball was nothing new in the 1840s.

analytics department to tell you that there is something wrong with this picture. Another problem is that there were many earlier interclub baseball games, including a Brooklyn versus New York City series in 1845. Consider also that over many years of research, whenever I run into a 19th-century newspaper story that calls baseball time-honored, traditional, or old-fashioned, I clip it and toss it into a file labeled "baseball has been old for a long time." It is full of clippings from the 1840s. That means that in the same decade when histories say baseball was invented, lots of contemporary observers thought of it as an old game. They are corroborated by mentions in print of baseball being played by adults in the 1820s, in the 1800s, and even earlier.

As different as they are, the Abner Doubleday and the Cartwright/Knickerbockers origin stories have the same primary propaganda objective: to assert that baseball is American. The Doubleday tale has a secondary purpose, to obscure the fact that baseball was born in New York City. The difference is context. The Doubleday origin story was invented during the Professional Era, fifty years later than the Knickerbockers version. In the mid-19th century, when baseball was competing with cricket for the favor of white Protestant Americans living in eastern cities, to be seen as the all-American brainchild of the solid and respectable Knickerbockers was a marketing feature. But at the turn of the

20th century, when cricket was going nowhere and marketing baseball meant selling it to all Americans as a patriotic national institution, baseball's identification with one not universally popular city became more of a bug. A faux-nostalgic origin tale set in a small town no different from hundreds of others from Massachusetts to Oregon filled the bill perfectly. The fact is that the game we call baseball was born and raised in New York City and Brooklyn. This is a part of its heritage that modern professional baseball has stubbornly and persistently disavowed.

IN 1876 A cabal of Midwesterners, including Albert Spalding, seceded from the New York–based baseball establishment and founded the National League, which in its first seven seasons had only one New York City or Brooklyn franchise, and that for only one season. In 1957 Major League Baseball let the Brooklyn Dodgers run away from home to Los Angeles because one rich man thought it would make him richer. Today Brooklyn's more than three million residents—five times the population of Milwaukee—are represented by a low minor league club in a ballpark that seats 7,000. Historically, all baseball roads lead back to New York. Later on, we will follow these roads in the opposite direction in order to understand how baseball spread to Philadelphia, Boston, and the rest of the country. But if you want to trace how baseball the national sport actually happened, you have to start in 19th-century New York City, which, together with Brooklyn (the two cities merged in 1898), projected its political, cultural, and economic power over great distances. The game went where New Yorkers went, out to the suburbs by train or streetcar, off to schools and colleges in other states, to New Orleans to buy cotton, to Nicaragua with William Walker, to Cuba with the sugar trade, to the California Gold Rush, to the upper Midwest via the Erie Canal, and to Washington D.C. to serve in the government. When New Yorkers went into battle in the Civil War, did business in Boston, Baltimore, and Philadelphia, or followed railroad and telegraph networks across the country, they brought baseball with them.

I ADMIT THAT I do not care much about the history of baseball as a folkway or children's pastime. It is a perfectly legitimate research topic but one whose significance, it seems to me, comes from what followed it, the game becoming a sport. If that had never happened, then baseball would be hopscotch. A brief definition of a sport would be a game played and taken seriously by adults—and therefore more sophisticated and more highly organized than a game. (The game of hopscotch, for example, has no formal rules, no governing body, no leagues, and no national championship criteria; the sport of basketball has all of these.) This began to happen to baseball in and around New York City between the American Revolution and the 1840s. It is hard to be much more specific than that. Part of the reason is that American society in the period that gave us the sport of baseball— pre–Industrial Revolution America—is so unlike the America of today. Much of its popular culture is lost and its values and customs are often incomprehensible to us. Trying to understand that time, it often feels as if we can make out broad shapes and movement, but little detail and nuance. We view both early baseball and the society that gave it to us as through a filter of age, ignorance, and lack of imagination.

One of the most important social developments of that time, the rise of the modern middle class, was vital to the spread of baseball. That is an understatement. Yet few baseball histories mention it. In the decades before the Civil War, New York and other American cities were going through a radical reordering of the economy and the class structure. When we look back at

New York City after the completion of this transformation, for example in the 1880s, we see a familiar social structure, containing something like today's upper class, middle class, and working class. Because it is hard for us to imagine a society that is organized in any other way, this sweeping social transformation is hiding in plain historical sight. The tip of the spear of the modern middle class was a group that historians have called the "emerging urban bourgeoisie." It is not an elegant phrase, but it is accurate. To avoid having to keep writing it throughout this book, we will call it the EUB. Appearing in the 1840s and 1850s, this class was made up of dynamic, resourceful urbanites including physicians, bankers, insurance men, manufacturers, and a striking number of entrepreneurs involved in transformative new industries (e.g., railroad, mass-market publishing, telegraph). Some were involved in more than one; baseball-promoting publisher and horseracing enthusiast George Wilkes pushed railroad expansion in America and was decorated by the Czar Alexander II of Russia for encouraging investment in the Trans-Siberian railroad. New York City was full of them. They were interested in amateur athletics—playing, not watching. Like any new social group, the EUB went through a process of class identification and self-definition. Sports played a role, bringing desirable people into the group and excluding others. Members of the EUB formed the Knickerbocker, Eagle, Gotham, and other New York City clubs of the 1840s and 1850s. Historians have exaggerated their wealth and status—hardly any were born into the upper crust—but they adopted baseball and lent it their energy, ambition, and respectability.

Another reason that it is difficult to trace the beginning of baseball is a different transformation that happened at the same

7. Wilentz, Sean. *Chants Democratic*. New York: Oxford University Press, 2004

34]

time, the rise of daily newspapers, or penny journalism. Earlier American newspapers had been dull weeklies that readers subscribed to by the year. Because an annual subscription cost $6 or $7, about a week's pay for a laborer in 1840, circulation was small and limited to wealthy landowners and merchants. These kinds of people wanted two things from a newspaper: financial data, and useful political and government news. Think of the *Wall Street Journal* without the interesting parts. In the 1830s and 1840s breakthroughs in printing technology like the steam-driven rotary press and inexpensive paper made large-circulation daily newspapers possible. They were cheap, hawked on street corners for a penny a copy. Because they depended on advertising, they marketed themselves to a wider readership and tried to catch the public's attention any way they could think of. (In 1835 the *New York Sun* broke circulation records by running fake stories, including pictures, about flying human-like creatures living on the moon.) Gradually, newspapers began to feature what we call reporting—on crime, theater, gambling, and gossip about celebrities. They also covered sports.

It is no coincidence that 1850s New York City, the place where the largest cohort of the emerging bourgeoisie was emerging— and ground zero of the penny journalism communications revolution—is when and where baseball appears first on our historical radar. 90 percent of what we know about this period comes from newspapers. This creates a pitfall for historians: the presumption that the penny newspapers were trying to portray contemporary urban life in a comprehensive way, instead of simply trying to sell newspapers to those who could afford them and were disposed to read them. Like all media, newspapers are fundamentally shaped by their consumers. A mainstream paper aimed at the white men of New York City's comfortable classes in the 1850s, for example, would typically avoid topics like the city's vast prostitution industry, efforts by feminists to encourage physical education for women, or anything that African Americans were doing or thinking. As for baseball, this raises a question. Were adult men playing baseball and forming clubs really a new thing in the 1840s and 1850s? To put it another way, did newspapers cover the Knickerbockers and their ilk because they were the first adult ballplayers, or because they were the first adult ballplayers who were the kind of people that their readers would be interested in?

BORN IN ENGLAND in 1824 and brought to America when he was 13, Henry Chadwick began his sportswriting career covering cricket. He had played baseball as a boy, but he preferred cricket and dreamed that Americans would adopt it and make it their own, as other former British colonies have. One day in 1856, however, he had an epiphany. As he told the story years later, it suddenly hit him that baseball, not cricket, was destined to become America's national sport.

> On returning from ... a cricket match on Fox Hill, I chanced to go through the Elysian Fields during the progress of a match between the noted Eagle and Gotham Clubs. The game was being sharply played on both sides, and I watched with deeper interest than any previous ball match between clubs that I had seen. It was not long before I was struck with the idea that baseball was just the game for Americans. . . .[8]

This story is usually interpreted in one of two ways. The first is that Chadwick realized in his eureka moment that baseball was better suited to the American character than cricket. The other

---

8. Chadwick, Henry. *The Game of Baseball.* 1868. New York: George Munro and Co., p. 10

is that he noticed that baseball had made great strides as a game while he wasn't paying attention. But neither one really makes sense. What opened Henry Chadwick's eyes that day was not the game of baseball itself, which was nothing new to anyone in New York in 1856—and certainly not to a man who had spent most of his life in Brooklyn—but *who* was playing it and *how*. He saw respectable New York businessmen and professionals of the EUB playing baseball like it mattered, practicing and trying their best to beat other clubs. If people like that were taking it seriously, then baseball had new and greater possibilities.

BEFORE THE 1850S newspaper sports coverage was mostly limited to New York–based national weeklies like the *Spirit of the Times*, which modeled itself on the English paper *Bell's Life in London*. The *Spirit of the Times* affected a faux-sophisticated, English editorial tone and promoted sports popular in England like boxing, thoroughbred horseracing, and cricket. It exaggerated attendance figures at American cricket matches and minimized or ignored Americans' negative feelings toward England. In 1843 the staff of *Porter's Spirit of the Times* (a successor to the *Spirit of the Times*) founded the New York Cricket Club, in part to promote the sport to native-born Americans. But the American dog wouldn't eat the English dog food. Starting in New York City in the 1850s the sporting papers, taking their cue from their readers, gradually switched sides from cricket to baseball. Journalism and baseball became allies. They fed off each other and appealed to the same kinds of people: the literate, the forward-looking, and the reform-minded.

Journalists not only covered baseball; in a stark conflict of interest they also played and promoted the sport. Journalists founded and joined baseball clubs. They invented the scoring system and the basic statistics that we still use. They served as umpires and scorers. Clubs made up of newspapermen played at the Elysian Fields in the 1850s and 1860s; in 1871 a baseball diamond was set aside for them exclusively. The early Eagle baseball club was full of newspapermen, printers, and even a publisher or two. William Cauldwell, whose *Sunday Mercury* was the first newspaper to have a full-time baseball reporter (Cauldwell himself) and cover baseball as news, cofounded the important Union club of Morrisania in 1855. Journalistic pioneer George Wilkes, who bought the *Spirit of the Times* and published it as *Wilkes' Spirit of the Times*, played baseball and was one of the first to grasp the sport's potential to sell newspapers. As they had with cricket, the newspapers sometimes exaggerated how many people played and went to see baseball games. They also exaggerated the sport's reach beyond the eastern urban centers. As *Harper's Weekly* wrote in 1859, "it is really worth inquiring whether [baseball] is or is not as popular as is commonly reported. . . . In New York, it is well known. . . . The same thing is true of Boston, Philadelphia, and perhaps one or two other cities. But is baseball so popular that it is a regular and well-understood diversion in most of the counties of the States of the Union? Do young men naturally learn baseball in Massachusetts, in Pennsylvania, in Wisconsin, and in Louisiana?" The difference between baseball and cricket was that with baseball, the public was buying the product. Five years later, the answer to both questions would be yes.

After his 1856 Milvian Bridge experience, Henry Chadwick covered baseball for too many publications to count and joined the Star club of Brooklyn. As a member of the rules committee of the NABBP and as an authoritative editorial voice, Chadwick acted as the young sport's *consigliere*. He is called the Father of Baseball on his gravestone, but in life he modestly declined the title. As the Brooklyn *Daily Eagle* put it in his 1908 obituary, Chadwick "succored [baseball] in its infancy, reared it in its youth, and kept it in the beaten path, jealously guarding it when assailed and bringing it to its present high standing, a scientific and lasting institution."[9] A tireless advocate, promoter, and marketer, he had a grasp of what appealed and did not appeal to members of the EUB, the class that baseball needed to reach to become a national sport. He fought hard to protect baseball from being associated with gambling, for example, knowing that gambling was repellent to the moralistic EUB. He came to realize that professionalism, if regulated and packaged correctly, would not be. After 1871 he made himself equally indispensable to baseball in the professional era. This is why Henry Chadwick is the only writer to be honored with a plaque in the main section of the Baseball Hall of Fame.

More than a century after his death, baseball fans still visit sportswriter Henry Chadwick's grave in Brooklyn's Green-Wood cemetery, some leaving behind an old baseball. Chadwick's marvelous monument features a grass and clay infield, marble bases, bronze baseball equipment and a plaque calling him "Father of Baseball."

9. Brooklyn *Daily Eagle*, April 20, 1908, p.3

BEFORE THE CIVIL War, popularizing baseball as a participatory sport became a national cause analogous to Abolitionism, Temperance, public health, feminism, and other contemporary reform movements. Hundreds of Amateur Era baseball men were involved in these as well. In the beginning at least, amateur baseball *was* a national reform movement. Both journalists and baseball men talked up baseball as a potential national sport. Today we take it for granted that there is such a thing as a national sport, but both the phrase and the idea itself were unheard of in the United States before the 1850s. In a recent search of databases of digitized newspapers, including the national sports weeklies, the earliest mentions of the phrases "national game" or "national sport" in this sense were from 1855. What was the point of wrapping the game in the American flag? It was effective marketing, so effective that baseball has never stopped doing it.

The baseball movement succeeded spectacularly. In 15 short years it went from a regional folk game to America's first national team sport. How did this happen? The answer to this and other fundamental questions of early baseball history lie not in box scores, in game accounts, or in baseball rules changes—and certainly not in baseball's own ridiculous creation tales—but instead in larger cultural, economic, and social trends and in the whole lives and times of the men who played, ran, and wrote about the game. The baseball players of the Amateur Era had careers, businesses, and lives outside of sports. Many of them saw themselves as guiding the development of a great country, industry by industry and institution by institution. One of these national institutions was baseball.

Members of the EUB did not invent the game itself. They invented an idea—an idea of who would play baseball, how it would be organized, and for what purpose. They made baseball in their own image, shaping it according to their values and ambitions. (One of these values was racism, but as we will see, organized baseball's whiteness did not go unchallenged in the Amateur Era.) Baseball went where they went and evolved as they evolved.

Lost in baseball's Horatio Alger story is a pair of accidental victories. Two of the most significant advances of the Amateur Era, the advent of the fan and the idea of sports as an entertainment business, were not part of baseball's original plan. Most of the first Americans to realize baseball's potential to make money were journalists, businessmen, or entrepreneurs, not players. Baseball's amateurs aimed to use baseball to persuade sedentary Americans to exercise and as an instrument to unify a fragmented nation. They succeeded in both. When the earliest professional leagues were founded in the 1870s, these organizations were innovative in many ways, but they did not have to create a sport. The amateurs who came before them had already done that.

A portrait of the New York Knickerbockers and their suburban satellite, the Excelsiors, taken after an 1859 game in Brooklyn. In the Amateur Era, the winning team kept the game ball as a trophy, but here Excelsiors president Dr. Joseph B. Jones, at center in the top hat, is about to offer the game ball to the losing team, the Knickerbockers, as a display of deference and respect.

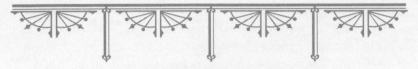

CHAPTER TWO
Wasps in the Attic

 HEN AMATEUR ERA BASEBALL told its own origin story, it started with the Knickerbocker baseball club. Here are three typical examples. (The bold type is added.)

Preamble to Constitution and Bylaws of the National Association of Baseball Players, March 1858:

> *The Knickerbocker Club, organized in 1845, was the **pioneer** organization, and for several years the only one in the field. Its first competitor was the Washington Club, which, however, only existed for a short period, many of its members taking part in the formation of the Gotham Club, in 1852. **The Eagle Club was organized in 18—**[sic].*[10]

New York *Atlas* newspaper, June 1858:

> *It is now only some thirteen years since the first attempt at **organizing** the game of baseball was made. The honor of being the **pioneers** in this movement, is due to the celebrated Knickerbocker Club, of this city, which was organized in the year 1845. The first club which followed the good*

---

10. *New York Clipper*, May 8, 1858, p. 5

example set them, was the Washington, but later became divided in itself, on the formation of the Gotham Club in 1852, and the majority of the members of the Washington joined the latter club. The Eagle was next organized, but we forget the year in which it was established.[11]

Brooklyn *Daily Eagle* newspaper, August 1865:

Baseball was not played to any extent, in its present form, much before 1851. The Knickerbocker Club of New York was the first organization, for the purpose of playing ball as it is now known, —and to the Knickerbocker belongs the honor and title of NESTORS OF THE GAME.[12]

As any marketing expert can tell you, to sell a product you need a story. The story doesn't have to be true. For almost as long as it has existed as an organized adult sport, the product baseball has been selling is itself. This is why baseball has been telling origin tales of varying heights since the 1850s. The original is the Knickerbocker story, which goes like this.

In 1845 a group of amateur athletes from New York City formed the first baseball club and published the first baseball rules. In some versions of the story bank clerk Alexander Cartwright was the driving force behind both. All of the Knickerbockers were white men; almost all of them were native-born Protestants. Among other rules innovations, the club was the first to outlaw the practice of "soaking," which meant smacking baserunners with a thrown ball in order to put them out. This was an important step forward in baseball's evolution from a children's pastime because adults preferred a game from which they did not have to limp home. Running out of playing space in New York City, the Knickerbockers wandered in the wilderness

---

11. New York *Atlas*, June 27, 1858
12. Brooklyn *Daily Eagle*, August 23, 1865, p. 2

until in 1845 they found a home on the Elysian Fields in Hoboken, New Jersey, 15 minutes by ferry from lower Manhattan. The Knickerbockers were influential gentlemen who popularized the game. Up sprang the Eagles, Gothams, and Empires. These were followed by more imitators in Brooklyn, New Jersey, and the greater New York metropolitan area. The first players were dilettantes who put more effort into postgame banquets than into vulgar pursuits like recruiting, training, or trying to win. The Knickerbockers ruled over baseball until, to their dismay, the game spread downward to the unwashed working classes. As it spread outward to Boston, Philadelphia, and the rest of the country, the Knickerbockers lost control over the sport that they had made, opening a Pandora's box of professionalism, gambling, and corruption.

Two parts of this story are true. Almost all of the Knickerbockers were white American-born Protestants and the Barclay Street ferry did get you to Hoboken in 15 minutes. As John Thorn explains in his wonderful 2011 book, *Baseball in the Garden of Eden*,[13] the Knickerbocker rules actually contain nothing new. They describe how the New York version of the game of baseball had been played for some time—quite likely by people of various ages, races, religions, and classes. Their rules were not the first written rules, merely the oldest set of rules that survives. Most Knickerbockers were merchants, professionals, and businessmen of some means, but they were not gentlemen in the mid-19th-century sense, that is, living on inherited wealth. They were influential, but their goal was not to make the game popular; if anything, it was the opposite. Like other clubs of the early Amateur Era, the Knickerbockers entertained themselves and visiting clubs with dinners—Knickerbocker dinners were

13. Thorn, John. *Baseball in the Garden of Eden*, New York: Simon and Schuster, 2011, pp. 71–77

the ones you wanted to be invited to—but this custom came from the world of the volunteer fire company, not high society. Finally, although gambling and professionalism were worrisome from a marketing point of view, it is far from clear that they were net negative influences on the sport of baseball itself. Gamblers promoted interclub play, helped spread baseball beyond New York, and pushed it toward greater organization and transparency. After the advent of fans, professionalism was inevitable. It brought in players who fell below the Knickerbockers' admissions standards, but it improved the quality of play, democratized the sport, and pressured it—for a brief time, successfully—to integrate racially.

IN 1936, WHEN the Amateur Era was a faded memory, the folks promoting the idea of a national baseball Hall of Fame dusted off Baseball Origin Tale 2.0, the so-called Abner Doubleday myth, to justify locating the Hall in Cooperstown, New York, where the future Civil War commander and memoirist may have attended prep school. This provoked a backlash from, among others, Robert Henderson, librarian of New York City's Racquet and Tennis Club, who argued correctly that baseball was far older than Doubleday, and descendants of Knickerbocker club member Alexander Cartwright, who claimed less credibly that Cartwright deserved the lion's share of the credit usually given to the Knickerbockers as a group. In order to avoid a public contretemps, the baby was apportioned. Cooperstown got the Hall and Cartwright, who for all we know was not even a particularly good player, got a plaque in the same room as real athletes like Babe Ruth and Christy Mathewson. If you visit the Hall of Fame today, you will read that Alexander Joy Cartwright Jr.—the "Father of Modern Baseball"—set the bases 90 feet apart, established nine innings as a full game, organized the

Knickerbocker baseball club in 1845, and carried the game to the Pacific Coast and Hawaii. We now know that he did not do any of these things, but you cannot edit a bronze plaque. That is why they make them out of bronze.

Today, the Abner Doubleday story has attained the status of

As MLB historian John Thorn once said, every word on Alexander Cartwright's Hall of Fame plaque is false, including "and" and "the."

ALEXANDER JOY CARTWRIGHT, Jr.
"FATHER OF MODERN BASE BALL."
SET BASES 90 FEET APART.
ESTABLISHED 9 INNINGS AS GAME
AND 9 PLAYERS AS TEAM. ORGANIZED
THE KNICKERBOCKER BASEBALL CLUB
OF N.Y. IN 1845. CARRIED BASEBALL
TO PACIFIC COAST AND HAWAII
IN PIONEER DAYS.

religious doctrine—everyone knows it, no one believes it. Ordinary baseball fans think that Cartwright, not Doubleday, was the real inventor of baseball. Those who take a serious interest in baseball history believe that the Knickerbockers were the first club, even if they may know that Alexander Cartwright's role as a club leader has been exaggerated. A few cognoscenti—a Society for American Baseball Research convention is a good place to look for them—know that while the Knickerbocker origin story is less embarrassing than the Doubleday story, it is still basically nonsense. You do have to give the Knickerbockers tale credit for staying power. The Knickerbockers' image as aristocratic founding fathers persists in the sports section of our cerebella like a dormant virus. Their name appears on the first page of just about everything written about early baseball. Once shorthand for anything associated with old New York, the word Knickerbocker lives on mainly through its sporting associations. New York City has a basketball team called the Knickerbockers. When the expansion 1962 New York Mets introduced their manager Casey Stengel to the press, one of the first things that came out of his mouth was: "It's a great honor to be joining the Knickerbockers."

Like the Doubleday tale, the Knickerbocker story was born in bad faith. In the 1850s, when the Knickerbockers were in their prime, men would rise to the podium at baseball banquets and pay homage to them as the first baseball club, the father of all baseball clubs, or, as sportswriter Henry Chadwick liked to put it, the "Nestors of our National Game." (In Homer's *Iliad*, wise King Nestor of Pylos coaches Achilles, a young star with a million-drachma spear and a ten-obol head.) But if you listen closely, you can pick up clues that this was not necessarily so—and that they knew it. The Knickerbockers are often called, vaguely, "pioneers" rather than founders; or the first "organized" club, rather than the first club, period. Always careful with words, journalist Henry Chadwick wrote in 1865 that the Knickerbocker club was "the first organization for the purpose of playing ball as it is now known."

The point of the hedges and qualifications was to avoid stating categorically that there was no serious adult baseball before the Knickerbockers. In fact, attending these 1850s baseball banquets were men who had played baseball and belonged to baseball clubs before the Knickerbockers existed. Referring to the Knickerbockers, Gothams, Eagles, and the rest of the 14 clubs who attended the first baseball convention in 1857, *Porter's Spirit of the Times* wrote, "Although many old baseball players were connected with the new clubs, it was generally conceded, and expected that the Knickerbockers would . . . take the lead in proposing the necessary reforms."[14] In other words, the Knickerbockers were not being deferred to because they were the first baseball players or the first club but for a different reason entirely.

One of the clubs that attended the 1857 convention, the Eagles, consistently claimed a founding date of 1840. Notice how this inconvenient fact is finessed in two of the quotations above. Acknowledging the Eagles' real age, of course, would undermine the Knickerbocker origin narrative. There is another problem with club founding dates. When trying to determine when a baseball club started, it is important to remember that those who joined the earliest known clubs had pre-existing social, occupational, or geographic ties. They did not come together solely for the purpose of playing baseball, the way athletes might join a club or team today. Typically, they were an existing set of friends from the firehouse, workplace, or neighborhood who decided to field a baseball team. These clubs very likely existed in a less organized form before their claimed founding dates, in some cases long before.

Another rival of the Knickerbockers, the Gotham Club, is a particularly interesting case. The Gothams were far from what we would call working class, but they were a more diverse, less uptight group than the Knickerbockers. Not all of them worked in an office. They put on chowder suppers, an unpretentious New York City tradition associated with three others: the firehouse, the militia company, and the political club. The Gothams did un-Knickerbocker-like things like organizing striped bass fishing outings in Long Island Sound. Officially founded in 1852, the Gothams were kin to at least two older clubs, the Washingtons and the New York Club that defeated the Knickerbockers

---

14. *Porter's Spirit of the Times*, March 7, 1857, p. 5

in 1846 in Hoboken. The New York Club announced a second anniversary celebration in 1845.[15] Whether this commemorated their second season at the Elysian Fields or their second year of existence or their second year using that name, this makes them older than the Knickerbockers as well. The Washington, New York, and Gotham clubs went through a series of schisms and reformations that probably underlie the name changes, but enough of the same names pop up in their box scores to show that they drew on a common pool of players.

The Knickerbockers also came out of this pool. In 1887 lawyer and Knickerbocker cofounder William Wheaton told the real story of the club's origins in an interview with the *San Francisco Examiner*. This interview is historical gold not only because it was given by a man who was there, but also because by joining the 1848 Gold Rush (like Alexander Cartwright) and moving permanently to California, Wheaton left the New York baseball scene before baseball had settled on an accepted origin narrative. In the 1830s, Wheaton recalled, he had played in a regular baseball game in lower Manhattan involving "merchants, lawyers and physicians." This is an important detail. Initially, the early baseball clubs played only among themselves and as was the case with Wheaton's game, which was formalized as the New York Base Ball Club in 1837, they were probably playing baseball before their stated founding dates. One of the leaders of the New York club was John Miller, an 1829 graduate of the College of Physicians and Surgeons, today the medical school of Columbia University. Descended from Quakers who had settled in Flushing, Queens, in the 1650s, Miller lived and practiced at 186 East Broadway, near the open spaces around Chatham Square in today's Chinatown, where Wheaton and others played before

---

15. New York *Daily Herald*, November 8, 1845, p. 3

they moved uptown to Madison Square. Quakers and doctors were both interested in public health reform, whose connection to baseball we will explore. The numbers of the club, Wheaton recalled, "soon swelled beyond the fastidious notions of some of us, and we decided to withdraw and found a new organization, which we called the Knickerbocker."[16]

HERE, FINALLY, IS a genuine Knickerbocker innovation: social exclusion.

The Eagles were made up largely of journalists, printers, and others with ink on their hands who worked on or near Nassau Street, Manhattan's publishing district. The Gothams also began as a neighborhood baseball game and evolved into a social organization, or perhaps vice versa. The Knickerbockers were less a community of place than one of class, values, and aspiration. Their fastidious notions included a code of personal conduct that was enforced with fines and admission criteria. Members were fined a few pennies, for example, for using bad language on the field. A clue to the importance of these fines is that they were written on the Knickerbockers' score sheets next to the offender's stat line. Becoming a Knickerbocker meant surviving a process of primary and secondary nomination by members, subject to anonymous blackballing, that was borrowed from another exclusive fraternity to which many Knickerbockers belonged, Freemasonry.

The Eagles and Gothams were not the only baseball clubs that were older than the Knickerbockers. They are merely the ones we know the most about and that were the most similar to the Knickerbockers in culture. These factors are not unrelated. Remember that the newspapers that covered early baseball had

---

16. *San Francisco Examiner*, November 27, 1887

an axe to grind. They were selling both sports and newspapers to the respectable EUB, who were positively allergic to drinking, gambling, and violence. This raises the question: How many baseball players and clubs were there that predated the Knickerbockers, but who were later ignored or forgotten by baseball history because they did not fit the image that baseball and the press were trying to sell?

The search for an answer to this question takes us back to a time that is strange to us, much of whose popular culture, including games and sports, is lost. In the 1840s and earlier, before penny journalism and the first regular journalistic sports coverage, newspapers are not much help. Like archaeologists sifting through potsherds and trying to reconstruct the shape and use of the object that they belonged to, we are faced with puzzling gaps in our historical knowledge. Sometimes the only way to bridge these gaps is to reason backwards from what did or did not happen at a later time. For example, one of the ways we know that baseball was widely played long before the first clubs appeared in newspapers is that the earliest mentions of the game are almost never accompanied by comprehensive explanations of what baseball is, or followed by letters to the editors of the national sporting weeklies asking basic questions about how it was played. The national press sometimes discussed fine points of the New York rules, but never the kind of basics that you would have to explain if you were teaching the game today to someone from France. Consider the fact that we know very little about baseball in Upstate New York before the late 1850s. But we do know that in the summer of 1860, when the Excelsiors of Brooklyn made the first multi-city tour, they had no trouble finding opponents in Buffalo, Albany, or Rochester. The Excelsiors were the best baseball club in the country or close to it. It is not surprising that they won every game, mostly by lopsided margins like 50–19 and 21–1. But in Troy, New York—behind their nearly unbeatable pitcher James Creighton—the Brooklynites defeated the local Victory club by a score of 13–7. By 1860 standards that was a nailbiter.

In another example, there is only scattered evidence that African Americans played baseball competitively in New York, Brooklyn, Philadelphia, and other cities in the 1840s and 1850s. But they must have been doing so because in the 1860s a world of competitive African American baseball suddenly appeared in newspaper sports sections. It could not have come out of nowhere. Baseball clubs made up of first-generation immigrants, for instance, did not suddenly appear at that time—or ever. The obvious explanation is that baseball is a cultural phenomenon. The skill and even the inclination to play the game develop organically over generations. Racism might have kept African American daily life out of mainstream newspapers for a long period of time, but it could not change African Americans' identity, culture, and essential Americanness.

As for early white baseball clubs of the wrong class, in 2007 John Thorn retrieved one example, the Magnolia baseball club, from history's deleted file.[17] The Magnolias do not appear in any later newspaper accounts, histories, or reminiscences. Given that they played in a conspicuous place, Hoboken's Elysian Fields, only two years before the arrival of the Knickerbockers, they could not have been left out of the historical narrative by accident. It is equally hard to believe that they were the only club of their kind. We have no list of members or box scores, but we do know that their club officers included a barkeeper, the holder of a political patronage job, and a man with a criminal record. These men had connections to the Empire political club,

---

17. Thorn, John. *Baseball in the Garden of Eden*, New York: Simon and Schuster, 2011, pp. 89 ff.

the power base of anti-Catholic and anti-immigrant Tammany Hall politico Isaiah Rynders. Two of them, Andrew Lester and Joseph Carlyle, were good friends of nativist firebrand and class warrior Mike Walsh. All of this tells a story—a story that those who later promoted baseball to the EUB as a clean and wholesome institution wanted to erase. As Thorn writes: "All three Magnolia officers had impeccable working-class, sporting, ruffian, and political associations. . . . Indeed, the Magnolia Ball Club was precisely the sort of poison for which the gentlemanly Knickerbocker Base Ball Club was created as an antidote . . . two years later." Men like the officers of the Magnolia club were held in disrepute more in retrospect than in their own time. Isaiah Rynders, for example, went from powerbroker in the 1840s to pariah in the 1860s as politics changed, but Thorn's point is well taken. The emerging urban bourgeoisie did not invent baseball; they adopted it and, in their minds, reformed it. The Magnolia club belonged to a dirty and disorderly New York that the EUB was emerging from, and was eager to leave behind.

There had to have been other Magnolia clubs. Consider the curious fact that there are two types of people that predominated in the baseball clubs of the 1850s—and that these two types are polar opposites. One we have already met, the EUB. Forward-looking, reform-minded, and economically versatile, they were on the cutting edge of the American economy's transition from merchant capitalism to modern industrial and finance capitalism. They were ready for the coming America that would be industrialized, corporatized, and knit together by new communication and transportation technology. Some of them were actively involved in making this happen. We modern middle-class baseball fans understand them easily because they are, in a word, us. The other type included craftsmen and artisans from the most conservative and traditionalist occupations of the time: butchers and other market traders, and shipwrights. For decades, men in these occupations waged a rearguard action against the modernity that the EUB was helping to realize—an action that ultimately failed. Unlike the EUB, as a social class they have no living descendants to understand them.

IN THE MIDDLE 1850s the New York City–style baseball club— certainly not the game of baseball, which was already there— crossed the East River to the then-independent city of Brooklyn. This was a giant step in baseball's evolution into a national sport, *the* national sport. It led to baseball's first and longest intercity rivalry. If we define a sports fan as a non-participant who regularly follows and supports a team without having a material interest, such as a bet, then the Brooklyn–New York baseball rivalry created America's first sports fans. According to the standard historical narrative, the Knickerbockers actively spread their kind of baseball. This is mostly false. The Knickerbocker club was directly involved in establishing one other club—the Excelsiors of Brooklyn—and only one. (Individual Knickerbockers helped to found baseball clubs in places where they moved for non-baseball reasons, but the same was true for the Gothams, Eagles, and many other clubs.) The close relationship between the Knickerbockers and the Excelsiors was unique. The Knickerbockers rarely played other clubs; most of the exceptions were games with their old Hoboken comrades the Gothams and the Eagles. But from 1858 through 1866 they played home and away series amounting to 15 games with the Excelsiors. The Knickerbockers ignored challenges from clubs like Brooklyn's Atlantics and, with one exception, never came to Brooklyn to play an opponent other than the Excelsiors.

The Atlantic and the Eckford clubs were both organized in Brooklyn in 1855, but there are no Knickerbockers in either club's pedigree. The Atlantics grew out of a pickup game played by butchers and tradesmen of the Atlantic Market, a public food market located at the corner of Hicks Street and Atlantic Avenue in Brooklyn. The Eckfords were men who worked in and around the shipyards of Williamsburg and Greenpoint. Eckford Club co-founder Frank Pidgeon called them "shipwrights and mechanics," a phrase that has been colossally misinterpreted. We know that historians have exaggerated the Knickerbockers' social status, but they also tend to label clubs like the Eckfords working class. This is anachronistic; there was no working class in the modern sense at that time, but it is also misleading. Among the Eckfords were shipbuilder and banker Joe Vanderbilt (etiquette authority Amy Vanderbilt's grandfather), a future newspaper editor, and several business owners. Shipwrights of the 1850s were skilled artisans with considerable social status, not laborers.

It is clear that the Knickerbockers and clubs like the Atlantics and Eckfords attracted different kinds of people, but it is less clear that the Knickerbockers were seen in their own time as belonging to a superior social class. We can say that there was little overlap between the aspirations and values of the EUB and those of Brooklyn butchers and shipwrights. These men had little interest in imitating the Knickerbockers in sports or in anything else. All three clubs eventually joined the NABBP, cooperated in many ways, and played baseball by the same rules, but the Knickerbockers never appeared on a baseball field with either the Atlantics or the Eckfords.

IF CLUBS LIKE the Brooklyn Atlantics were not descended from the Knickerbockers, then where did they come from? Sifting through the scattered potsherds that constitute our knowledge of adult baseball before the Knickerbockers, we find associations between baseball and particular neighborhoods and institutions. Baseball seems to have been played at a very early date at Columbia College, perhaps as long as 75 years before the beginning of formal intercollegiate baseball in the 1860s. Another example is the relationship between baseball and New York City's food markets, in particular the butchers of the Washington Market. It is probably not a coincidence that both Columbia and the market were originally located only a few blocks from each other, just west of New York's City Hall Park. Before 1842 City Hall Park was a parade ground and common where baseball had been played for years. One of New York's oldest markets, Washington Market was located on a site overlapping that of the present World Trade Center. It lasted in various forms from the end of the 18th century until 1962, when it was torn down and its tenants moved to Hunts Point in the Bronx. All that is left today is a public park northwest of the corner of Greenwich and Chambers Streets and three brick buildings on Harrison Street just west of Greenwich Street. In early 19th-century New York, butchers and wholesale grocers were not semi-skilled laborers paid by the hour by large corporations. They were independent businessmen who controlled the large covered markets in which they worked through something similar to a medieval guild. Here is how they were described by George G. Foster in his 1849 book, *New York in Slices*.

> The butchers form a powerful and respectable body of citizens, and are thoroughly organized into a Mutual Benefit Association, which regulates prices and enforces its rules strictly.... They are among our most quiet and amiable citizens, and are in no wise responsible for the goings-on of the "butcher-boys," [i.e., nativist thugs] with whom they are often ignorantly confounded.... Such a thing as a lean butcher, or a butcher in want, has never been heard of.[18]

18. Foster, George G. *New York in Slices*, New York: W. F. Burgess, p. 42

Butchers were pillars of New York's antebellum artisan and tradesman class—spiritually and, in many cases, literally heirs of the Sons of Liberty, who fought for and won American independence. They were proud of their role in creating and shaping American democracy. Like other members of their class, the butchers formed militia companies, volunteer fire companies, and political clubs. William "Bill the Butcher" Poole was a butcher at Washington Market. The portrait of Poole as a gangster in Herbert Asbury's 1927 book *Gangs of New York* is sensationalized beyond all recognition. Martin Scorsese's film of the same name goes even further. It paints Poole (called Bill Cutting) as something out of a slasher film, as well as moving him to a later historical period in order to blame American-born white Protestants, not Irish immigrants, for the racist violence of the 1863 Draft Riots. The reality is that no political faction or ethnic group in mid-19th-century New York had a monopoly on racism; New Yorkers drank it in with their Sunday chowder. The real Bill the Butcher, who died in 1855, was a tough character, but hardly atypical of his time and place and not in any sense an underworld figure. He swam in the mainstream of Whig politics, did some boxing, and served as a volunteer firefighter with the Bowery B'hoys of Red Rover Engine Company 34. After his murder, which resulted from a gambling dispute with another boxing politician (and baseball man), John Morrissey, Poole was buried in Brooklyn's Green-Wood cemetery, the preferred final resting place of New York's EUB. Today he lies alongside hundreds of respectable Amateur Era baseball players, including dozens of Knickerbockers. No subterranean rotations have been reported.

The butchers were a fun-loving bunch. Washington Market butchers and other food tradesmen competed in sports ranging from rowing to pedestrianism (speed walking) to baseball.

Like most contemporary adult American males, they did a lot of drinking and gambling. Two Washington Market butchers once bet $1,000 (more than triple a laborer's annual salary) on who could kill and dress 125 sheep the fastest. Remember that one of the early incarnations of the Gotham baseball club was named the Washington club. Many prominent Gotham baseball club members, including Leonard Cohen, Seaman Lichtenstein, Richard Thorn, and Robert Forsyth and his two sons, worked in the Washington Market. The Atlantic baseball club of Brooklyn was rooted in the same New York City market culture that produced the Gothams, not in any ties to the Knickerbockers. That culture spawned other early baseball clubs such as the Baltics, who were organized in 1855 by W.H. Taylor, Jacob Varian, and the Cornell brothers, Robert and Charles. All were butchers in the Washington and other markets. Robert Cornell was important enough to play a role in the abortive first attempt to form a baseball governing body. The connection between butchers and baseball survived the Industrial Revolution, the professionalization of baseball, and the corporatization of the meat industry. As late as the 1920s, New York butchers played baseball in their own amateur leagues.

CHOWDERS DEMOCRATIC

Before clubs like the Knickerbockers introduced the elaborate postgame banquet, baseball games were followed by a simple chowder. An 1843 announcement in the New York *Herald*, for example, informs members of the Magnolia club that their baseball game would start at the Elysian Fields at one o'clock and the chowder at four. The traditional New York chowder did not have milk or cream like New England clam chowder, or tomatoes like modern Manhattan clam chowder. In fact, it was clamless. The word chowder comes from the French word for stew pot, *chaudiere*, which is what it was cooked in. Going back to the late 1700s, chowders were a popular way to feed large crowds at political meetings, firehouses, and militia excursions. While well-off merchants and bankers slurped snapping turtle soup at meetings of the exclusive Hoboken Turtle Club (you had to kill the turtles yourself, although the hired help cleaned and cooked them), artisans, mechanics, tradesmen, members of the early baseball clubs and their families ate chowder.

Every published recipe from the pre–Civil War years has onions, potatoes, salt pork, cod or other cod-like fish, and hardtack. It is a clue to the dish's maritime origins that all of these ingredients could be found in or caught from an 18th-century ship. Issued to soldiers and sailors for centuries, hardtack is a dense cracker that is baked over and over again in order to make it virtually unspoilable; today a museum in Denmark proudly exhibits a piece of hardtack that is probably no more inedible now than it was when it was made in 1851. It is easy to see how modern clam chowders may have descended from this kind of fish chowder. When cod and other white-fleshed, meaty fish became scarce and expensive, dirt-cheap clams were added or substituted. Milk or cream replaced crushed hardtack as a thickener. To make up for the loss of protein and substance, flavorings like tomatoes, beer, and stock were sometimes added.

In 1841 Sarah Josepha Hale, editor of *Godey's Lady's Book*, a nationally popular women's magazine, published a famous chowder recipe. She also published the writers Washington Irving, Nathaniel Parker Willis, and Thomas Fitzgerald of the Philadelphia Athletics baseball club. This is the same Sarah Hale who cofounded Vassar College, campaigned for women's entree to all-male workplaces and professions, and convinced Abraham Lincoln to declare Thanksgiving a national holiday in 1863. She had a darker side; she wrote "Mary Had a Little Lamb." Here is Hale's chowder recipe, with my added cooking notes in brackets.

> To Make Chowder – Lay some slices cut from the fat part of pork [i.e., salt pork; thick cut bacon is a good substitute], in a deep stewpan, mix sliced onions with a variety of sweet herbs [such as savory, thyme, and parsley], and lay them on the pork; bone and cut a fresh cod into thin slices, and place them on the pork, then put a layer of pork, on that a layer of

biscuit [zwieback or rusks work fine], then alternately the other materials until the pan is nearly full, then season with pepper and salt, put in about a quart of water, cover the stew pan very close, and let it stand, with fire above as well as below, for four hours [this seems crazy long; if using the top of the stove I would cut this down by at least two hours]; then skim it well, and it is done. This is an excellent dish and healthy, if not eaten too hot [go ahead, eat it hot].

IN THE CASE of the Eckfords, baseball New York City–style took yet another route to Brooklyn. The patriotic pride of pre–Civil War Americans was their shipbuilding industry, which traced its beginnings to the naval vessels built by Henry Eckford during the War of 1812. Eckford taught the next generation of great American shipbuilders, including Isaac Webb, John Dimon, and John Englis, whose yards lay along the New York City side of the East River near Corlear's Hook. The shipyards of New York, Boston, and other East Coast cities struck a blow for American economic independence by ending decades of British domination of long-range commercial shipping. Their primary weapon was the American clipper. These magnificent sailing ships set speed records to Europe, the West Coast, and the Far East. Running out of space in the 1840s and 1850s, the New York City shipyards relocated to the sparsely populated farms and orchards of Greenpoint and Williamsburg on the Brooklyn side of the East River. Thousands of shipwrights and workers in dependent industries went with them, moving to Brooklyn from the 7th, 10th, 11th, and 13th Wards of New York. They brought their culture, including, according to legend, the peculiar way of talking that became known as Brooklynese. (If you go today to Greenpoint, where I am typing these words, and talk to a local over 50, you can still hear "south," "boiler," and "there" pronounced "sowt," "burluh" and "deh-ah.") In 1855, Frank Pidgeon, William H. Bell, and others formed the Eckford baseball club, named in honor of Henry. Like most of the original Eckfords, Pidgeon and Bell grew up around the New York shipyards. For a while the Eckfords straddled the East River, working and playing in Greenpoint while some continued to live in Manhattan. Pidgeon was a dock builder. Bell was a physician, but members of his family worked in shipbuilding. We cannot trace a definite connection between baseball and shipwrights further back than that. Remember, however, that baseball was played in the 1830s in Chatham Square, the onetime location of the pickup game that begat the New York, Washington, and Gotham clubs—the predecessors of the Knickerbockers. Chatham Square lies on the western edge of both the 7th and 10th Wards.

Historians credit the Knickerbockers with the idea of calling a convention of baseball clubs, which was a first step toward creating a national baseball infrastructure. As the story goes, the Knickerbockers called the first convention in 1857 and made it an annual event starting in 1858. These annual conventions allowed the Knickerbockers and their allies to modify the playing rules, enforce rules on amateurism, oversee the spread of baseball, and otherwise speak and act for the sport as a whole. But a closer look at the timeline suggests that the Knickerbocker club's leadership role has been exaggerated. Far from aspiring to rule over baseball, for most of their existence the Knickerbockers were internally divided over how to interact—and even whether to interact—with the rest of the baseball world. Baseball clubs had been playing and evolving more or less independently of one another until about 1854. That year the Gothams and Eagles met at a Knickerbockers club meeting and decided to play by the Knickerbocker rules. Whose idea this was we do not know. Common rules were needed for practical reasons. This was not necessarily because the Gothams and Eagles rules were so different from those of the Knickerbockers, but because as clubs played more interclub matches even small differences were inconvenient. Today, there is only one rules difference between the two major leagues—the designated hitter—and in interleague and postseason games baseball has struggled to handle it in a way that makes everyone happy.

A YEAR LATER, in 1855, something interesting happened—or rather didn't happen. Representatives from the fourteen or fifteen principal New York–area baseball clubs were publicly invited to meet at the Gotham public house, a hangout for nativist politicians and sporting types on the Bowery. The meeting was to be presided over by Thomas Van Cott of the Gotham club and its purpose was "to make arrangements for a banquet and a ball, and to establish general rules for the various clubs."[19] Only eight clubs came. Among the no-shows were the Knickerbockers. The meeting was adjourned, as it turned out, permanently.

Baseball picked up again in the spring and continued as usual in the summer of 1856. Then at a September 5 contest between the Knickerbockers and Gothams, a big game for the two old rivals, former Gotham Joseph Pinckney reappeared in the Gothams lineup and helped the club to a 21–7 victory. The problem was that Pinckney was an active member of a third club. The grumbling reached the ears of *Porter's Spirit of the Times*, which reported, "Some dissatisfaction was expressed by members of the Knickerbocker club and their outside friends, at the introduction

19. *New-York Tribune*, December 10, 1855, p. 7

of Mr. Pinckney, a superior player, from the Union club of Morrisania into the club of the Gothams for this occasion. . . ."[20] What are "outside friends?" Also known as "fancy characters," "the fancy," and "the sporting fraternity," outside friends meant gamblers, who were understandably upset to see this kind of lineup change after odds had been set and money wagered. Was Pinckney innocently doing his ex-teammates a favor? Was he a paid ringer? Did he have a bet down on the Gothams? We do not know. But there is reason to think that it was at least one of the last two.

Suddenly, baseball's reluctant Solons showed a renewed interest in making rules for interclub play. In early December 1856 President Daniel "Doc" Adams of the Knickerbockers called for a convention of baseball clubs in January 1857. After electing Adams as its president, the 1857 convention voted to substitute nine innings for the old 21-run rule, which as defense improved was causing an embarrassing number of games that were cut short by darkness. It addressed the ringer problem by requiring all players in interclub games to be members of one of the participating clubs—and no other club—and the gambling problem by prohibiting betting on games by any participant.

In the following year another, larger convention established the National Association of Base Ball Players, or NABBP, which would serve as baseball's national governing body for the rest of the Amateur Era. But the historic 1858 convention was called jointly by the four Elysian Fields clubs—the Knickerbockers, Gothams, Eagles, and Empires—not by the Knickerbockers alone. According to sportswriter Charles Peverelly's 1866 book *American Pastimes*, the 1858 convention was actually the Empire club's idea.[21] That convention elected William Van Cott of

---

20. *Porter's Spirit of the Times*, September 13, 1856
21. Freyer, John and Rucker, Mark. *Peverelly's National Game.* Charleston, SC: Arcadia, 2005, p. 18

the Gothams, Thomas Van Cott's brother, to replace Doc Adams as president. From then on, no Knickerbocker held a major NABBP office outside of the rules committee, which was chaired by Doc Adams until 1862. And if there is one element of baseball whose importance baseball historians consistently overrate, it is rules. Today, Adams is making a comeback as a possible replacement for debunkable founding father Alexander Cartwright, but as early as 1895 the Montpelier, Vermont, *Argus and Patriot* called him "the recognized father of baseball."[22] Despite Adams's enthusiasm for "grand matches," after a few years the Knickerbockers gradually withdrew from formal interclub competition, soon stopping completely. In 1867 longtime Knickerbocker James Whyte Davis, while serving on the NABBP nominations committee, helped draw baseball's first color line by authoring a blanket ban on African American players and clubs. But he shares that disgrace with others.

THE KNICKERBOCKERS' PICKINESS about opponents is often attributed to their supposed high social status. But the Knickerbockers were not bluebloods and they never pretended to be. Exaggerating their social status was not necessary for the original purpose of the Knickerbockers origin story—to promote amateur baseball. It was professional baseball, long after the fact, that converted the Knickerbockers from would-be gentlemen into the real thing. As baseball's Amateur Era faded from memory, the real Knickerbockers were replaced by caricatures. In 1911 Albert Spalding, major league baseball's most powerful owner and the man who bought and paid for the Abner Doubleday story, wrote the first attempt at a full history of baseball, *America's National Game*. The book's first printing of 5,000 copies sold

---

22. Montpelier *Argus and Patriot*, August 28, 1895, p. 3

out in 60 days; it sold 90,000 more in six months. Spalding's book has shaped baseball's historical narrative in a lasting way. In the chapter on the Knickerbockers, Spalding converts socially ambitious urban white-collar workers interested in physical fitness into upper-class twits in knickers and tri-corner hats. "In 1842," he writes, "a number of New York gentlemen—and I use the term 'gentlemen' in its highest social significance—were accustomed to meet regularly for baseball practice games. It does not appear that any of these were world-beaters in the realm of athletic sports. ... Let us not forget that the men who first gave impetus to our national sport ... were gentlemen 'to the manor born,' men of high tastes, of high ability, of upright character."[23] Toned down a bit, you can still read this kind of thing today, minus the out-of-date clothing. In his 1983 book *American Baseball*, David Voigt calls the Knickerbockers "aristocratic" and compares them to the snobbish Marylebone Cricket Club, which has controlled English cricket for more than two centuries, and which owns the copyright on the sport's official rules.

Pre–Civil War New York had no aristocrats in the British sense of titled nobility, but it did have an old-money class whose wealth typically came from family trading firms or land. Members of this class liked to gamble, and they preferred horseracing and yachting to team sports. Some envied the English aristocracy and dreamed of replicating its social and economic domination in the New World. They had little interest in the American game of baseball. Knickerbockers pitcher (and cricket bowler) Richard Fowler Stevens was an exception. He belonged to the Stevens family that owned most of Hoboken, New Jersey. The Stevenses were different. Like other members of their social class, they sent their sons to Columbia College, raced horses,

23. Spalding, Albert. *America's National Game*. San Francisco: Halo Books, 1991, p.37

sailed yachts, and developed real estate. Less typically, they liked to work. The Stevenses were shrewd, entrepreneurial businessmen interested in cutting-edge transportation technologies like steam ferries and railroads—building them, not merely financing them. Another uncle of Richard F. Stevens, the inventor and engineer Robert L. Stevens, ran the Camden and Amboy Railroad, which connected New York and Philadelphia. It also connected two sporting cultures—the New York game of baseball and its Philadelphia counterpart town ball. Colonel John Stevens and his sons John C. and Edwin built and operated the Elysian Fields, a private park and resort in Hoboken, which from the 1840s onward provided playing space to cricket and baseball clubs, including the Knickerbocker club.

John C. Stevens and eight others founded the New York Yacht Club in 1844, a year before the New York Knickerbockers were formed. The two organizations soon became neighbors at the Elysian Fields. The reason was the Stevens connection. Comparing their memberships demolishes the idea that the Knickerbockers were in any sense upper-class. All nine founders of the New York Yacht Club were the genuine article, old-money aristocrats. The list includes financier Hamilton Wilkes; rich socialite William Edgar; John C. Jay, grandson of Founding Father and first Chief Justice of the Supreme Court John Jay; George L. Schuyler, a grandson of Revolutionary War General and Senator Philip Schuyler, who married Alexander Hamilton's granddaughter; and industrialist James M. Waterbury, a descendant of the New York Livingston dynasty and father of international polo stars Monte and Lawrence Waterbury. There is no one on this list who would have joined the Knickerbocker baseball club. With the exception of Richard F. Stevens, his cousin Richard Conover, and at most one or two others, the Knickerbockers lived in a different social universe from the founders of the New York Yacht Club.

COTTON CAPITAL

James Wenman was the son of firefighting legend Uzziah Wenman, who battled temperatures of 17 degrees below zero and high winds to put out New York's Great Fire of December 16, 1835, a disaster that razed 700 buildings and wiped out much of old New Amsterdam. Young James was there, too. In the middle of the night, a fireman found him and his brother, who had snuck out of the house to help fight the fire, wet and shivering. He wrapped them in blankets and left them in a sheltered doorway. When James Wenman grew up and became a fireman himself, he made the newspaper front pages with a daring rooftop rescue of a shop girl named Lizzie Sullivan. He also joined the Knickerbocker baseball club. Over time, with the help of his baseball, firefighting, and political associations, James Wenman moved up in New York society. In the 1840s he belonged to the Gulick Guards, a Bowery B'hoy militia company full of volunteer firemen. Twenty years later he had risen to the 7th New York State Militia, once a blue-blood unit, but by Wenman's time made up mostly of members of the EUB, including many baseball players from the Knickerbockers, Eagles, Gothams, and Empires.

James Wenman's business was cotton. After the 1840s most of the world's cotton was grown and picked by slaves in the American deep South. The mills that turned it into fabric were in England, France, and New England. The great distances between producer, buyer, and seller were a problem, which New Yorkers solved by financing production and shipping costs with loans and by building the ships that brought the raw cotton from New Orleans, Mobile, Savannah, and Charleston to New York. For a commission, they handled sales and transportation to Liverpool and Le Havre. Their ships returned from Europe with finished textiles; after being offloaded in New York, they were reloaded with tools, machines, and other goods manufactured in New York or New England to be taken to the southern cotton ports and sold. Today, the tiny emirate of Dubai serves as the financial heart of the energy-producing Persian Gulf even though it has virtually no oil or natural gas of its own. In a similar way, 19th-century New York used its location, its financial resources, and its status as a communications and transportation hub to become indispensable to the cotton trade without planting a single cotton seed.

James Wenman was not the only cotton dealer in Amateur Era baseball. During the Civil War Harry Polhemus, centerfielder for the Excelsiors of Brooklyn, made a fortune selling cotton duck to make tents for the U.S. Army. In 1861 Wenman founded the New York Cotton Exchange and served as president through 1870. By financing every stage of cotton growing, shipping, and manufacturing, the exchange inserted itself deep into the global cotton business, capturing 40 cents of every dollar spent on cotton. It was an amazing success story. It would have been more amazing if it hadn't been built on a foundation of human misery. James Wenman spent the first part of his career profiting from the sweat of slaves. He continued to make a good living in the cotton trade for decades after slavery was abolished. The same was true of hundreds of other members of the New York Cotton Exchange. There is no reason to think that the institution of slavery presented any moral dilemma to them.

THE KNICKERBOCKERS WORKED mostly as insurance men, merchants, stockbrokers, or in other financial sector jobs; quite a few practiced medicine or law; and two or three were engineers. This may not sound glamorous, but in the mid-19th century innovators in these now stodgy fields were building a bridge to New York's and America's future. The Knickerbockers' first president, Duncan Curry, was an insurance executive in the formative years of that industry. Pioneered by New Yorkers like Curry, fire, life, and other kinds of insurance were advances that lubricated the economy and fostered growth by spreading risk. Knickerbockers William Grenelle and Alex Drummond were customs house brokers and commission merchants. Another New York innovation, commission merchants streamlined trade and shipping, and helped make the city the dominant American seaport. James Wenman cofounded the country's first Cotton

Exchange. Financial sophistication and lots of available capital are the reasons why this happened in New York. The cotton dealers of New York didn't grow cotton, manufacture textiles, or make clothes. They inserted themselves into the lucrative international cotton trade by financing the buying of seed, equipment, and human beings.

The key to understanding the Knickerbockers' self-conscious assertions of amateurism and enforced gentlemanly behavior is that they expressed social aspiration, not actual high social position. Real aristocrats do not advertise their gentility or fine each other for using four-letter words. Like other members of the EUB, most of the Knickerbockers' parents and grandparents came from the humble artisan, mechanic, and tradesman class. Still, the

The Knickerbocker club, shown here at an 1862 dinner, did not invent baseball but, for better or for worse, they left their mark on the game. Seated second from left is Doc Adams, who as baseball rules committee chairman gave us nine-inning games and nine men on a side. Seated next to him at center is James Whyte Davis, who did his best to keep amateur baseball all-white.

Knickerbockers' deck contained a few wild cards. Club member John Clancy, for example, was an Irish American politician and newspaper publisher born in New York's Sixth Ward, home of the infamous Five Points slum (although the Five Points achieved maximum infamy after he left). Clancy was an unusual Knickerbocker for two reasons: his religion—Catholics were unusual in early Amateur Era baseball—and his political associations. Democrats were not rare in either the Knickerbockers or their social class, but Clancy had friends in low places, like radical provocateur Mike Walsh and Mayor Fernando Wood, a racist demagogue who argued that New York City should secede from the United States rather than fight the Confederacy. The presence of John Clancy suggests that in the mid-1850s baseball had not yet entirely exorcized the spirit of the Magnolia club, and that the class identity of the Knickerbocker club was still under construction.

FOR MOST OF THE PAST CENTURY AND A HALF, the Knickerbockers have been credited with inventing the game, organizing the first club, and writing the first rules. This was never true, but only recently has anyone dared to point out that the emperor wasn't wearing any knickers. However, back in the 1850s, when the Knickerbockers were alive and playing, their contemporaries knew firsthand that the Knickerbockers were not the first baseball club. Why did they go along with the story? The likely main reason is that they understood the Knickerbockers' usefulness to the sport as a brand. Another may lie in what is called (admittedly only by me) the "Ray's Pizza" phenomenon. In the 1980s Manhattan was full of competing slice joints called Ray's. At some point in the past, a naming war had broken out. One called itself Original Ray's. There was also Famous Original Ray's—and World-Famous Original Ray's. Curiously, although someone filed a lawsuit over who owned the trademark, none claimed to be the original original Ray. The actual first Ray's, a Little Italy pizzeria where wise guys (allegedly!) sold heroin out of the basement, was long out of business. None of the later Ray's pizzerias was the first and everyone knew it. It is possible that something like this was going on in the 1850s. Baseball's promoters decided to make the Knickerbockers the face of the expanding sport. Calling them the first baseball club lent verisimilitude to an otherwise bald and unconvincing narrative. The Gothams, Eagles, and others could not make a credible counterclaim because in the 1850s, too many people were alive who knew that none of them was the first club either.

AT FIRST GLANCE the Knickerbockers are hard to distinguish from their contemporaries. Many of what are called the first baseball clubs were made up of white, successful, upwardly mobile New Yorkers. Nearly all were American-born Protestants with a common set of beliefs and values. There were a handful of players from New York's long-established Jewish community, but their beliefs and values were so compatible with those of the American Protestant mainstream that their presence in baseball—however surprising it may be to us today—was not so much as remarked upon at the time. But the Knickerbockers really were seen as different by their contemporaries. The respect and deference given to them by the rest of the baseball community was sincere. Why? The obvious first place to look for an answer is on the baseball field.

Were the Knickerbockers the best baseball club of their day? This sounds like a simple question, but it isn't. Today we judge baseball clubs by how many games they win or lose, taking into consideration the quality of their opponents. But the Knickerbockers hardly ever played outside opponents, especially in their early years. From 1845 through 1850, the club played over 200 games, but only three of these were matches against other clubs. The rest were intramural games played between impromptu lineups made up of Knickerbocker members. There is one unsettling anecdote from 1849 in which a random party of journalists visiting the Elysian Fields, possibly including George Wilkes, challenged an unnamed group of Knickerbockers for a chowder supper and defeated them, 11–4.[24] Presumably, this was not the Knickerbockers' starting lineup, or "first nine." The Knickerbockers played outside opponents 40 times between 1851 and 1860, but that is not a large enough statistical sample to tell us much. When the Civil War started in 1861, the Knickerbockers stopped playing completely for two seasons. After that, they remained permanently behind baseball's competitive curve, in later years serving as a kind of living museum of the early Amateur Era game. As Charles Peverelly drily observed in 1866:

> No person can obtain admission in the [Knickerbocker] club merely for his capacity as a player; he must also have the reputation of a gentleman; and hence arises one of the causes of its not being what is called a match-playing club.[25]

We have no useful statistics by which to evaluate the Knickerbockers, but we do have the opinions of contemporary sportswriters. They tell us that the Knickerbockers were acknowledged as the best club in baseball for the first decade or so of their existence. They also tell us that other clubs were catching up with them in the mid to late 1850s. The December 6, 1856 issue of *Porter's Spirit of the Times* writes, "Until the present season, [the Knickerbockers] deservedly stood pre-eminent." In July 1858 the *New York Clipper* expressed surprise that the

---

24. *National Police Gazette*, June 9, 1849
25. Freyer, John and Rucker, Mark. *Peverelly's National Game.* Charleston, SC: Arcadia, 2005, p. 11

Knickerbockers had lost to the young Excelsiors, "for it is well known that the veterans of the Knickerbocker have long been the champions of the 'base' as a club." A month later the New York *Atlas* reported that the rubber match of a three-game series between the Knickerbockers and Eagles "resulted most unexpectedly in the hollow defeat of the former club."

The 1856 *Porter's* article contains another tantalizing detail. Whoever wrote it—my guess would be someone from the world of cricket—criticizes the Knickerbockers hitters for upper-cutting the ball. "No club," he writes, "strikes with greater power, but from their habit of striking high, they give too many chances for such excellent clubs as the Gotham and Eagle."[26] It may be that this is true, that outfield defense had improved to the point that too many of the Knickerbocker power hitters' long fly balls were being turned into outs. Another possibility is that the Knickerbockers had figured out what Babe Ruth figured out in the 1920s, what Ted Williams preached in the 1940s, and what major league hitters have re-rediscovered today, that the way to produce runs in baseball is not to hit down on the ball—as high school coaches told me, my father, and my grandfather to do—but to drive it in the air as far as possible. As unapologetic upper-cutter and AL MVP Josh Donaldson once tweeted, "Just say NO . . . to ground balls."

Pioneers of launch angle or not, the Knickerbockers played most of their games among themselves. In modern terms, they were a regular pickup game. The key element of a good pickup game is stability. No one wants to travel all the way from Wall Street to Hoboken to find out that only 12 players had shown up. Peverelly writes that the early Knickerbockers addressed this by having two or three of their members, "go around in the

---

26. *Porter's Spirit of the Times*, December 6, 1856

forenoon of a pleasant day and muster up (Knickerbocker) players enough to make a match." Another is strong leadership. The Knickerbockers seem to have been a stable organization with effective leadership over a long period of time. This may be a false impression, a by-product of the fact that so many of their records have been preserved. But it is probably the other way around; that their records were preserved *because* of their organizational stability.

Another indication of the quality of Knickerbockers games is the high quality of the transient players they attracted, players who joined the club not for social reasons but because they were looking for a challenging game. Among them was Napoleon Bonaparte McLaughlen, a lanky Vermonter whose parents somehow knew from birth that he would be an outstanding military officer. A baseball pitcher and cricket bowler, McLaughlen spent a couple of years in New York City as a recruiter for the 2nd U.S. Dragoons. Other examples include Lewis Wadsworth, who switched from the Gothams to the Knickerbockers in 1854 and switched back again in 1858, and Richard F. Stevens, who played briefly for the Knickerbockers before moving to the Philadelphia area and playing for a top club there. Harry Wright belongs in this category, too. A professional cricketer, he played with the Knickerbocker club for the competition, not for any social benefit. Wright left the Knickerbockers for the Gothams when the Knickerbockers shut down because of the Civil War. During the 1858 Fashion Course series in which New York City played against Brooklyn, Wright played for New York City. Both sides were made up of the top players in each city as chosen by committees of baseball men. In 1858 the Knickerbockers as a group may have been past their peak, but three of them—Wright, catcher Charles DeBost, and outfielder James Whyte Davis— were judged to be among the best players in New York.

To FIND THE real source of the Knickerbockers' prestige, however, we need to look not at how they played on the field, but who they were off it. Like almost all early Amateur Era clubs, the Knickerbockers had roots in the volunteer fire department. But even as firefighters, the Knickerbockers were a hose of a different color. Several important early members belonged to Oceana Hose No. 36, located near the corner of Madison Street and Rutgers Street—not far from the site of the ancient baseball game that spawned the Gotham, New York, Washington, and Knickerbocker clubs. This includes merchant and future capitalist Alonzo Slote and his brothers Henry and Daniel. In 1867 Daniel Slote roomed with author Mark Twain on the package tour of Europe and the Middle East that inspired *The Innocents Abroad*. This book portrays Slote (who Twain later accused of swindling him in a business deal) as the kind of American tourist who tries to communicate with non-English speakers by yelling. Future Knickerbockers including businessman William Woodhull, stockbroker James Whyte Davis, and the banking Cartwright brothers, Alexander and Benjamin, also belonged to Oceana Hose No. 36. A 19th-century history of New York City firefighting describes them this way:

> Oceana's crew were an exclusive set, who prided themselves upon possessing one of the finest looking carriages in the Department and in being able to make the most attractive appearance on gala occasions. Not unnaturally they were regarded with jealousy by some and with a feeling akin to contempt by others, who dubbed them "the quills" because they were mainly merchants and merchants' clerks. They were the "dudes" of the Department.

> They wore fancy uniforms, held the best banquets and—most important to romantic success—drove a carriage that was "richly

plated and ornamented with silver."[27] They provoked worse than contempt. In 1851, while returning from a fire, Oceana members were ambushed by "a gang of rowdies who made [a] cowardly and unprovoked attack upon the members." Violence was part of volunteer firefighting culture, in particular when companies were racing each other to a fire, but this incident has overtones of pure class conflict. When their enemies spread rumors that the attack had been staged, Oceana responded not with their fists but with a public notice complaining of the "injuring [of] its reputation in the eyes of the public" and denouncing the attack as "unmanly in the extreme."[28] This kind of concern for reputation, correct behavior, and appearances was typical of the Knickerbockers as a club and of the EUB as a class.

Early baseball clubs like the Gothams and Eagles looked up to the Knickerbockers for the same reason that rival fire companies envied Oceana No. 36. They had style. The Knickerbockers were the first club to design and wear playing uniforms. They may have been the first club to put on annual dinners and to hold annual organizational meetings, but even if they weren't, Knickerbocker events were finer and more elegant. In 1854 a young stockbroker named John Suydam, impressed by the Knickerbockers, formed a club in Brooklyn originally called the "Jolly Young Bachelors' Base Ball Club," but soon renamed the Excelsiors. In the mid-1850s, when New York baseball men felt the need to discuss issues affecting the sport as a whole, the venue they chose was a Knickerbocker club dinner. From the mid-1850s on, the Knickerbockers held some of their club dinners at an expensive Barclay Street hotel restaurant owned by a man named Francis Fijux. (A French speaker, he probably pro-

27. Costello, Augustine. *Our Firemen*. New York: Pub. By author, 1887, pp. 441 ff.
28. New York *Daily Herald*. March 8, 1852, p. 4

nounced his name "fee-ZHOOKS," but the best his anglophone customers could do was "Fish Hooks.") The Knickerbockers usually held business meetings at an ordinary hotel, but they met at Fijux's when the evening's focus was on food and drink. This deceptively trivial detail tells us a little more about who the Knickerbockers were.

TODAY FORMAL PUBLIC dining is a common way to display sophistication and assert social status. It was far less common in the early 19th century. Antebellum New York had a thriving restaurant scene for the same reasons it does now—a combination of prosperity and large numbers of busy single people living in cramped apartments or kitchen-less rented rooms. But most New York restaurants were simple lunch counters, takeout joints, or bars serving one type of food, such as chowder, oysters, or donuts. Dining in the European style, with waiters, formal table service, and meals ordered *a la carte*, was rare. As late as 1866, *Trow's New York City Directory*, a guide for travelers, lists only four restaurants in this category. One is Delmonico's, a name that is still synonymous with good steak. The city's first fine dining restaurant, Delmonico's was opened in the 1830s by two brothers from the Swiss canton of Ticino. Famous for its high standards and even higher prices, it was the first restaurant ever reviewed by *The New York Times*. Francis Fijux came to New York to work for the Delmonicos, but later opened his own hotels and restaurants in New Orleans and New York. A New York newspaper described Fijux's restaurant on Barclay Street as "an eating house that rare gastronomers in the fashionable society of the time lauded to the skies." This included poet, editor, and gourmet Robert Barry Coffin, who (under his pen name Barry Gray) praised Fijux's in the pages of *The Table*, one of the earliest American publications devoted to food. Coffin had sophisticated and well-travelled literary friends like Edgar Allan Poe, Fitz-Greene Halleck, and the Irish Fenian John Savage. In the days before airlines and the democratization of tourism, few New Yorkers had been to France and even fewer knew enough to appreciate genuine French cooking. Among the exceptions were epicures like Coffin and his circle—and the members of the Knickerbocker baseball club.

The real Knickerbockers may not have been truly upper class, but they were a class act. They threw the best parties and were the envy of early Amateur Era New York baseball. Some of them were good athletes. But the Knickerbocker club's main contribution to the wider baseball movement was its usefulness to baseball's marketing effort. The Knickerbockers' style, social exclusivity, and strict amateurism helped to sell baseball to the moralistic Protestant EUB as a participant sport and as an all-American alternative to cricket. Both the Knickerbockers and the New York game of baseball had something that the bat-and-ball games played in Boston, Philadelphia, and elsewhere did not have: ambition. The New York game was the only one of the three to create a governing association with the word "national" in its name, and it was the only one to invent origin stories. The Knickerbockers that we know from baseball history were not agents of baseball's ambition as much as products of that ambition.

PANORAMA OF NEW YORK AND VICINITY.

An imaginary "bird's-eye view" by John Bachmann. Bachmann lived in Jersey City and often added a bit of his home state to views of New York. If you look in the darkness of the left foreground of this 1866 example, you can see live baseball action from the Elysian Fields in Hoboken, New Jersey.

CHAPTER THREE
Escape from the City

 LL BASEBALL FANS have the same memory of their first big-league game. You enter the grandstand, way up in the cheap seats. When you look down, you see a shimmering green island, surrounded by an ocean of brick, concrete, and asphalt that stretches to the horizon. You realize that the green island is a baseball field. The incongruity of it stays with you.

Maybe this is why, when we are told that the sport of baseball was born in the country and imported to the city, we believe it. The truth is that it was the other way around. In 19th-century America, of course, children played bat-and-ball games in the country as well as in the city. There are stories of rural adults playing them when they got together on holidays like Election Day, July 4th, or one of many local feasts of thanksgiving; this may explain why some baseball-like games were called "town ball." But playing baseball in a serious, organized way—with clubs, practices, uniforms, statistics, championships, and umpires—required the abundance, leisure, and freedom of city life. The cities that gave us the sport of baseball were not the concrete and steel metropolises of today's Chicago or New York. They were low-rise cities with easy access to open spaces. And they were small enough that that you could get around them without wheels. In 1840 almost all of New York City's 312,000 residents lived between the Battery and Houston Street, which is about a half an hour's walk. The tallest building was Trinity Church, whose 281-foot spire is now comically dwarfed by office towers. That sunlit field of our memories is not a piece of the country magically transported to the city. Rather, it is a remnant of the pre-automobile, pre–mass transit walking city where baseball was born.

NEW YORK BEGAN to lose its open space in the 1840s and 1850s, at the same time that the growing sport of baseball was about to need a lot more of it. The reason was a sudden, massive economic expansion. In 1825 the city's economy had taken a dose of performance-enhancing drugs in the form of the Erie Canal, which redirected to the Hudson River and the port of New York much of the wealth that had previously flowed from the upper Midwest down the Mississippi. By the middle of the century, a building boom had eaten up the last of lower Manhattan's undeveloped land. Industrialization and pollution had ruined estuaries and waterways where New Yorkers once rowed, sailed, and fished. Brooklyn grew from a ferry landing to the country's third-largest city in 25 years. A battalion of city blocks marched up Manhattan Island, conquering sleepy Greenwich Village and then setting its sights on the outlying villages of Yorkville, Harlem, and Bloomingdale. Sports and games had already been crowded out of downtown public spaces like City Hall Park, Washington Square, and Chatham Square. The city's baseball and cricket players fled to the open spaces around Madison Square, but soon had to pick up and move again. The Knickerbocker baseball club sought refuge on the Stevens estate across the Hudson River in Hoboken, New Jersey.

The St. George cricket club, nicknamed the Dragon Slayers,

went to Hoboken, too, but not before finding a temporary home at the Red House, a country tavern and resort north of the city, near Third Avenue and 105th Street. This was a 10-mile round trip for most New Yorkers. In the 1830s the Red House shuttled its customers to and from the city in horse-drawn stagecoaches. Soon they had a faster option—the New York and Harlem Railroad, which ran up Fourth Avenue, now called Park Avenue, on tracks laid at street level. By 1844, powered by steam engine above 14th Street and by horse in the populated parts of the city below, the NY&H extended from near New York City Hall through Harlem and the Bronx to White Plains in Westchester County.

If you were taking the train from lower Manhattan to the Red House, you got off in the village of Yorkville at 86th Street and Fourth Avenue on what is now Manhattan's Upper East Side. Harry Wright must have done that often. Two blocks from the Yorkville station was the Episcopal Church of the Redeemer, where in 1858 the 23-year-old Wright married Mary Fraser, the 17-year-old daughter of a Scottish carpenter. The son of Englishman Sam Wright, cricket professional of the St. George club, Harry was a promising cricketer who had recently started dabbling in baseball with the Knickerbockers (the Dragon Slayers' neighbors after they left the Red House for Hoboken in 1857). He was employed as a jeweler at Tiffany and Co., but he would not have to work a day job for long. The Knickerbockers did not pay players, but cricket clubs did. The money for this came from wealthy backers and club dues, not ticket sales. Ordinary cricket matches attracted little or no spectator interest in the United States; paying to watch any kind of game was unheard of before 1858. In 1860, the St. George cricket club was mocked by the *Clipper* for experimenting with a 10-cent admission charge for spectators, "with such an attractive game as baseball to rival cricket."[29] In 1861 the Knickerbockers gave Wright, the father of a two-year-old, a novel "benefit game" in which cricketers played baseball against baseball players. The original idea of the benefit game, which was borrowed from cricket, was to raise funds for a player in need; neither sport considered it a violation of the amateur ethic. If Harry Wright had cash flow problems in 1861, the obvious reason was the Civil War, which caused many New York baseball and cricket clubs to shut down for a year or more.

In 1862 newspapers reported that Harry Wright, "the well-known professional cricketer," had opened a cricket batting cage in a former racquet (an ancestor of squash) court at 233 Bowery. There he taught young men how to guard the wicket for 25 cents an hour, afternoons and evenings, seven days a week. In 1866 he went to Cincinnati to work as a cricket professional. Shortly after that, he was hired away by the Cincinnati Red Stockings baseball club. Harry Wright's career move was cricket's loss and baseball's gain. The Red Stockings assembled a quasi-all-star team of salaried baseball mercenaries. In 1868, 1869, and 1870 Wright led the Red Stockings on a series of tours from coast to coast. They played 84 games in a row without a loss, creating a national sensation. In 1953, six major-league pennants and 26 professional seasons later—12 of them as manager of the National League Philadelphia Phillies—Harry Wright was inducted into the Baseball Hall of Fame.

Most of the fields where Harry Wright played cricket and baseball are long gone. When today's city-dwellers need open space, they can visit one of America's great urban public parks. We take these parks for granted, but they are not all that old an idea. New York's Central Park was completed in 1873; Brooklyn's Prospect Park opened in 1867; and Philadelphia's Fairmount Park was not

---

29. *New York Clipper*, June 16, 1860

completed until 1876. Before that, cities had pleasure gardens or pleasure grounds like the Red House. These were smaller, privately owned resorts where people escaped the city and spent evenings, holidays, and hot summer weekends. They offered green space; food and drink; concerts and shows; and sports and games. Some were big enough for baseball, bowling, and other sports. The earliest examples were in the center of the city or close to it. In early 19th-century New York there were pleasure gardens near Battery Park and in what is now Tribeca and Soho. By the 1840s, increasing density encroached on them or pushed them out of lower Manhattan entirely. The Red House lasted longer because it was located far north of the city in rural Harlem. If we could travel through time and visit one of these pleasure grounds, we would be struck by the mix of people there—all ages, sexes, races, and ethnicities, and all classes except the very rich and the very poor—and the amazing array of activities and attractions on offer. Many of us today prefer to do as little as possible in our precious time off, but our 19th-century ancestors liked their leisure mixed with plenty of action. Cooled by East River breezes, the Red House's 50 acres had shady groves where patrons strolled, picnicked, played, and were entertained.

The Red House was also a mecca for lovers of harness racing, or trotting—the stock car racing of the 19th century. It added baseball diamonds in the 1850s. Every big city in the United States had pleasure gardens offering at least some of the features of the Red House. They were modeled on and often named after famous European urban resorts like London's Vauxhall and Paris's *Jardin de Tivoli*. New York, Boston, New Orleans, Philadelphia, Charleston, and Richmond all had at least one Vauxhall Garden. New Orleans, Philadelphia, and Charleston had a Tivoli. New Orleans's Tivoli Garden along the Carondelet Canal (now filled in and called the Lafitte Greenway), for instance, featured "choice trees and shrubbery beneath which were benches and tables, and amid which were latticed bowers and arbors. There were buildings for barrooms, ice cream cakes, coffee ... musicians poured forth German waltzes...." There was bowling. A mysterious game called *les quatres*—possibly another name for the baseball variant "old cat"—was played there, too.

IN THE EARLY 1800s one man, Colonel John Stevens, owned all of what is now Hoboken, New Jersey. Stevens and his descendants directed the development of Hoboken for generations and provided vital support to the American sports movement. Separated from Manhattan by a narrow section of the Hudson River, Colonel Stevens's property was four miles closer to 14th Street in Manhattan than the Red House. Stevens himself lived in an estate atop Castle Point, a bluff overlooking the Hudson River and Manhattan that was covered by gardens and lawns, but the rest of Hoboken was undeveloped. Much of it was a mosquito-ridden swamp containing more snapping turtles than people. (It took a few decades, but humans evened the score by eating them as the main ingredient of Hoboken's celebrated turtle soup.) The colonel and his sons shared interests in engineering, real estate development, and sports. In the 1820s they began to drain and fill Hoboken's marshes. In the drier, more elevated section along the Hudson River on either side of their estate, they started work on a new kind of pleasure grounds. The purpose of places like the Red House was to sell food, drink, and entertainment, but the Stevenses were thinking bigger than that. Like other pleasure grounds, theirs would provide a place for the growing number of New Yorkers who were not wealthy enough to own or rent country places, but who had enough money and leisure time to escape summer in the city for an afternoon or weekend. Along with Stevens's Hudson River ferries, it would also serve as an amenity to help sell land in his envisioned "new city" of Hoboken.

It was an act of philanthropy as well, if philanthropy can be profitable. The Stevenses' pleasure grounds, later named the Elysian Fields, became New York City's main playground for much of the 19th century. It provided New Yorkers with something their government could not or would not provide, ample green park space, including grounds for baseball, cricket, and other sports—for free. One by one, the top New York City baseball clubs gravitated to Hoboken. And the Stevenses' pleasure grounds helped sell a lot of real estate. Income from the ferries only minimally offset the capital and operating costs of the Elysian Fields, which did not charge admission. But John Stevens's real estate sales and the Hoboken Land and Improvement Company, formed in 1838 and owned by Colonel Stevens's son Edwin, made an astronomical amount of money. When Edwin Stevens died in 1868 the real estate company's holdings were valued at $20 million, a figure that did not include the Elysian Fields and other waterfront land worth an additional $15 million, for a total of $35 million.[30] To give some perspective on that number, the U.S. Navy budget for 1868 was $16.6 million. Today's Navy budget is $172 *billion*.

All that is left of the Elysian Fields today is a triangular sliver of a park at Washington and 11th Streets with creaking swing sets and, of course, a "No Ball Playing" sign. For most of the 20th century a Maxwell House coffee plant, topped by a giant neon coffee cup yielding its final drop, stood where Knickerbocker infielders smothered daisy cutters with their bare bankers' hands. In 1992 the plant was torn down and replaced by a "condominium community." Life may be short, but real estate wealth is eternal. The

---

30. Louisville *Courier-Journal*, September 25, 1868, p.4

city of Hoboken lives on and so does the great family fortune that it helped create. The Stevenses have scores of well-off descendants. Among them was New Jersey Republican Congresswoman Millicent Fenwick, the pipe-smoking patrician feminist who inspired a character in the cartoon strip *Doonesbury*.

The Stevens that matters most to baseball history is Congresswoman Fenwick's great, great uncle and Colonel Stevens's eldest son, John C. Stevens. He viewed sports both as an instrument for unifying a young nation and as a way for America to prove itself against England, the sporting motherland. Even though his personal tastes ran to cricket, horses, and yachts, he and his brothers were open to any sport that caught the public imagination. John C. Stevens is best remembered today for his 1851 upset victory in the Royal Yacht Squadron's Isle of Wight race, which had never before been won by a foreigner (and which the United States would successfully defend for the next 132 years). The winner's trophy was renamed the America's Cup, not after Stevens's country but after his yacht. A departure from conventional design, the 90-foot schooner *America* was built in Greenpoint by shipbuilder George Steers, a friend of Eckford baseball club founder Frank Pidgeon. Stevens cofounded the New York Yacht Club at the Elysian Fields and was the godfather of American yacht racing.

John C. Stevens was also a patron of thoroughbred horseracing, which was becoming an arena for the rivalry between the northern and southern states. He persuaded New York State to legalize horseracing in Queens County and then worked to raise northern thoroughbred racing to the level of its southern counterpart. His partners included his brother Edwin Stevens and Virginia-born Alexander Botts. Owner of the Union Racecourse in Woodhaven, Queens, Botts was baseball writer and advocate Henry Chadwick's future father-in-law. In 1823 the owner of the southern champion *Henry* proposed a race with the northern champion *American Eclipse*. John C. Stevens put up the $20,000 purse. Tens of thousands of people, among them President Andrew Jackson, went to the Union Course by carriage or train and saw *Eclipse* win the decisive heat with three lengths to spare. Not long after, *American Eclipse*, unlike Jackson, retired undefeated. Ultimately, staunchly nativist 19th-century New Yorkers preferred the homegrown sport of harness racing to thoroughbred racing, although both survive today. This was not a problem for Stevens, who built a harness racing track near the Elysian Fields.

PLEASURE RAILWAY AT HOBOKEN.

The Pleasure Railway was an amusement ride invented in the 1820s by John Stevens, whose family operated the Elysian Fields as a kind of laboratory of transportation, leisure and recreation. Disneyland, Central Park, Coney Island and the modern baseball park can all claim the Elysian Fields as an ancestor.

[89

SUCCES DE STEAM

When the American Revolution was won, Colonel John Stevens of the Continental Army looked around him and saw not a unified country, but, in the words of his biographer Archibald Turnbull, "thirteen disjointed, virtual independent republics." This was also true when it came to sports. The idea of a national sport was a non-starter when it took a week to get from Philadelphia to Boston.

Colonel Stevens and his sons spent the next three quarters of a century using mass transportation and sports to further the dream of national unification. In 1790 Colonel John Stevens pushed Congress to pass the first law protecting patents in order to encourage new technology and to prevent transportation monopolies. Stevens's crusade against the innovation-stifling monopoly on Hudson River steam ferries that New York State granted to Fulton and Livingston led to the 1824 Supreme Court decision *Gibbons v. Ogden*. This gave the Federal Government, not the states, the power to regulate navigation.

In 1852 President Charles King of Columbia College—which male Stevenses attended for generations—said of John Stevens, "Born to affluence, his whole life was devoted to experiments, at his own cost, for the common good." The Elysian Fields, donated in part by the Stevenses to the cause of building American sports, was one of those experiments. In 1806 Stevens drew up plans for another, a tunnel linking New York and New Jersey underneath the Hudson riverbed. It was a good idea, but ahead of its time; the Holland Tunnel opened in 1927. In 1804 he and his son Robert L. Stevens built a boat with the first-ever underwater twin-screw propeller and motored over to the Battery on the southern tip of Manhattan. Astounded New Yorkers could not understand how it moved. This technology replaced paddlewheels, but not for another half-century. In 1811 Colonel Stevens built the *Juliana*, America's first steam ferry, to bring passengers to and from Hoboken and lower Manhattan. Another son, Edwin A. Stevens, founded the Stevens Institute of Technology on the site of the family estate in Hoboken. It is still there today.

In 1815 New Jersey granted Colonel Stevens America's first railway patent, which became the Camden and Amboy Railroad, the first mass transit link between New York and Philadelphia. In 1823 he obtained another patent that became the mighty Pennsylvania Railroad. At that time canals were thought to be the coming transportation technology. The purpose of the "circular railway" that Colonel Stevens built in Hoboken in 1825 was to convince the public that railroads were the real future. Of course, he was right.

After Colonel Stevens died in 1838, the Camden and Amboy Railroad was run by Robert L. Stevens and his nephew Richard F. Stevens, who played baseball with the Knickerbockers at the Elysian Fields. Robert L. Stevens manufactured railroad engines; he also designed T-rails, the hook-headed railroad spike, and other railroad technology that is still in use. Today Amtrak's Northeast Corridor runs on the original Camden and Amboy line for 43 miles. The railroad brought Richard F. Stevens to the railroad's offices in Camden, across the Delaware River from Philadelphia. Employees of the Camden and Amboy formed a baseball club. In 1860 Stevens pitched for the Equity club, one of the first Philadelphia clubs to switch from town ball, the local bat-and-ball game, to baseball, the future National Pastime.

THE STORY OF Hoboken and the Stevens family—a relationship that was indispensable to the success of baseball and American sports in general—begins at the end of the American Revolution, when state governments decided to punish Americans who had supported the king by seizing and selling off their property. (This was also done to my ancestors.) New Jersey's Commission of Forfeitures confiscated Hoboken from William Bayard, the son of a New York City mayor and a descendant of Peter Stuyvesant's sister. George Washington's chief of staff Baron von Steuben helpfully suggested that it should be given to him as a present, but in 1784 John Stevens, ex-colonel in the Continental Army and the father of John C. Stevens, bought all 800 acres for $90,000. In 1804, the year in which Aaron Burr shot Alexander Hamilton in a duel on Weehawken Heights, then part of Hoboken, John Stevens began advertising building lots for sale. His unique selling proposition was not location, location, or location. It was health. Hoboken, the ads said, was "free from the danger of Yellow Fever and the restrictions of quarantine."

Welcome to 19th-century America, where outbreaks of yellow fever, typhoid fever, and cholera killed tens of thousands, almost all of them in cities. Yellow fever struck New York City in waves between 1795 and 1803. Cholera killed roughly 3,500 New Yorkers in 1832, 5,000 in 1849, and 2,000 in 1854. The 1849 outbreak killed former President James K. Polk. Cholera spreads when sewage contaminates sources of drinking water. New York City had no public water system until 1842, when the first stage of the Croton system opened. Before that, those who could afford it had pure water delivered from the country in barrels; everyone else used brackish or polluted wells. (Aaron Burr's private Manhattan Water Company laid down a few wooden pipes for show, but his water company was really a subterfuge to get around state banking regulations; it became the Chase Manhattan bank, later absorbed by the present J.P. Morgan Chase and Co.) Until the 1850s New York had no city-wide sewer system (don't ask). Street levels rose an inch a year because of compacted horse manure and whatever garbage was rejected by the city's thousands of feral pigs. This is why the city's brownstones and row houses were built with stoops and raised parlor floors. Wealthy women carried vinaigrettes, silver or gold compacts containing a sponge soaked in vinegar and herbs that they could hold to their noses to mask the general stink. In 1855 Mortimer Thomson testified that "the filth in Broadway gets so deep as to stop the stages [horse-drawn coaches, the buses of the mid-19th century]."

New York was not significantly unhealthier than most other American cities, merely bigger. For most of the 1800s, moving from the country to any American city lowered your life expectancy. Like a sport, epidemic disease had a season. During July and August the well-to-do got out of town. Downtown areas grew quiet. Conventional medical theory held that cholera and other infectious diseases were caused by vapors given off by decomposing organic matter; sudden changes in temperature; or eating unripe fruit. Contemporary newspapers are full of stories blaming negligent mothers for risking their children's lives by letting them eat green apples. Conventional medical theory was, of course, wrong. Without a scientific understanding of how contagious diseases work, doctors and public health officials had little to fight them with but offices and titles. American city dwellers lived in fear that the next epidemic might take away their lives or their loved ones.

A public health movement sprang up in the early and mid-19th century that offered hope. It was mostly false hope, but hope just the same. Rationalists like English public health revolutionary Sir Edwin Chadwick (Henry Chadwick's older half-brother, he did not emigrate to the U.S. with their father), believed that disease could be prevented by maintaining a healthy body and by reforming social and governmental systems. Public health reformers advocated free vaccination and medical treatment for the poor, as well as fresh air, exercise, and public parks. Colonel John Stevens was speaking their language when he pitched Hoboken as "a place of general resort for citizens, as well as strangers, for health and recreation. So easily accessible, and where in a few minutes the dust, noise and bad smells of the city may be exchanged for the pure air, delightful shades and completely rural scenery. . . ."[31] When initial land sales were slow, Stevens decided to improve the Hudson River ferries and manufacture reasons for New Yorkers to take them. In 1821 he launched a fast, steam engine–powered ferry service to replace the old horse-driven boats. It ran back and forth to lower Manhattan every day until (not a misprint) 1967.

31. Winfield, Charles H. *Hopghan Hackingh*. New York: Caxton Press, 1895, p. 34

In 1824 Colonel Stevens proposed that the city of New York buy the future site of the Elysian Fields from him and use it as a public park. It was a typical Stevens idea—unconventional, intelligent, and decades ahead of its time. Two of his wealthy friends, John Jacob Astor and Dr. David Hosack, would finance the purchase. Hosack was the physician who had cared for Alexander Hamilton after he was fatally wounded in the famous duel with Burr. He was also a pioneer in the treatment and understanding of yellow fever, an early advocate of universal vaccination, and New York City's chief public health official. The city rejected Stevens's proposal, but he did not give up; in the end he made most of it happen himself. Until the creation of Central Park and for some time afterwards, the Stevens-owned Elysian Fields gave New Yorkers a pleasant escape from the city. Persistence is a Stevens family trait. By 1900 the Elysian Fields were long gone and there was no nature in Hoboken left to save, but in that year New York State and New Jersey created the Palisades Interstate Park Commission to preserve 2,500 acres of undeveloped woodland on the west side of the Hudson, six miles upriver from Hoboken. New Jersey's representative on the commission was Colonel Stevens's grandson, Edwin A. Stevens Jr.

IN THE 1820S Colonel Stevens's ferries let their passengers off in Hoboken on the same spot where the ferry docks today. Visitors would then walk up a short path to a hotel and bar at the corner of Washington and 1st Streets called the '76 House, the only remaining structure from the Bayard farm. Nearby was a wide green, extending to the river, where the Stevenses installed a progressively more exotic series of novel fun machines. The Elysian Fields became a laboratory for mass leisure, amusement, and recreation; this eventually included baseball and other organized sports. Stevens's first riverside attraction was a "circular railway" that ran on a loop. Built in 1825 to educate the public about new railroad technology, Colonel Stevens's other great passion, it was powered by a steam locomotive built by Stevens himself. He later converted the exhibit into a "pleasure railway" on which riders raced hand cars on parallel tracks. In 1829 he built a machine called a *montagne russe*, based on a ride that his son Richard Stevens had enjoyed at the Folie Beaujon pleasure garden while studying medicine in Paris. French for "Russian mountain," the *montagne russe* was a mechanical recreation of the undulating sled run that was built, using mounds of snow, for Russian Empress Catherine the Great at her palace near St. Petersburg. The Stevens version was America's first roller coaster. Over the years they added a merry–go–round, a bowling alley, a gallery of wax figures of famous people, a camera obscura (a round building that uses a lens to project an image of the surrounding landscape onto an interior wall), and a whirligig. A whirligig was a kind of turbocharged Ferris wheel that rotated riders through the air with "sickening velocity." One day the famous P.T. Barnum made the trip from Manhattan to take it for a spin. "It's a great invention," he said, "you go so far and so fast, and yet are so near home when you are done."

In 1829 Hoboken's permanent population reached 500. Two years later the Stevenses expanded and upgraded their pleasure grounds to raise the tone and appeal to the discriminating EUB. This is when they began using the name Elysian Fields, after the paradise of classical mythology where earthly heroes somehow spent a blissful eternity without whirligigs. The wooded section north of the Castle Point site of the Stevenses' Italianate villa was cleared and landscaped. The Stevenses carved out an old iron mine to create the Sybil's Cave, a fake grotto that functioned as a folly and refreshment stand. Here visitors strolling along the river walk stopped to buy water that supposedly came from a spring in the cave, and supposedly had health-giving properties. A wink to the waiter would bring you hard liquor instead. The cave was later accidentally sealed up by debris from the construction of the Pennsylvania Railroad and forgotten. In 2007 it was rediscovered and re-excavated. (You can go there today, but it is strictly BYOB.) 19th-century New Yorkers could also get a drink at a new restaurant and bar called the Colonnade Hotel, which had a portico with Doric columns and lovely river views. Colonnaded pavilions were a typical feature of pleasure gardens on both sides of the Atlantic. In the 1840s and early 1850s the Colonnade became known as "McCarty's" after its manager, Michael McCarty, and was a favorite hangout of baseball players. McCarty joined the Knickerbocker club and played in at least one of their games.

In 1832 writer Frances Trollope, English novelist Anthony Trollope's mother, published a description of the new and improved Elysian Fields: "[Colonel Stevens] has restricted his pleasure grounds to a few beautiful acres, laying out the remainder simply and tastefully as a public park. It is hardly possible to imagine one of greater attraction."[32] The landscape got top billing, but the Stevenses continued to provide entertainment as well. In 1833 they put on a stag hunt west of the Colonnade on Fox Hill, the future site of the cricket grounds. In 1834 they built the Beacon harness racing track on the same site. There were walking and running races, rowing competitions, ox roasts, concerts, boat races, and a cattle sale. P.T. Barnum picked up a herd of adolescent bison cheap and brought them to the Elysian Fields for what was advertised as a "buffalo hunt." A big crowd turned out, but things went wildly wrong. Spectators burst out laughing when they saw how small the bison were. The spooked

---

32. Philadelphia *National Gazette and Literary Register*, June 18, 1832, p.1

animals broke free and stampeded into the streets of Hoboken, killing one man and injuring several.

The Elysian Fields drew weekend day crowds of 20,000 and more. A newspaper wrote that it was now "the" popular resort for New Yorkers. In the 1830s a band of Native Americans, Penobscots from Maine, arrived. They stayed for a decade, staging "Indian dances" and canoe races for entertainment, and selling particularly fine handwoven baskets to tourists—which Penobscots still do. The Penobscots make a surprise appearance in the life story of Seaman Lichtenstein, a wholesale grocer and mainstay of the Gotham baseball club. Born in 1824 and orphaned at a young age, Lichtenstein lived by his wits, doing odd jobs. When he was 11 he found work in the Washington Market sweeping out butcher's stalls. (The butchers may have exposed him to baseball.) He was paid in meat trimmings, mostly beef and pork fat, which he took to Hoboken on the ferry and sold, according to his obituaries, to "Indians." Lichtenstein's customers were undoubtedly the Penobscots, whose cuisine, which featured wild game dishes and baked beans sweetened with maple syrup and cooked in a pot buried underground (this is the origin of Boston baked beans), required lots of added fat.

What were the Penobscots doing in New Jersey? Going back to the 1600s the tribe had enjoyed friendly relations with the Massachusetts Bay Colony and the Commonwealth of Massachusetts. The Penobscots were early converts to Christianity and fought on the American side in the Revolution. Massachusetts returned the favor by honoring, to an unusual extent, treaties that protected their land rights and their hunting and fishing grounds. This changed when Maine split from Massachusetts and became a state in 1820. After allowing whites to steal the Penobscots' traditional sources of food and much of their territory, the state of Maine fraudulently sold several of their villages in 1833. The Elysian Fields group may have been among the dispossessed. The Penobscots went to Hoboken for the same reason that a band of gypsies showed up there in 1851, to do business with the crowds of visitors the Elysian Fields attracted. Incidentally, Louis Sockalexis, the major leagues' first Native American ballplayer, was a Penobscot. He played in the late 1890s for the first Cleveland club to be nicknamed the Indians.

FROM THE 1830S through the 1850s the Elysian Fields were touted by tourist guidebooks as a "must see." Some American and international visitors who wrote about the Elysian Fields were slumming. The pretentious and educated tended to look at the Elysian Fields the way New Yorkers who summer in the Hamptons look at Jones Beach. Others were puritans who hated to see people having a good time. Visiting from Boston in 1842, the pious Samuel Ward admitted that the Elysian Fields was "truly a lovely spot" before saying (you can almost hear him sniff), "There were a great many people here, male and female, but in my opinion few respectable ones."[33] In New York City, Ward had to be dragged kicking and screaming to the theater, which he considered morally perilous. In 1851 the *Christian Advocate* complained that "Sabbath breaking [here] is practiced beyond a parallel.... Twenty thousand persons have crossed the ferries on a single Sabbath." The *Advocate* blamed Catholic immigrants and their permissive European ideas on how to spend a Sunday. Even worse, the Elysian Fields was a known spot for lovers to meet for a little whirligig and chill. "A little walk," one visitor wrote, "meanders through a shady grove, and has received the deserved appellation of 'lovers' path'.... Leaving aside the realms of Cupid...." Finding a place for non-connubial sex could be tricky in

33. *The New-York Historical Society Quarterly Bulletin*, Vol. XXI No.4, October 1937, p. 114

early 19th-century American cities; some restaurants advertised "private dining rooms for gentlemen and their guests" with discreet side entrances, but that kind of privacy was costly.

Some came to slum and had fun despite themselves. The oh-so-refined Mrs. Trollope disliked almost everything about America (you didn't want to get her started about tobacco chewing and spitting), but she called the Elysian Fields "a little Eden" during her visit in the early 1830s. "It is true," she writes, "that at Hoboken, as everywhere else, there are *reposoires* [sic], which as you pass them, blast the senses for a moment, by reeking forth the fumes of whiskey and tobacco, and it may be that these cannot be entered with a wife or daughter. The proprietor of the grounds, however, has contrived to render these abominations not unpleasing to the eye; there is one, in particular, which has quite the air of a Grecian temple, and did they drink wine instead of whiskey, it might be ascribed to Bacchus; but in this particular, as in many others, the ancient and modern Republics differ."[34] (She is referring to the future baseball players' hangout, the Colonnade.)

In 1843 popular magazine writer and aesthete Nathaniel Parker Willis spent "a very amusing afternoon" with 10,000 of his fellow New Yorkers at the Elysian Fields. His high-society girlfriend was less amused, perhaps because of the cheap thrill Willis got from meeting a Native American girl who was not wearing a corset or any other underwear.[35] "The first object of attraction on landing was an encampment of Penobscot Indians. . . . A very pretty and very rosy squaw of sixteen honored the grass with her pressure in one of the tents. . . . The aboriginal beauty was dressed in a fashionably made calico gown, presented to her probably by some visitor or neighbor, but as she wore it strictly *au naturel*,

34. Philadelphia *National Gazette and Literary Register*, June 18, 1832, p.1
35. Newark, NJ *Centinel of Freedom*, July 11, 1843, p. 3

allowing it 'to rise and fall as nature not cotton pleases,' she had, I must say, a most unfurnished air." Willis declared the Elysian Fields to be "the finest public pleasure ground in the world.... In the neighborhood of the Pavilion [another name for the Colonnade], on the open lawn, jugglers and rope dancers were performing in their spangled dresses; the great proportion of the crowd scattered through the sun-flecked fields and groves, as far as the eye could see, were dressed on gay colors or in white.... I was quite enchanted by the whole spectacle, but for my superfine companion who *would not* permit me to ride round on the flying horses, nor swing in the great yellow gondola, nor eat oysters at the 'crib,' nor speak to the Penobscot squaw.... I am rather surprised, by the way, that the patent-leather class of our country do not frequent these charming resorts. If it were only as a variety after their 'velvet friends,' I should think they would like an occasional Saturnalia, as indeed, in all other countries, gentlemen do." Saturnalia was an ancient Roman holiday, a celebration of social slumming, on which masters switched places with their servants.

ENTERTAINMENT, SPORTS AND other leisure activities may promise escape from reality, but they did not entirely deliver in the 19th century, any more than they do today. New Yorkers came to the Elysian Fields to escape the dark side of the city—crime, disorder, and disease—but they could not escape the darkness that was inside them. American cities of the time had almost no social safety net, no public health system, and no effective mental health treatments. Alcohol was cheap, unregulated (until the late 1850s), and available everywhere. So were opiate drugs like laudanum and morphine. The suicide rate in the United States climbed throughout the 19th century. The Elysian Fields became a popular suicide spot at about the same time that it became a popular resort.

In 1834 a young man with gambling debts that he could not pay crossed the Hudson from Manhattan, swallowed a vial of morphine, uttered the words "happy nonentity," and drowned himself in the river. In 1835 S.H. Dyer, a music composer and apparently a relative of the Dyer who managed the Colonnade, hanged himself there, despondent over the death of his wife and child. In 1843 a newspaper wrote that the "suicide business has commenced for the season over at Hoboken," referring to two recent deaths at the Sybil's Cave and several others that had happened earlier. In 1852 Michael McCarty, the Knickerbocker baseball club member who took over as manager of the Colonnade from Dyer in 1841, died while bird shooting. The newspapers said that he had picked up a loaded shotgun by the business end and accidentally shot himself through the heart, but it is hard to imagine a hunter doing that, even a drunk one. In that time suicides, especially by people with influence or friends in the press, were commonly reported as hunting or gun-cleaning accidents in order to protect victims' families from shame, as well as to allow a full Christian burial. The newspapers reported numerous Elysian Fields suicides in the 1860s, 1870s, and 1880s. In 1884, the *Jersey Journal* wrote, "The bodies of suicides found dangling from the trees and those washed ashore during the past three decades would give the [Elysian] Fields a startling record as a morgue, as during that period more than 300 corpses were found in that locality." That may be an exaggeration. It may not.

The most sensational Elysian Fields death of them all took place in 1841. The body of Mary Rogers, a 21-year-old salesgirl in a Manhattan tobacco shop, was found floating in the river near Sybil's Cave. Rogers was already a celebrity because of her spellbinding beauty—non-smokers lined up to buy cigars just to stare at her—and because she had been on the front pages before. Three years earlier she had gone missing from home, raising a stir and newspaper circulation figures. She returned a day or two later without explanation. The police wrote off that disappearance as a publicity stunt by her employer, but this time they had a body. It looked like murder, but several months later, they had not identified suspects or a motive. The police were not even sure about the crime scene. Rogers's body may have been dumped at the Elysian Fields or it may have floated there from somewhere else. It was rumored that Mary Rogers, who was engaged to a respectable young man, had been seen crossing the river with a mysterious older lover who sounded suspiciously like the mustachioed military officer who seduced and abandoned virgins in contemporary melodrama. Another rumor claimed that Rogers had died during an abortion and that her body had been mutilated to delay identification (which it did) and throw the police off track.

To make things more confusing, Rogers's fiancé killed himself near where her body had been found, leaving a suicide note that expressed guilt but didn't say exactly for what. The case fascinated Edgar Allan Poe, who less than a year earlier had published *The Murders in the Rue Morgue*, the first detective story ever published. His 1842 sequel, *The Mystery of Marie Roget*, transfers the Mary Rogers story to Paris, where Chevalier Auguste Dupin, the cerebral fictional detective who inspired the creation of Sherlock Holmes, investigates the case. Dupin ruled out both a gang attack and the theory that the fiancé was the killer. Poe's short story leaves the murder unsolved, but it is interesting to say the least that it omits any mention of abortion, a subject which may well have been beyond the pale for Poe's publisher. One of the reasons that the abortion business flourished in Poe's time was that while it was disapproved of, the subject was so taboo as to be virtually undiscussable in a public forum. Neither Chevalier Dupin nor the real police ever figured out what really happened to Mary Rogers. But perhaps Poe did.

LIKE OTHER PUBLIC SPACES, the Elysian Fields had their share of isolated robberies, brawls, rapes, and prostitution arrests, but they also became the site of broader ethnic, religious, and racial conflict. In the 1850s large numbers of German and French immigrants moved to the growing city of Hoboken. The Elysian Fields opened the Otto Cottage, a beer hall catering to Germans, but not everyone was as welcoming. "The place is half-Germanized already," complained the New York *Evening Post* in 1851. "The amusements witnessed in the Elysian Fields are from the Rhine and the Danube—men and women dance on the turf or under the trees to the sound of the hand-organ or fiddle."[36] An influx of lager-drinking musical Germans accompanied by women and children may not sound menacing, but 1850s America was gripped by a fear of immigrants, particularly Catholics. Most contemporary German immigrants were Catholic, as were nearly all of the Irish potato famine refugees who came in the late 1840s and early 1850s. Many of the Irish and virtually all of the Germans stepped off the boat unable to speak English. Protestant native-born Americans worried that the Irish and Germans, accustomed to following orders from princes, kings, and popes, would not be able to carry out or even comprehend the responsibilities of free citizens in America's fragile young democracy.

Today nativism is synonymous with bigotry. Bigotry certainly fed 19th-century American nativism, but there were also more legitimate contributors, such as frustration with the effects of unregulated immigration. Until the late 19th century the U.S. had some restrictions on who could be naturalized, but none at all on how many immigrants could enter the country. In 1840 the population of New York City was a bit over 300,000. Between 1847

---

36. New York *Evening Post,* July 31, 1851, p. 2

and 1851, 1.8 million immigrants arrived in New York harbor.[37] As a proportion of the total population this would be the equivalent today of one million desperately poor refugees landing at JFK airport every month, *for four years*. The immigrants' sheer numbers challenged America's institutions, infrastructure, and identity. A political backlash came in the mid-1850s, when the nativist Know-Nothing movement sprang up, its chief goals being to stop future immigration and to prevent or delay the naturalization of existing immigrants. The vast majority of Amateur Era baseball players were born in the United States; virtually none were adult immigrants. Many were nativist in politics. There was also a non-political response. In New York, Philadelphia, and other cities, gangs of nativist thugs, including young men called "short boys," terrorized immigrants, vandalized Catholic churches, and broke up ethnic parades and celebrations.

On May 6, 1851 thousands of Germans came to the Fox Hill cricket grounds in Hoboken to celebrate *Maifest*, a celebration of spring centered on the *maibaum*, a kind of maypole, and, of course, free-flowing beer. Among them were turners, members of turnvereins, or German gymnastics clubs. A gang of short boys came over on the ferry from Manhattan to make trouble. A fight broke out. The physically fit turners quickly organized themselves into an effective fighting force; the short boys retreated but were soon backed up by local reinforcements. A massive riot spilled into the Elysian Fields proper and the streets of Hoboken. Heads were cracked, windows were broken, and Michael McCarty had to defend his family and the Colonnade by firing shotgun blasts into an angry mob. There were several deaths and hundreds of injuries. Sixty Germans were arrested. Murder charges were brought, but the Germans were

---

37. Glazer, Ira and Tepper, Michael, *The Famine Immigrants*. Baltimore: Commercial Pub. Co., 1983 and 1984

A favorite watering hole of baseball players, the Elysian Fields' Colonnade hotel exemplified the contradictions of race relations in mid-19th-century New York. Its customers excluded African Americans from their baseball clubs and enjoyed blackface minstrel shows at the Colonnade, but when the management replaced the hotel's beloved African American waiters with white men, so many customers protested that they were rehired.

acquitted on the grounds that they were defending themselves and their families. The judge in the case, however, lectured the defendants with words that echo nativist ideology. "[No one] can deny that they had many wrong causes of provocation that day; nevertheless they should remember that genuine gallantry is not at all inconsistent with moderation and mercy, and that in the absence of the latter the former spirit may easily degenerate into an exclusiveness wholly opposed to Republicanism."[38] The Knickerbockers were playing baseball on the day of the riot. Their scorebook notes that in the fourth inning the game was "broke up by the Dutch fight."

About a year later, another hate crime occurred at the Elysian Fields, but this one was all American. After Michael McCarty

---

38. *New-York Tribune*, May 31, 1851, p. 5

died in early May 1852, his widow took over as manager of the Colonnade. One of the attractions of the Colonnade was its corps of veteran African American waiters. At that time many professions were closed to African Americans; among the exceptions were barbers, cooks, and waiters. White immigrants also faced job discrimination; some organized to take these jobs away from African Americans. A few months after her husband's death in 1852 Mrs. McCarty was pressured to fire her waiters and replace them with Irishmen. When the Colonnade's regular customers protested, she fired the new waiters and rehired the African Americans. A few days later, the re-unemployed Irish waiters returned to the Elysian Fields in an ugly mood. Twenty of them attacked four African Americans who were on their way to the Sybil's Cave. One stabbed a 24-year-old waiter named Charles Williams in the chest; Williams cried, "Oh God, I am a dead man," and collapsed. The murderer was caught and convicted.

This episode is a cautionary tale about the complexity of racial and ethnic relations in mid-19th-century America. The Colonnade manager who had hired the African American waiters in the first place, Michael McCarty, also booked white actors who performed in blackface. Even in its time, this was considered a particularly low-brow kind of entertainment. "Mr. McCarty begs leave," runs an ad from 1845 "to announce ... THE ETHIOPIAN OPERATIC BROTHERS AND SISTERS ... Billy Whitlock, the great Locomotive Nigger and accomplished banjo player. OLD DAN EMMETT, the celebrated Violinist and Old Virginny Nigger ... "[39] and so on. Emmett and Whitlock, both white, were two of the Virginia Minstrels, the group that invented the genre of the blackface minstrel show in New York City in 1843. There are few Americans today who cannot whistle

---

39. New York *Daily Herald*, September 6, 1845, p. 3

the Northern-born Emmett's hit song "Dixie," which was both the unofficial anthem of the pro-slavery Confederacy and the favorite song of Abraham Lincoln, the man who ended slavery. It is possible that some of the New Yorkers who watched the minstrel show in 1845 were among those who demanded that Mrs. McCarty bring back their favorite African American waiter in 1852. Some of them may have been baseball players. Many Amateur Era baseball players were Abolitionists and hundreds, if not thousands, of them risked or lost their lives to defeat the slave-owning Confederacy in the Civil War, yet not one of their baseball clubs was integrated. Irish immigrants of the time are routinely stereotyped as racists, even by serious historians, but in New York City in 1853—a year after the murder of Charles Williams—African American and Irish American waiters joined together to strike for higher wages. They won.

AT THE END of the Civil War the Elysian Fields began to lose space, prestige, and the patronage of the EUB. Sports clubs disbanded or departed. In 1865 the St. George Cricket Club abandoned its grounds on adjacent Fox Hill. The cricketers hoped to find playing space in Manhattan's new Central Park; the National Association of Base Ball Players tried to negotiate the same thing for America's new national pastime. "This," wrote the *New York Clipper* in April 1869, "is probably the last season of the once famous Elysian Fields as a place of resort for our metropolitan ball clubs."[40] Encroached on by the shoreline railroad tracks laid down by the Pennsylvania Railroad, the New York Yacht Club relocated to Rosebank on Staten Island in 1868. (In 1903 the yachtsmen accepted the railroad's offer to return their original clubhouse, on the condition that they move

---

40. *New York Clipper*, April 24, 1869

it somewhere else; it stands today in Newport, Rhode Island.) In the mid-1890s the Colonnade hotel was knocked down and the baseball fields gave way to piers, warehouses, and more railroad tracks. Newspapers ran obituaries for the Elysian Fields pleasure grounds, which died in its early 70s of unnatural causes. One cause was the opening of Central Park; another was New York's expansion into upper Manhattan, which made Hoboken too long a trip for most New Yorkers. More importantly perhaps, the Elysian Fields were no longer needed to help the Stevens family sell Hoboken real estate. "Hoboken was divine," reminisced the New Orleans *Times–Picayune* in 1889, "for had it not the Elysian Fields stretching away in a vista of idyllic loveliness? . . . From the moment a land and improvement company began to despoil the Elysian Fields the age of unrest set in."[41]

But it was not only the Elysian Fields that closed at around this time; pleasure grounds in general were going extinct. The reason was changing ideas of what an urban public park should be, particularly among the EUB, the class that made the decisions about urban planning and the design of places like Central Park. James Wenman, an important member of the Knickerbocker baseball club, was a city parks official and a Central Park Commissioner. (He was instrumental in bringing Cleopatra's Needle to the park.) Ironically enough, his Central Park Commission voted down allowing cricket or baseball grounds in the park. Sports, entertainment, and whole other categories of fun were judged incompatible with the idealized un-nature of Olmsted and Vaux's park design. "All were welcome, regardless of rank or wealth," the architects of the park said, to stroll and drive expensive carriages—but not to play baseball, throw a group picnic, or barbecue. Adults wanting to play team

---

41. New Orleans *Times–Picayune*, October 13, 1889, p. 7

sports in Central Park would have to wait for the Great Depression of the 1930s, when parks commissioner Robert Moses laid out the park's first baseball and softball diamonds (and the Parks Department moved the descendants of Olmsted and Vaux's sheep out of the Sheep Meadow out of fear that hungry New Yorkers would eat them).

IT IS HARD for us today to make sense of the ratatouille of different uses that the Elysian Fields were put to in their prime. What were baseball, cricket, theater, music, amusement rides, bars, restaurants, fake Roman ruins, stag hunts, and landscaped walkways all doing in the same place? Not to mention riots, Native American dances, sex, murder, and minstrel shows? It wasn't simple lack of space that brought all of these together; pleasure grounds existed as far back as the 18th century, when cities were smaller and less dense. Tellingly, almost the same mix is found in contemporary sporting weeklies like the *New York Clipper* and the different incarnations of the *Spirit of the Times*. The Elysian Fields, Harlem's Red House, and other pleasure grounds hosted baseball, cricket, horseracing, pigeon shooting, yachting, competitive walking, boxing, and militia and target company outings. All of these were extensively covered in the sporting weeklies.

Pleasure Grounds hosted theatrical productions and spectacles, ethnic celebrations like the *Maifest*, panoramas of famous places like Niagara Falls, technological wonders, and exhibitions of exotic and agricultural animals. These, too, routinely appeared in the pages of papers like the *New York Clipper*. There were episodes of ethnic and racial conflict, as well as racist entertainment. The sporting weeklies catered to racism and bigotry; they covered blackface minstrel shows in depth and included racist jokes told in mock African American dialect, along with ethnic humor featuring the whole gallery of 19th-century American stereotypes: thick-headed Germans, violent Irishmen, hard-bargaining Jews, devious Yankee traders, and penny-pinching Scots. Places like the Red House and the Elysian Fields offered secluded places for lovers to stroll, picnic, and have sex. They were also the scene of sexual crimes like prostitution and rape. The weeklies provided their male readers with notices of "model artists' exhibitions" (a quasi-porn show), sexually suggestive serialized fiction, and dirty jokes. Their back pages sold sex manuals and advertised remedies for male wet dreams, sexual impotence, and venereal disease.

In the early 19th-century leisure was a rarer and more valuable commodity than it is today. It occupied a narrower cultural space. Leisure was a specifically urban phenomenon and less than 10 percent of the U.S. population lived in cities—more than a third of those in only two cities, New York and Philadelphia. Pleasure grounds aimed their attractions at the small minority of American men who had the money, time, and inclination for leisure activities. The sporting weeklies offered the same thing to the same demographic, but in black and white and in two dimensions. Both changed in the 1860s and 1870s, when leisure in America started to become democratized by the growing size and wealth of the middle class. The passion for rationalizing, reforming, and organizing that characterized the EUB and its descendants set in motion a great sorting out. The sporting weeklies folded or narrowed their focus to theater or particular sports like boxing, baseball, or horseracing. The pleasure gardens did not vanish as much as literally disintegrate. Their component parts live on today in dedicated public places that none of us would think to put in the same place or category. The Elysian Fields, the Red House, and the other pleasure grounds and gardens were the anteced-

An 1866 championship game at Philadelphia between the Athletics and the Brooklyn Atlantics. A comparison of this illustration to that of an early match at the Elysian Fields on page 14 tells the story of amateur baseball's rapid journey from participant sport to entertainment business. A big game in 1856 attracted no more than a few dozen gamblers and friends of the players; in 1866 there are stands holding thousands of paying spectators, including one reserved for women. There are journalists, star players whose names we are expected to recognize, bookmakers, food vendors, a pickpocket and fans keeping score.

ents of amusement parks like Coney Island, which appeared in the 1880s as the pleasure grounds were on the way out; faux-wild landscaped urban parks like Central and Prospect Parks; theme parks like Disneyland; indoor sports arenas like Madison Square Garden—and that city baseball park where you saw your first major league game.

THE SPORTS HEYDAY of the Elysian Fields was the two decades between the mid-1840s and the mid-1860s. After Colonel John Stevens died in 1839, his heirs, John C. and his brothers, began to provide dedicated space for team sports. It was in 1844 that the New York Cricket Club was founded there. In 1859 an eleven made up of some of the best cricketers in England made a North American tour, hoping to promote the sport to Americans. The highlight was an October match at the Elysian Fields against a side made up mostly of New Yorkers. The three-game event drew an estimated 25,000 total (non-paying) spectators, but the English thrashed the Americans so badly that cricket supporters worried that it had actually set back the cause in America. It probably did. Baseball-playing members of the EUB arrived in 1845, when John C. Stevens or some other clairvoyant arranged a New York versus Brooklyn baseball series. The games did not generate a lot of public interest, but only because this was an idea that was ahead of its time. The Knickerbockers relocated to Hoboken in 1845 and never left.

As more New York City baseball clubs moved across the river in search of playing space, the Elysian Fields expanded to two and then three baseball diamonds. The Knickerbockers, Gothams, Eagles, Empires, Mutuals, Actives, and others took turns practicing (usually two times a week after work) and playing games there. Their presence, side-by-side with cricket grounds, sent a message. Here was a native alternative to the English sport of cricket; the people playing it were respectable New Yorkers, men of substance. The baseball diamonds advertised baseball in the same way that Colonel Stevens's circular railway advertised the railroad. The message was received. Both Henry Chadwick and John Suydam, cofounder of Brooklyn's Excelsiors, for example, had their come-to-baseball moments at the Elysian Fields. Harry Wright spent the summer and fall of 1857 walking past Knickerbockers games on his way to the St. George cricket grounds. One day he decided to join in. There were certainly others. In 1855 a newspaper noted that the Elysian Fields were now "surrounded by great crowds of the 'fancy' [i.e., gamblers], attracted by matches of baseball and cricket." Until around 1858, when the Brooklyn clubs caught up with the Knickerbockers and other elite New York clubs, Hoboken was the center of the baseball world. The Elysian Fields were a showcase where baseball, its elite clubs, and their EUB members were on public display.

The Elysian Fields clubs played against each other a little more frequently in the mid-1850s and there were stirrings of interclub rivalry. But baseball changed surprisingly little between 1845 and 1855. It survived, but in a kind of suspended animation; the players played, but few new clubs were formed and almost no one watched or wrote about it. There were changing rooms for the baseball players behind the Colonnade, but there were no stands or facilities for spectators in the 1840s or 1850s. The Mutuals, a top New York club that had renovated one of the Elysian Fields diamonds in 1865, adding stands to accommodate spectators, left Hoboken in 1868. They went to Brooklyn, where the fans were and where the money was. Brooklyn's Union Grounds was the first ballpark to regularly charge admission and the clubs that played there took a cut. The old Elysian Fields quartet of the Knickerbockers, Gothams,

Eagles, and Empires stayed in Hoboken into the 1870s, but in a coma of competitive irrelevance. "Thus the old Knickerbocker Club, once so powerful and for those days, so skillful, where are they now?" asked the *Clipper* in 1869. "So with the Gothams, Empire and Eagle clubs, they too have sunk down to a lower grade...."

Next to but not part of the Elysian Fields, the Fox Hill cricket grounds outlasted the Elysian Fields as a sports venue. In 1887 and 1888 the Cuban Giants, an African American baseball club run by the brilliant Stanislaus Kostka Govern, an immigrant from St. Croix in the Danish (now U.S.) Virgin Islands, played some of their home games there. In 1888 the Cuban Giants won the opening game of the "colored championship of the world" on the cricket grounds, which by then had wooden stands. This game must have sold a lot of tickets, because in 1901 the major league New York Giants played a game at Fox Hill that provoked an intra-monopoly dispute with the Brooklyn Dodgers over the territorial rights to Hoboken. Used in the 1890s and 1900s for college football, today much of the old St. George cricket grounds is still open space. It is the site of a city park, Columbus Park, and Hoboken High School's sports field, John F. Kennedy Stadium.

A striking thing about the accounts by visitors to the Elysian Fields from the 1840s and 1850s is how many of them do not mention baseball. Whatever interclub rivalries did develop in the Elysian Fields did not lead to the next evolutionary steps— the first fans, the first ticket sales, or the first for-profit baseball park. All of these happened later and elsewhere. Why? Spectators become fans because they identify with a team that represents their city, neighborhood, or community. The Elysian Fields clubs played in one city and lived in another; they represented only themselves. And the landlords of the Elysian Fields, the Stevenses, had no interest in making money from baseball. Like almost everything else on the menu at the Elysian Fields, baseball and other sports were a loss leader intended to bring people to Hoboken. As much as they helped and supported the cause of American sports, ultimately the Stevenses were in the real estate business and the transportation business, not the entertainment business. Baseball's next big leap forward would happen in another city on a different river, reached by a different ferry—Brooklyn.

Nativism fed both the rise of baseball and a political movement, whose supporters flew flags like this one. The slogan "twenty-one years" on the ballot box beneath the American eagle refers to a nativist proposal to deny the vote to immigrants until their 21st year of residency in the United States.

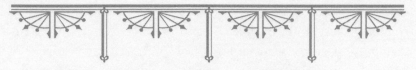

CHAPTER FOUR
What Makes a River

 SPORTS MOVEMENT ran through 19th-century America like a great river. As it ran, it adapted itself, in the words of historian Foster Rhea Dulles, to "the nature of the country through which it flows, the main stream continually augmented by tributaries, and the river-bed itself ever growing broader and deeper."[42] Gaining momentum over many decades, this movement gave us baseball. As far back as the 1820s, a loose coalition, including at different times and in varying combinations physicians, journalists, ministers, entrepreneurs, and visionaries, advocated adult exercise. Advocacy, however, was not enough. What was needed was a sport that would persuade a wide cross-section of Americans to take better care of their bodies.

The movement tried boxing, then gymnastics, and then cricket. Boxing won the most popularity of the three, but it was chiefly a spectator sport and it was too violent and too cozy with gambling for the Protestant EUB. Not a fan, *New-York Tribune* editor Horace Greeley called boxing the sport of "the grog shops and brothels and low gaming Hells." Gymnastics

---

42. Dulles, Foster R. *America Learns to Play*. New York: D. Appleton-Century Co. 1940, p. vii

were too physically demanding and required an indoor facility with elaborate equipment. As a team bat-and-ball sport that was played in sunlight and open air, cricket was a promising candidate. Cricket also had a developmental head start over baseball; in the 1850s cricket was a maturing international sport when baseball was one of many regional bat-and-ball games. But cricket, boxing, and gymnastics had the same ultimately disqualifying drawback. They were imported from Europe and popularly associated with England, the country that had fought one bitter war to deny Americans their freedom and humiliated them by burning down the White House in another. Remember that when taken down to their essence, both of baseball's made-up origin stories, the Doubleday myth and the Knickerbockers tale, are appeals to American exceptionalism. Their main point is that baseball, like *Hiawatha*, the Constitution, and cornbread, is wholesome, purely American, and uncorrupted by foreignness.

The sports movement and baseball found each other in the 1850s. Why baseball and not one of America's other bat-and-ball games is an interesting question. Historians often answer that the influential New York–based sports weeklies were biased toward baseball. After a certain point, they probably were, but that did not stop them from giving extensive coverage to the Massachusetts game and Philadelphia's town ball, as well as cricket and more obscure local bat-and-ball games like wicket and *les quatres*. The weeklies depended on their readers around the country for scores and game accounts, and the weeklies routinely printed what they were sent. Some turn to the rules or other intrinsic qualities of the game to explain why baseball ultimately defeated cricket or why the New York version of the game won out over the others. But these are ripples on the surface. There is no reason to think that the New York game of baseball was inherently better to play than other bat-and-ball games. And rules are nothing more than rules. Does anyone really think that baseball history would have followed a different course if a baseball convention had voted for seven-inning games (which it nearly did), five-ball walks, or fast overhand pitching (which was how they played in Boston)?

The secret of baseball's success was extrinsic: who played it. In 1790 New York, with 33,000 people, was the largest city in the United States, but not by much. Philadelphia was second at 28,500—actually number one if you count urban districts outside the city limits. Boston was third at 18,000. By 1820 New York was first in population with 124,000; Philadelphia narrowly edged out Baltimore for second, 64,000 to 63,000; Boston was fourth. By 1840 New York's population of 313,000 was more than three times that of the next-largest city, Baltimore. In 1860 New York had grown to 814,000; Philadelphia was a distant second at 566,000, even after consolidating with the Northern Liberties, Southwark, and Spring Garden. Brooklyn was third at 267,000, but coming up fast. The swelling size, wealth, and influence of metropolitan New York, baseball's home, themselves formed a powerful tributary.

Why did the baseball-playing cities of New York and Brooklyn grow so much faster for so much longer than other American cities? The answer is an alloy of geography, culture, and history. New York's harbor is much larger than those of Boston and Philadelphia; it is one of the largest natural harbors in the world. Even though it is south of one and north of the other, New York's harbor is the only one that never (well, hardly ever) freezes in winter. Boston is colder and Philadelphia's port, located 61 miles from the ocean on the Delaware River, freezes at higher temperatures because of its shallowness and low salinity. The advantage of 12-month port access is obvious in a time when goods and people moved mostly by ship. New York and Brooklyn are also located near the easily navigable Hudson River, a resource that New York State maximized in 1825 by opening the Erie Canal, which connected the port of New York to western New York, the Great Lakes, Canada, and the upper Midwest. The Erie Canal is where New York's geographical and cultural advantages met. The canal was made possible by a receding glacier that during the last Ice Age carved out the Mohawk Valley, the widest gap in the 1500-mile-long Appalachian mountain range. Thanks to more than a million years of erosion, the 363-mile-long Erie Canal has to lift its traffic only 565 feet. Except for this gap, the Appalachians stretch from Alabama to Maine, walling off Boston, Baltimore, and Philadelphia from the upper Midwest, where more and more of the economic action was in mid- and late 19th-century America. But gap or no gap, the Erie Canal would never have happened without the outrageous ambition of the Empire State's leaders.

In 1825 the longest canal on the planet was the Grand Canal, built by generations of Chinese emperors between the 5th and 17th centuries. The second longest, the Erie Canal, was built in eight years *by the state of New York*. Even today it is the longest canal in the Americas and the sixth-largest anywhere. Fed by trade with the Midwest, greater New York City added roads, bridges, and railroads, creating a massive transportation hub that pulled in trade, immigration, and manufacturing. After a long chase, in the 1920s New York passed London as the world's largest city outside of Asia. Since then New York has seen times of decline, decay, and disaster but it has handled them and bounced back. New York and Los Angeles are the only American cities in the top 10 in population in 1930 that are larger today.

Historians have argued that New York's mercantile heritage and its ethnic, cultural, and religious diversity gave it a further economic advantage. Perhaps they did. Both Boston and Phila-delphia were founded by religious refugees; religious communi-ties, especially those formed by persecution, are naturally less open to people and ideas from the outside. This is truer of Bos-ton than of Philadelphia, but New York was the outlier. It was born as a Dutch fur-trading station and originally ruled by a corporation, not by a king. Then called New Amsterdam, the city had an official seal that featured the North American bea-ver, the animal that gave its waterproof pelts by the millions to cover the heads of Europe. In the 1840s beaver hats went out of fashion, but making money remained the city's reason for being. New York was about trade, not about constructing a city upon a hill or expanding its territory through settlement. Yet New York is where most immigrants to America went.

Trade favors diversity. In 1638 New Amsterdam's 500 inhabit-ants famously spoke a combined 18 languages.[43] It was the site of America's first Jewish congregation, Shearith Israel, founded in 1654 by Spanish and Portuguese refugees and still going strong. The result was that New York—more open to outsiders, more materialistic, and more pragmatic—accumulated a deep reser-voir of commercial and financial savvy. As economist Edward Glaeser put it, "New York's remarkable survival is a result of its dominance in the fields of finance, business services, and corpo-rate management."[44] Perversely, New York also made a virtue of its lack of space. "The success of finance and business services on the island of Manhattan," Glaeser writes, "hinges critically on the advantage that the island has in bringing people together and speeding the flow of knowledge." In other words New York

43. Shorto, Russell. *The Island at the Center of the World*. New York: Vintage Books 2005, p. 107
44. Glaeser, Edward. *Urban Colossus: Why is New York America's Largest City?* FRBNY Economic Policy Review December 2005, p. 7

owes its wealth and its unusual ability to adapt to fires, wars, economic downturns, and technological change to its advantageous location on an island densely packed with smart, resourceful, and ambitious people. The better we get to know the people who played it, the less surprising it becomes that New York's game succeeded.

WE COULD HAVE chosen cricket as our national sport. The idea sounds absurd today. Present-day Americans are surprised to learn that baseball players in pre–Civil War America also played cricket. Richard F. Stevens, Harry Wright, George Wright, James Creighton, and other Amateur Era baseball players moved easily back and forth between the two sports. But social and historical tides pulled them toward baseball. Baseball emerged in a time of great ambition and expectation. America in the 1840s and 1850s was a game underdog that had gone 1–0–1 in wars against the world's greatest military. Americans were convinced of their own exceptionalism and eager to spread their egalitarian and democratic ideas throughout the world. No idea was too new or too radical to be contemplated. In 1837 journalist John L. O'Sullivan wrote: "All history is to be re-written; political science and the whole scope of all moral truth have to be considered and illustrated in the light of the democratic principle."[45] O'Sullivan coined the phrase "manifest destiny," the slogan of the Young America movement, which advocated American expansionism, radical social reform, and support for democratic and anti-aristocratic movements at home and abroad. These were national movements, but New Yorkers were often on the front line. Pre–Civil War New York had what amounted to its own foreign policy. Often in defiance of the Federal Government, New York

45. *United States Magazine and Democratic Review*, Washington, D.C.: Langtree and O'Sullivan, 1838, Vol. 1 No. 1, p.14

volunteers fought for the independence of Texas, helped annex parts of Mexico, and invaded Nicaragua under William Walker. During the Dorr Rebellion in 1842, New York politician Mike Walsh sent armed militiamen to Rhode Island to support fellow workingmen who were fighting for their right to participate in the government of their own state. As the country stumbled and blundered toward civil war in the 1850s, New York City's political leadership was so uninterested in fighting the South, an important trade partner, that Mayor Fernando Wood threatened to pull Manhattan, parts of Long Island, and Staten Island out of the Union and form an independent country called the Free City of Tri-Insula. Maybe the problem was the name.

The monied upper classes of New York and other eastern cities suffered from congenital Anglophilia, but not the trendsetting EUB. To most native-born Americans, anything that smacked of old Europe, from hereditary aristocracy to Catholicism to English stage actors, was suspect. At least eight pre–Civil War clubs were named Young America. The Young America movement's ideas colored the writings of poet Walt Whitman and fed the rise of baseball at the expense of cricket. Baseball fit well with Whitman's themes of celebrating American originality and promoting physicality, fraternity and health. His words from 1888, "Baseball is our game, the American game: I connect it with our national character,"[46] are often quoted without appreciating that Whitman had played a part in *making* baseball the American game. As a journalist he championed the sport as far back as the mid-1840s, before anyone dreamed that it might become a national institution. According to William F. Ladd, a founding member of the Knickerbockers, "the reason [we] chose the game of base-

---

46. Whitman, Walt quoted (1888) in Traubel, Horace. *With Walt Whitman in Camden*, vol. 2, New York: Mitchell, Kennerley, 1915, p. 330

ball instead of—and in fact in opposition to—cricket was because [we] regarded baseball as a purely American game; and it appears that there was at that time considerable prejudice against adopting any game of foreign invention."[47]

Its deep-seated anti-Englishness is one of the greatest differences between 19th-century America and the *Downton Abbey*–besotted nation that we live in today. In 1842, the English novelist Charles Dickens wrote *American Notes for General Circulation*, a travelogue about his visit to the United States. This was not an original idea. Books like Dickens's and Frances Trollope's sold well on both sides of the Atlantic. The English were curious about their dynamic former colony; and no matter how much they resented the English, Americans never tired of hearing what the English thought of them. In the book Dickens tells of walking through lower Manhattan and encountering something odd. "You wonder," Dickens deadpans, "what may be the use of this tall flagstaff in the by-street, with something like Liberty's head-dress on its top: so do I. But there is a passion for tall flagstaffs hereabout, and you may see its twin brother in five minutes, if you have a mind."[48] As Dickens knew perfectly well, these were Liberty Poles, totems of the Sons of Liberty, kept standing sixty years after the last shot of the Revolution had been fired. Into the early 1900s Boston and New York City were still putting on grand military parades on "Evacuation Day" to celebrate the final departure of occupying British troops. Philadelphia, the city that wore its occupation by the British Army most easily, never had an Evacuation Day of its own. Not coincidentally, Philadelphia is where cricket sank its deep-

47. Ladd, William F. quoted by John M. Ward in *Spalding's Official Baseball Guide*, New York: American Sports Pub., 1907, p.44
48. Dickens, Charles. *American Notes for General Circulation*, London: Chapman and Hall, 1842, p. 198

est American roots. Cricket maintained its popularity there into the 20th century. The cricket club of Haverford College in the Philadelphia suburbs was founded in 1833 and is still breaking for tea today, although most of its current players are from India, Pakistan, and Bangladesh.

In most parts of the United States the hard feelings left over from the Revolutionary War and the War of 1812 lingered well into baseball's Amateur Era. In New York in 1849 a feud between fans of the leading English Shakespearean of the day and an American rival got 30 people killed. There was already bad blood between the English actor William Macready and the American actor Edwin Forrest when in May 1849 they found themselves playing the same part on the same night in the same city. By then,

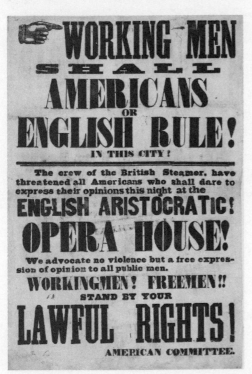

The intense anti-Englishness of 19th-century America prevented cricket from becoming our national sport. How intense? In 1849 dozens of New Yorkers were shot dead in a riot sparked by the rivalry between America's greatest Shakespearean actor and his English counterpart.

the rivalry had taken on political and class dimensions. On May 7 supporters of Forrest broke up Macready's performance of *Macbeth* at New York's Astor Theatre with a shower of rotten eggs and inexpensive produce. The incident had been instigated by Empire Club boss Isaiah Rynders and nativist Edward Judson, who wrote dime novels and roused rabbles under the name Ned Buntline (a buntline is a sailor's knot). Their aim was to embarrass the ruling Whig Party and its elite Anglophile patrons. Macready decided to cancel the remaining performances and go back to England. New York Mayor Caleb Woodhull should have let him go, but instead he drew a line in the sand. A public petition was circulated among New York's cultural elite, asking Macready to stay and return to the stage. Herman Melville, then known for his popular whaling tales *Typee* and *Omoo*, and Washington Irving, the creator of Rip Van Winkle, both signed it. Tragically, Macready agreed. On the evening of the next performance, May 10, Mayor Woodhull mobilized an extra 100 policemen and National Guard units to guarantee Macready's safety. This level of force was provocative; so was a rumor that the Mayor would allow Royal Marines from a British navy ship anchored in New York harbor to come ashore to help. Ned Buntline's Order of United Americans, a predecessor of the nativist Know-Nothing Party, put up posters that shouted: "WORKING MEN, SHALL AMERICANS OR ENGLISH RULE! In this city!"

What followed was a classic police riot, an excessive show of force that incites rather than prevents violence. As ten thousand people gathered in the streets near Astor Place—many of them to see what the commotion was about—Macready's *Macbeth* was broken up again. When the actor ran off after the first act, police clashed with demonstrators who were determined to set the theater on fire. The silk-stocking 7th National Guard regiment—not a judicious choice from a class point of view—arrived, for some reason bringing artillery. The crowd was ordered to disperse and responded by throwing stones and building barricades. The Guardsmen fired warning shots in the air, then fired into the demonstrators' legs; this only made the demonstrators angrier. Faced with an advancing mob that was raining cobblestones down on their heads, the troops defended themselves by shooting to kill. Thirty civilians died, all demonstrators, and over a hundred were wounded, including soldiers, police, women, and passers-by. Awakened in his house near Astor Place, War of 1812 and Mexican War hero General Winfield Scott became so agitated that his wife (whom he apparently addressed as "Madam" when they were alone together) asked him if he was frightened. "Am I a man to be frightened, Madam?" he replied, "It is *volley* firing, Madam—*volley* firing. They are shooting down American citizens!"[49] The next night a mass protest rally filled City Hall Park. Isaiah Rynders called Mayor Woodhull and his administration "murderers" and "tools of British aristocrats and Tories." Leftist politico Mike Walsh said that the authorities had "excelled the most despotic acts of the Czar of Russia, who, before shooting armed insurrectionists, fired three blanks." Militia units patrolled the streets of downtown Manhattan amid sporadic rioting. Fifty-three New Yorkers were arrested, including Ned Buntline, who got a $250 fine and a year in the Tombs.

Nativism was the defining characteristic of Bowery B'hoy culture, which formed another tributary to the movement that made baseball a national sport. The Bowery itself was a New York street lined with theaters, pleasure gardens, and beer halls patronized by artisans, tradesmen, and mechanics—many of whom were also volunteer firemen. The Gotham Inn, where

---

49. Headley, Joel Tyler. *The Great Riots of New York, 1712-1873.* New York: Thunder's Mouth Press, 2004, p. 88

early baseball players hung out, where the baseball convention of 1856 was supposed to take place, and where the baseball convention of 1858 did take place, was at 298 Bowery. The old racket court that Harry Wright used as a cricket batting cage was at 233 Bowery. Bowery B'hoys—the spelling attempts to reproduce their distinctive New York accent—was a New York term, but other cities had their equivalents. To be a Bowery B'hoy was to share the muscular egalitarianism and defiance of authority of the native-born Protestant American of the early and mid-19th century. The Bowery B'hoys were and are often reduced to a crude and false stereotype, even to the ridiculous extent of making them Irish. (It sometimes seems as if any drunk, violent, or racist 19th-century American—even an American-born Protestant nativist—has been assumed by at least one historian to be Irish.) As early as 1847, Walt Whitman wrote, "It is too common among supercilious people to look on the Firemen as a turbulent noisy fold, b'hoys for a row and 'muss' only: this does the great body of them a prodigious injustice."[50]

Bowery B'hoys were a street gang and a style of dressing and talking; they embodied an elbows-out brand of patriotism and held anti-immigrant and anti-elitist beliefs. The classic Bowery B'hoy wore the red shirt of a volunteer fireman, marched with a militia unit or target company, and enjoyed communal chowder suppers. He wore a cocked beaver hat and greased his hair to hold curls in the fashion known as "soap locks." What it meant to be a Bowery B'hoy broadened over time from an urban subculture to a popular political movement aimed at defending artisans whose status was threatened by the incipient Industrial Revolution. Their culture and their distinctive slang thrived in

---

50. Brooklyn *Daily Eagle*, January 7, 1847, quoted in Bergman, Hans. *God in the Street*, Philadelphia: Temple University Press, 1995, p. 76

the urban markets where many of them worked; market traders, as we know, had a long association with baseball. Somewhat appropriately, the most famous Bowery B'hoy of them all was fictional. He was Mose the Fireman, the hero of Benjamin Baker's 1848 hit play, *A Glance at New York*, and its—count 'em—eight sequels. Illustrations frequently show Mose at the Washington Market or another New York market. The other main characters were Mose's "Bowery G'hal" Lize, a fan of minstrel shows, and Mose's loyal sidekick Sikesy. Not only did Bowery B'hoys play baseball before what are now called the first baseball clubs, but they also spread the game beyond New York. The Gold Rush of 1848 brought hundreds of Bowery B'hoys—and the game of baseball—to California.

Politically, the Bowery B'hoys were soldiers in a decades-long struggle to pry power out of the hands of the wealthy elites that controlled city governments through property requirements for voting and other anti-democratic mechanisms. Bowery B'hoy

Mose, the archetypical Bowery B'hoy of Benjamin Baker's hit 1848 play, *A Glance at New York*. In the first half of the 19th century, native-born, aggressively egalitarian urban young men nicknamed "Bowery B'hoys" formed the backbone of New York's volunteer fire companies, citizen militias and baseball clubs.

F S CHANFRAU IN THE CHARACTER OF "MOSE"

culture, nativism, and Tammany Hall politics had many points of intersection. All of these overlapped with European radical leftism and the American reform movements that indirectly fed the rise of sports and baseball. Disorderly and dysfunctional Tammany Hall, called by its friends "the Democracy," fought the battles of the Bowery B'hoy and the mechanic until the 1860s, when it switched sides and became a disciplined political machine catering to immigrants. This, of course, is how it is remembered today. Isaiah Rynders of the Empire political club, infamous as the man whose "shoulder hitters" coerced, bought, and fabricated the votes that made James K. Polk president in 1844, was a Democratic Party insider until his brand of anti-immigrant and anti-Catholic hatred was dropped by Tammany Hall.

THE MOST OUTRAGEOUS figure of an outrageous time was Mike Walsh. Walsh belonged to Engine Company No. 34, "Red Rover," the firehouse of well-known Bowery B'hoy champions Bill "The Butcher" Poole, Dave Broderick, and Harry Howard. Broderick managed a bar named for Mike Walsh's newspaper, the *Subterranean*. Broderick joined the Gold Rush and went to San Francisco, where he became rich and where an early San Francisco baseball club was named for him. Broderick's chief political strategist in California was another baseball-playing New Yorker, journalist George Wilkes. The man who brought pari-mutuel betting to the United States, Wilkes helped put Dave Broderick in the U.S. Senate in 1857. When Broderick was killed in a duel while in office, he left his large fortune to Wilkes. George Wilkes used the money to launch the sporting weekly *Wilkes' Spirit of the Times*, one of the first newspapers to promote baseball on a national level. Like Wilkes, Mike Walsh had one foot in politics and the other in journalism. Around 1840 he founded the Spartan Band, which backed his political program with muscle.

It was members of this group that went to Rhode Island in 1842. Walsh's politics were a mixture of attacks on greedy elites, hyperpatriotism, and demands for social and economic justice for the American workingman.

You could add racism. Like every American movement of the time except for Abolitionism, the radical left split on the issue of race and slavery. Karl Marx, a foreign correspondent for Horace Greeley's *New-York Tribune*, argued that a successful workers' movement was incompatible with slavery. Walsh disagreed, believing that entertaining Abolitionism would divide and weaken the campaign for the rights of white workers, many of whom were pro-slavery. A magnetic speaker and a fiery polemicist, Walsh inspired loyalty in his followers, fear in New York's powerful, and anxiety in Tammany Hall. His politics are a fascinating blend of reactionary and visionary ideas. The nativism of the Bowery B'hoy arose from a desire to protect the fragile American democracy and American culture from foreign influence and from business interests that used unlimited immigration to undermine the labor union movement. Walsh feared that the coming industrialization and corporatization of the American economy, fueled by an unlimited supply of cheap foreign labor, would create wealth inequality, corrupt American democracy, and turn workers into serfs. Walsh knew what he wanted America's future to look like and, as his intelligent critique of modern capitalism shows, he also knew what he didn't want it to look like. Not much that has happened in the 150 years following his death would have surprised him.

In the early 1840s Mike Walsh covered Washington and national politics for the *Aurora*, which was edited by Walt Whitman. In 1843 Walsh launched the *Subterranean* with help from George Wilkes. The title refers to the working poor who lived in cramped, dank basement apartments, a feature of New

York City life that endures despite modern building codes. The newspaper proclaimed itself to be, like the archetypical Bowery B'hoy, "independent in everything—neutral in nothing." The front page of issue number one features a poem by Walt Whitman. Walsh published for two years before he was convicted of libel, a long time considering his journalistic style. The story that sent him to prison falsely accused a politically connected New York businessman of supplying the White House with furniture recycled from brothels. Walsh and Whitman were united in their celebration of American self-assertion and their rejection of the snobbery, cynicism, and decadence of the Old World. As Whitman wrote in *Democratic Vistas*, "*Vive,* the attack—the perennial assault! *Vive,* the unpopular cause, the spirit that audaciously aims—the never-abandoned efforts. . . ."[51]

Walsh served a term in Congress but in 1855 his political career ended in the most ironic way possible. It was discovered that he was not an American citizen. Born in the charming port city of Youghal in County Cork, brought to America as an infant and never naturalized, he had claimed to have been born in the United States because he hoped one day to run for president. Mike Walsh's life came to a sudden and expected end. In March 1859 he spent an ordinary evening and night drinking with politician William Wilson (political patron of pitcher James Creighton's brother John), boxer Tom Hyer, and the ubiquitous George Wilkes. In the morning, he was found dead at the bottom of a flight of stone steps. He was 48. The police ruled it a homicide, but no one was ever charged. Perhaps there were too many suspects.

---

51. Whitman, Walt. *Democratic Vistas*, facsimile edition Iowa City: University of Iowa Press, 2010, p.29

WALSH WAS A close friend of shipbuilder George Steers, the designer of John C. Stevens's yacht *America*. Steers was a colleague and childhood playmate of Frank Pidgeon, who cofounded the Eckford baseball club. A remarkable number of early baseball men had personal connections to radical and reformist movements, among them Abolitionism, Temperance, public health reform, the labor union movement, and land reform. This is not an accident. These movements overlapped ideologically and attracted similar kinds of people; both amateur baseball and the wider American sports movement were stars in the same reformist constellation. American reform movements also took in stray Chartists, Fenians, Socialists, and others who had fled or been kicked out of Europe. Even some of these had baseball connections. A leftist English newspaper editor who had roomed in Paris with revolutionary propagandist Thomas Paine during the French Revolution, Henry Chadwick's father James Chadwick moved to America in 1838 after annoying too many powerful people. (James Chadwick's father Andrew Chadwick was a disciple of John Wesley, the founder of Methodism, which itself was a reform movement.) Thomas Ainge Devyr was an Irish-born Chartist who raised three baseball-playing sons; the best of them was politician and newspaper editor Thomas Devyr Jr., a star player for the Eckfords and Mutuals.

The Chartists were political reformers in England who advocated proportionate voting districts, the secret ballot, salaries for legislators, and eliminating property qualifications for voting. If their program does not sound radical today, it is because they accomplished all of these reforms so long ago that we take them for granted. Devyr belonged to a fanatical Chartist cell that was caught plotting violent attacks in the northern English city of Newcastle; he fled to America in 1840 to avoid arrest. In New York he cofounded the National Reform movement with

Mike Walsh and English land reformer George Henry Evans, and helped lead the Anti-rent War, which achieved its goal of breaking up New York State's vast quasi-feudal estates and giving ownership of the land to former tenant farmers. Their efforts led to the Homestead Act of 1862, which distributed unimproved government land in the West to settlers.

Evans was also a key player in the American labor union movement, one of whose leaders was New York chairmaker John Commerford of the National Trades' Union, America's first national labor organization. Commerford was also a nativist and an Abolitionist. His son Charles Commerford played shortstop for the Gothams and Eagles, helped bring baseball to Connecticut, and was a good friend of Henry Chadwick. Mike Walsh seems to have had less personal involvement in baseball than his friends George Wilkes and Walt Whitman, but the New York game makes a tantalizing appearance in an early issue of his *Subterranean*. Boasting of his proletarian tastes, Walsh writes, " . . . as soon as I am Mayor, I'll play ball in the park and have a chowder in the 'Mayor's Office,' every Sunday." As the

Leftist politico, journalist and firebrand Mike Walsh, who promised, if he ever became Mayor of New York City, to spite the city's Anglophile ruling classes by playing baseball in City Hall Park.

readers of the *Subterranean* were assumed to understand, the sport for a true Bowery B'hoy and man of the people was not thoroughbred horseracing, yachting, or cricket. It was good old American baseball. This was written in 1846—the year in which generations of baseball fans have been told that the first baseball game was played.

THE NAMES OF the early baseball clubs contain clues to the ideologies behind the rise of amateur baseball in the 1850s. In modern professional sports, club names have little meaning. The name Dodgers, for example, short for "trolley dodgers," refers to Brooklyn pedestrians' fear of the fast, electric streetcars introduced in the mid-1890s. Almost no one in Los Angeles today knows or cares why the club is called the Dodgers. It is simply a brand. This was not so in baseball's Amateur Era. The earliest baseball clubs were self-constituted membership organizations. In other words, they were actual clubs. Because club names were chosen by their members, they tell us who the Amateur Era players were, what they believed, and what both have to do with baseball.

What stands out first about the club names from the early Amateur Era is how few of them are related to sports. The main exceptions are the Athletic club of Philadelphia and several Olympic clubs. After excluding the minority of names which, like the Portlands of Portland, Maine, tell us only where the clubs were located, there were about 240 pre-1860 amateur baseball clubs that we know of whose names were used more than once. Most were located in New York State, New Jersey, Connecticut, and Massachusetts, but clubs from Louisiana, Rhode Island, Minnesota, Illinois, Michigan, Pennsylvania, Vermont, and Kentucky make the list. Forty-one of the names were political. There were 21 named Union, eight named Young America, three each named Lone Star and Live Oak, and two Magnolias.

In the 1850s, to name a baseball club Union was to take sides in the great national debate over slavery. Southern efforts to expand slavery to the western territories were seen as threatening the sacred Constitutional order with "disunion," a threat that was realized with the shelling of Fort Sumter in 1861. If there is any doubt that the name Union was a political statement, consider that only one of the 21 Union clubs was located south of New Brunswick, N.J.—the Union club of Sacramento, California. The Union clubs were full of nativists, Republicans, and Abolitionists. David Milliken, for example, cofounder and president of the Unions of Morrisania, now part of the Bronx, was an important early member of the anti-slavery New York State Republican Party. So was the club's star player Joseph Pinckney.

The live oak tree was the symbol of nativist demagogue George "Live Oak" Law, a Trump-esque figure who ran for vice president in 1856. The native American tree *Magnolia Makrophylla* was a symbol of nativist Kentucky statesman Henry Clay. There were clubs called Empire in New York City and in Albany, New York, which might suggest New York's nickname, the Empire State, but there were also Empire clubs in Newark and New Orleans. The empire in question is the American empire envisioned by advocates of manifest destiny. The Lone Star is the symbol of Texas, which seceded from Mexico in 1836 with the support of the Young America movement.

The single largest category is patriotic names. There are 17 Washington or Lady Washington clubs, eight Columbia or Columbians, seven Nationals, and seven Independent or Independence clubs, as well as Star, Pioneer, Eagle, Liberty, and American. There are 33 clubs named Washington, Lafayette, Franklin, Hamilton, Wayne, Warren, or Marion. All were named after heroes of the American Revolution. Two clubs were named Lawrence. War of 1812 martyr James Lawrence was in command of the *USS Chesapeake* in action against a British warship when, fatally wounded, he spoke the words, "Don't give up the ship," that have gone down in history as an American rallying cry.

Fifteen club names refer to the occupations of their members, including eight Mechanic clubs. Some names belong to more than one category. The three Franklin clubs, for example, took the name of Revolutionary War figure, polymath, and printer Ben Franklin, but they were also made up of printers. Shipbuilder Henry Eckford was a hero of the War of 1812, but clubs named Eckford were made up mostly of men who worked in shipbuilding and associated industries like ironworks, sail making, and dock building. Clubs in shipbuilding cities often adopted the names of ships, like George Steers's *Niagara* and *Adriatic*. There were seven Enterprises, as well as Baltics, Arctics, and Orientals. All are names of other famous ships.

19th-century Americans were intensely proud of their shipbuilding industry. Pre–Civil War New York newspapers reported on the progress of ships being built in local yards with the detail and fervor of financial news today. Large crowds of spectators gathered to watch ships in New York harbor. On June 28, 1860 Brooklynites had a choice. They could watch the world's best pitcher, James Creighton of the Excelsiors, take on the Star Club in Brooklyn's Carroll Park, or go down to the waterfront to see the arrival of the British steamer *Great Eastern*, built by the competition but an impressive sight. At 692 feet in length, it was the world's largest ship. The baseball game drew a disappointing crowd of 500.[52] According to *The New York Times*, the *Great Eastern* attracted a "multitude" that crowded the harbor in row boats, tugs, and private yachts like "porpoises after a whale."

---

52. Brooklyn *Daily Eagle*, June 29, 1860, p.3

The militia or target company, the volunteer fire company, and the baseball club formed the holy trinity of pre–Civil War American urban culture. In the days before a large standing army and professional fire departments, the first two were civic necessities. In the 1840s and 1850s in New York, Brooklyn, Philadelphia, and Boston, nearly every able-bodied adult male belonged to one, two, or all three of these kinds of volunteer organizations. Twenty-six baseball clubs had names that were commonly used by volunteer fire companies: Niagara, Atlantic, Alert, Active, Zephyr, Harmony, Americus, and Mutual. The culture of firefighting profoundly shaped baseball. Many of the designs of the first baseball uniforms, such as those with shirt fronts protecting the buttons, were borrowed from fire company outfits. Decades before the first regular interclub baseball matches, fire companies held competitions of firefighting skills. These would often involve travel to another city and post-competition banquets given by the host company; the favor would then be returned. Amateur Era baseball clubs adopted these customs. Well into the 1860s, home and away baseball series included postgame dinners with music, cigars, toasts, and speeches. There was also much overlap between particular volunteer fire companies, militia units, and baseball clubs. They often had the same members and used the same name.

Founded in 1831, the Olympics of Philadelphia were arguably the first enduring club that played a bat-and-ball game. Ten other clubs used that name. The Olympics originally played town ball, Philadelphia's now extinct baseball variant, but in 1860 they switched to the New York game of baseball. Strictly amateur, the Olympic games of ancient Greece were a form of religious observance, not entertainment and certainly not a business. Though sometimes rewarded for victories, the participants were ordinary citizens, not professional athletes. The same was true for most, but not all of baseball's Amateur Era players.

If it is hard to imagine a modern baseball club being named after a war hero, it is even harder to imagine one being named after a writer or work of literature. But there were at least 28 early Amateur Era clubs with literary names, including Waverley, Irving, and Hiawatha. Seventeen clubs alone were named Excelsior. It has been argued that some of them were named after the Brooklyn Excelsiors, the first club to use the name, but most were founded before the Brooklyn Excelsiors achieved national fame in 1860. Like the Brooklyn club, the majority were named after Henry Wadsworth Longfellow's massively popular 1841 poem, *Excelsior*. The subject of the poem is a young man who is grimly determined to climb a mountain in the Alps, carrying a mysterious banner with the word "Excelsior," a Latin word meaning ever onward and upward. Ignoring warnings of avalanche and bad weather, he refuses offers of shelter, comfort, and female company, only to be found dead of exposure, clutching the banner with frozen fingers. Young men of the Amateur Era were attracted to the poem's themes of masculine courage, independence, and pioneer spirit. The 1814 historical novel *Waverley* by Sir Walter Scott struck a sympathetic chord in Americans with its themes of egalitarianism and social progress. Longfellow's omnium gatherum of Native American mythology, *The Song of Hiawatha*, published in 1855, attempts to create a fully American work with no obvious English or European model. It was, or tried to be, the baseball of epic poems.

A TARGET EXCURSION

Service in target companies or citizen militias was a fact of life for pre–Civil War American men. These volunteer organizations were sometimes mocked for their drinking, lack of military discipline, and nativist pretensions. In 1855, humorist Mortimer Thomson, writing under the pen name Q.K. Philander Doesticks, P.B. (which stands for Perfect Brick, i.e., numbskull), described a target excursion taken by a fictitious New York City militia unit named "The Lager Bier American Volunteers, and Native Empire City Shillelagh Guards," which was "composed of Irish, Dutch, Spaniards and Sandwich Islanders, the only Americans in the company being the colored target-bearer and the undersigned." Thomson's portrait is a caricature, but it gives us some idea of what ordinary militia units, volunteer fire companies, and baseball clubs may have been like—as well as a clue to why the armed forces and fire departments were reformed and professionalized after the Civil War. It also shows us how comfortable mid-19th-century America was with racism.

> Here, the target companies are composed of all sorts of people—fire companies, express companies, policemen, gangs of men from all kinds of mammoth shops—for wherever thirty or forty men work in one shop, they form themselves into a military company, and once or twice every year go to Hoboken and shoot for whisky and other prizes. . . . In these companies there are always more officers than men, and more epaulettes than muskets—always a big band of music, and two darkies to carry the target. . . . They go forth in the morning in high spirits, and return at night, surly, dusty, discontented, dilapidated and drunk. . . . As these excursions come off just before [an] election, the candidates for office generally pay for the prizes. . . . Next came the shooting. Nigger set the target at twenty paces. . . . As the brandy had circulated pretty freely, some of the shots were rather wild—several missed the target entirely and knocked their heads against the trees; one bored a deep hole in a sand bank, and the first lieutenant was put under arrest for trying to tap the captain. . . . Finding that shooting was no use, captain adopted the usual plan . . . blindfolded the men and each one charged on it with an auger, where the point happened to hit, he bored a hole. . . . Marched home in as good order as circumstances would allow—the darkey bearing in proud triumph the perforated target, which had so many hits near the center, as to excite the admiration of the deluded public, which, as a general rule, in such cases, can't tell a bullet mark from an auger hole.[53]

---

53. Thomson, Mortimer (AKA Q.K. Philander Doesticks, P.B.) *Doesticks' Letters: And What He Says*, Philadelphia: T. B. Peterson and Bros., 1855, pp. 75 ff.

THE NAMES OF the two most important baseball clubs of the early Amateur Era were literary references: the Gothams and Knickerbockers. Both come from the works of the same writer, Washington Irving. Irving's career was a point of pride for Americans, who felt the sting of inferiority particularly sharply in the realm of literature. Washington Irving gave Americans an answer to English critic Sydney Smith, who famously asked in 1820 (two months before the English publication of Irving's *The Legend of Sleepy Hollow*), "In the four quarters of the globe, who reads an American book?"[54] Taken from an English nursery rhyme about a village whose residents pretend to be crazy in order to hoodwink the king, Gotham (whose etymological meaning is "Goatville") was first used as a nickname for New York City in an 1807 issue of Irving's magazine *Salmagundi*. Two years later Irving created the character of Diedrich Knickerbocker to serve as the fictitious author of *A History of New York*, which pokes fun at New York's less than heroic origins as a Dutch trading post. Knickerbocker quickly became a popular nickname for old New Yorkers, or anything associated with their Anglo–Dutch ways. In the United Kingdom today, women's underpants are called knickers, short for knickerbockers, because they once resembled the baggy breeches worn by men in illustrated editions of Irving's book. For 200 years, all sorts of things associated with New York, from ships to bottled beer to hotels to a chronically mismanaged basketball team to an avenue in Brooklyn, have been called Knickerbocker.

---

54. Smith, Sydney in the *Edinburgh Review*, January 1820, p. 69

Looking at the names of the early baseball clubs, themes emerge that paint a composite portrait of the amateurs who founded America's first national team sport. On the positive side, there is patriotic pride; belief in America's exceptionalism and destined greatness; and faith in republican democracy. On the negative side runs an undercurrent of keenly felt cultural inferiority to the English, hostility to monarchy and elitism, and fear of the superior political and military power of Great Britain. This fear was very real. Consider that the United States had to fight two wars against the British in order to win and maintain its independence, and that a British army had invaded the United States less than thirty years before the founding of the Knickerbocker baseball club. The War of 1812 might not be remembered by ordinary Americans today, but they stand up and sing about it before every professional baseball game.

ANOTHER TRIBUTARY TO the baseball river was public health reform. In an 1896 interview Daniel "Doc" Adams, who moved to New York after his 1838 graduation from Harvard Medical School, recalled playing with the New York Club in 1839, before he and "several of us medical fellows" switched to the newly formed Knickerbockers in the autumn of 1845. He did not name names, but the Knickerbockers' membership records include several prominent physicians, including William B. Eager, Chief of Staff of the City Hospital on Blackwell's (now Roosevelt) Island and Professor of Gynecology at Bellevue, and Francis Upton Johnston Sr., a trustee of the College of Physicians and Surgeons, the medical school of Columbia College. Both of these men had professional connections to Adams and to the cause of public health reform, one of whose central beliefs was that Americans needed more exercise, fresh air, and sunlight. Doc Adams became the

Knickerbockers' president and most influential member. He and his fellow reformist physicians found an ally in the press. Henry Chadwick wrote that baseball could be, "a powerful lever ... by which our people could be lifted into a position of more devotion to physical exercise and healthful outdoor recreation."[55] In 1846 Walt Whitman wrote in the Brooklyn *Daily Eagle*, "In our sundown perambulations, of late, through the outer parts of Brooklyn, we have observed several parties of youngsters playing 'base,' a certain game of ball. We wish such sights were more common among us. In the practice of athletic and manly sports, the young men of nearly all our American cities are very deficient. . . . The game of ball is glorious—that of quoits is invigorating—so are leaping, running, wrestling, &c. &c."[56]

Early 19th-century American physicians like Doc Adams were neither as technically accomplished nor as well paid as today's doctors. Lacking modern antibiotics, anesthetics, and surgical technology, they had pitifully few weapons to fight sickness and disease. But they did have a social conscience and a strong sense of mission. Inspired by the ideas of Englishman Sir Edwin Chadwick, the father of public health science, the favorite disciple of Utilitarian social reformer Jeremy Bentham— and Henry Chadwick's half-brother—they believed that physical and social ills could be cured by reforming human systems. They campaigned to clean up American cities' polluted water, foul air, and medieval sewage and garbage removal. They also believed that physical fitness not only prolonged and improved life, but also offered protection from tuberculosis, cholera, and other common diseases. A key goal of public health reformers was to put physicians, not political appointees, in charge

55. Chadwick, Henry. *The Game of Baseball*. 1868. New York: George Munro and Co., p. 10
56. Brooklyn *Daily Eagle*, July 23, 1846, p. 2

of public health. "Are officers of our government, employed in the conservation of public health, competent persons?" asked legendary surgeon Dr. Valentine Mott, cofounder of the NYU School of Medicine. "Not men of science, not of learning, but some political artist, some worker in the dark caverns of political villainy, is always the chosen one for this task . . . [is] it not necessary that medical men should be employed to divine and arrest the causes of disease?"[57]

A CURE FOR CHOLERA

In the mid-19th century, public health reformers believed that clean living, fresh air, and physical exercise could protect Americans from dreaded killers like typhoid fever, yellow fever, and cholera, diseases that we know now are caused by bacterial or viral infection. Their ideas helped drive the rise of baseball. The United States had terrible cholera outbreaks in 1832, 1849, and 1866. In 1866 the New York *Sunday Mercury*, which was published by William Cauldwell, a founder of the Union baseball club of Morrisania, claimed that the way to avoid cholera was to play baseball. This sounds crazy, but no more so than the recommendations of mainstream medical authorities of the time, who blamed cholera on humidity, miasmas (unhealthy vapors), and eating unripe fruit.

> The columns of the dailies for some time have been filled with notices of cholera-specifics, in which drugs of various kinds are the principal ingredients. Now we happen to know of one cholera-specific which we can recommend to the patronage of every man and boy in the land, and that is baseball. No sanitary measure that can well be adopted—in addition to the practice of temperance and cleanliness—is so calculated to induce that healthy condition of the system which forms a barrier to the progress of this disease, as baseball exercise every fine afternoon. The free perspiration induced, and the active and healthy circulation of the blood to the surface of the body, consequent open air exercise,

57. *The New York Times*, November 13, 1858, p. 2

and the relief afforded the over-taxed lungs and bowels by this healthy action of the skin, together with the vitality and strength derived from the inhalation of the pure oxygen of the atmosphere of a ball-field, and the vigor imparted by open-air exercise, in which every muscle of the body is brought into play, are all conducive to a high degree of health, and of course prove strong obstacles to the approach of disease, especially of those of epidemic form, like cholera, which finds its first victims among those enervated by the lack of those very promoters of health. It is scarcely necessary to add, that anything like the extremes some enthusiastic members of the fraternity sometimes rush into, are to be avoided as evils having a reverse effect; but temperance, in connection with daily exercise on a ball-field, will almost make a man cholera-proof.[58]

WHEN THE ANSWER from the New York City political estab-lishment was a resounding no, New York City doctors created a public health system by themselves. By the 1830s, often work-ing without pay and independently of the government, they had divided the city into health districts, each with a dispen-sary that provided free treatment and medicine to the poor, including vaccinations, and collected public health data. This was a time when there were no hospitals in the modern sense. The wealthy bought medical care from private physicians and the poor relied on charity. In 1847 the New York dispensary system served 28,277 patients, more than 5 percent of the to-tal population of the city. Free from the exigencies of politi-cal patronage, it did so at the shockingly low cost of $3,476. Supported by private charity, these dispensaries are the direct ancestors of modern public hospital systems and municipal health departments. Behind the story of the forgotten dis-pensary system, there are connections to baseball. Wealthy

---

58. New York *Sunday Mercury* quoted in Philadelphia *City Item* June 2, 1866

Quaker watchmaker Samuel Demilt, a major dispensary benefactor, was a relative of William W. Demilt, a member of the Gotham baseball club. The Quakers' interest in public health and social reform led some of them to baseball; an important figure in pre–Knickerbocker Era baseball was Quaker physician John Miller. In 1840 two Knickerbocker Club M.D.s, Doc Adams and Francis Upton Johnston, supervised the central New York Dispensary at the corner of White and Centre Streets. In the 1850s Doc Adams became medical director of the dispensary. On his staff was another Knickerbocker, Dr. William B. Eager.

The effort to convince American adults to exercise was a long campaign, not all of whose battles were won. Before the sports movement succeeded with baseball, it had failed with boxing and gymnastics. In some cases, the same men were involved in two or even all three sports. In the 1820s and 1830s, boxing gyms opened in Boston, Philadelphia, and New York. They tried to market the sport to respectable gentlemen as the "manly art of self-defense." But the general public never embraced boxing as a participant sport. Physicians and entrepreneurs made another attempt to sell exercise by importing gymnastics and weight training from Great Britain and the Continent. In 1833 Englishman William Fuller opened one of the first New York City gymnasiums to feature gymnastics at 29 Ann Street, near City Hall. He took out this advertisement in the *New York Evening Post*:

> We esteem exercise, as an essential means to the preservation of health, and as one of the most certain prophylactics against those innumerable diseases, which result from a want of it. We, therefore, cordially recommend all seden-

tary persons, whose professional avocations debar them from the pursuit of health by the more common forms of exercise, to resort to this Gymnasium. . . ."[59]

Not only was Fuller using the language of public health reform, but he also added a testimonial—"We fully concur in the value of Gymnastic exercises"—signed by Dr. Valentine Mott and nine other pillars of the New York City medical establishment. In the 1840s, Charles Ottignon, another Englishman, taught gymnastics on Canal Street and later on Crosby Street. In 1852 Ottignon held a gymnastic competition in which prizes were won by Knickerbocker baseball club members James Montgomery and Edward Cone. Another prize winner, Henry Bogart, may be the Knickerbocker of the same name. In 1856 Ottignon went into partnership with Montgomery, who was also an early proponent of weightlifting. It is no coincidence that we find the same people involved in boxing, gymnastics, weightlifting, and firefighting. These overlapping activities formed the cutting edge of the American sports movement. And amateur baseball represented that movement's fulfillment. The success of baseball as a national participant sport fundamentally and forever changed American attitudes toward sports, exercise, and health.

THE TRIBUTARIES OF public health reform, rapid urban growth, and the civic unrest of mid-19th-century New York also combined to steer the course of the sports movement in a new direction, toward the city of Brooklyn. In 1849 a ship captain's son named Joseph B. Jones opened Brooklyn's first state-of-the-art gymnasium at the corner of Pineapple and Fulton Streets in what is now Brooklyn Heights, a five-minute walk uphill from

---

59. New York *Evening Post*, April 17, 1833, p. 1

the New York ferry landing. Jones was a good amateur boxer and an excellent gymnast who judged competitions and performed at Ottignon's gymnasium. Dr. Jones energetically promoted his new business to a skeptical public with advertising and public lectures—sometimes too energetically. When Jones hired trousers-wearing English feminist Madame Beaujeu Hawley to teach women and girls, he provoked a backlash from Brooklynites who considered it indecent for men to see women work up a sweat.

Jones's response was like something out of modern Tehran or Riyadh. He promised to keep the sexes strictly separate at his facility and published a statement in the *Brooklyn Daily Eagle* from Abolitionist preacher Henry Ward Beecher and other prominent Brooklyn mullahs endorsing the moral probity of gymnastics for women and girls. Beecher was an adherent of a Protestant movement called Muscular Christianity, which held that exercise and physical education were not a distraction from religion but, on the contrary, a religious imperative. This was the ideology that created the Young Men's Christian Association, which started in Great Britain in 1844 and crossed the Atlantic Ocean to America.

American YMCAs built gyms and from the 1850s on, sponsored baseball clubs. But like boxing, gymnastics did not reach enough people. Jones sold his gym and entered the College of Physicians and Surgeons in New York City. There, he switched his focus to baseball. Graduating in 1855, he opened a medical practice in Brooklyn and joined a baseball club called the Esculapians, who played near the present site of Brooklyn's Carroll Park. As its name suggests, this club was made up of physicians and medical students. Its members included doctors who staffed and ran the Brooklyn Dispensary, Long Island College Hospital, Brooklyn Medical Association, and other institutions; as well as public health officers and Kings County coroners. The very existence of the Esculapian club, the earliest baseball club made up entirely of members of a single profession, testifies to the special relationship between early baseball and medicine. Brooklyn's first New York City–style baseball club, the Excelsiors, was founded in 1854. Late in 1857, however, Dr. Jones and his medical and physical fitness allies took over the club in a bloodless coup. What they did with it changed baseball and America.

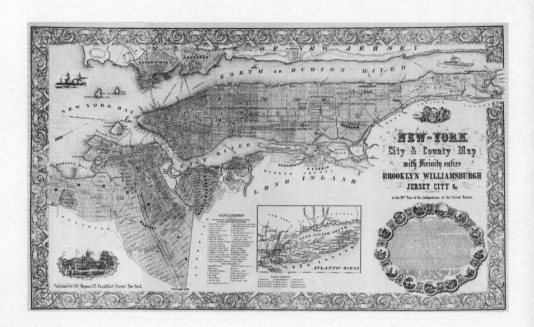

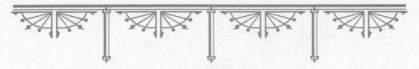

CHAPTER FIVE
It Happened in Brooklyn

HERE IS THE REAL BIRTHPLACE of baseball? If you open up five history books, you will find at least four answers to this question. Depending on how old the book is, it might be Cooperstown, New York, where a teenage Abner Doubleday supposedly laid out the first diamond; Hoboken, New Jersey, where the Knickerbockers supposedly played the first baseball game; New York City, where the men who supposedly formed the first baseball clubs lived and worked; maybe even England, the home of rounders, baseball's supposed ancestor. But the best answer may be none of the above: Brooklyn.

Humor me.

Once two independent cities, New York and Brooklyn are separated by the East River, a body of water about 1,500 feet wide. In the early 19th century, when Brooklyn was the place where the ferry landed that connected New York to Long Island, people moved from one to the other, but they rarely worked and lived on different sides of the river. That changed in the 1840s and 1850s, when prosperous urbanites decided to get out of dirty, dangerous, and disorderly New York, where they made their money, and raise their families in Brooklyn, a fast-growing city where blocks of rowhouses were swallowing up the small towns and farms of Kings County. They moved for the same reason that people like them were moving to Harlem, the Bronx, and New Jersey. It was not the desire that was new; it was the ability. No one who worked in New York was willing to live outside Manhattan if it meant depending on horse-powered vehicles or plodding ferries twice a day, five or six days a week. Horse-drawn streetcars and railways were fine if the terrain was flat, bodies of water were bridged, and the distances weren't too great. Every mid-19th-century city had so-called streetcar suburbs. Many of them are still around, but they are now considered city neighborhoods, some of them even inner-city neighborhoods, not suburbs. New York had Yorkville and Harlem. Philadelphia had Spring Garden, Penn, and Hamilton Village. There were hundreds of others. But thanks to advancing steam technology and expanded ferry and railroad service, it was now practical for those who could afford it to buy a house in a distant residential neighborhood and commute to the office.

A different type of suburb, popular in England, had freestanding, one-family houses set back from the street and hidden by trees and hedges. The idea caught on in Boston, which in the 1830s and 1840s built the radial railroad network that made Boston, "The Hub," a literal hub. ("Hub Fans Bid Kid Adieu" is the name of John Updike's 1960 essay in *The New Yorker* magazine on Ted Williams's final game at Fenway Park.) Most early American railroads were built to carry freight, but Boston railroad companies realized that they could add to their profits by selling discounted, or "commuted," fares for daily short trips to people travelling for work to and from Boston and outlying towns such as Dedham. This is where the word commuter comes from. In 1848, about one-fifth of Boston businessmen commuted to work from the suburbs by railroad. The early

New York City bedroom community of Morrisania, in a part of Westchester County that is now the Bronx, followed this model.

Spacious lots and detached houses, however, were expensive. A key to the viability of this kind of suburb was a financial innovation imported from the birthplace of the suburb, England—the building society. Later called savings and loans in the United States, these organizations enabled people to pool their savings in order to finance home construction and mortgages. Soon after the New York and Harlem Railroad crossed the Harlem River, Republican politician and real estate developer David Milliken and his partners divided the country village of Morrisania into building lots. As a trustee of the Greenwich Building Society, Milliken helped thousands of New Yorkers to finance a suburban house on a quiet street in a leafy neighborhood. Places like Morrisania were impossible without building societies, but they were also impossible without the railroad. As the *New York Express* wrote in 1852, "The high rents of the city, the crowded habitations, etc., will drive thousands from the island. Morrisania has grown from a wilderness, almost, in three or four years, to a town of four thousand inhabitants, under the system of cheap railroad fares."[60] Suburbs like Morrisania promised the best of both worlds, urban and rural.

A feature of city life that New Yorkers did not want to leave behind was baseball. David Milliken made a living in real estate development and finance, but he was also the cofounder of the Union baseball club and an important national baseball figure. Milliken served as Union club president for years; in 1861 and 1862 he was also president of the NABBP. His plan for Morrisania included playing grounds for the Unions near 163rd Street, within walking distance of the Melrose station

---

60. New York *Express* quoted in Wheeling *Daily Intelligencer*, September 20, 1852, p. 2

on the New York and Harlem Railroad line. The club pursued talented players like Gothams star (and Republican Party official) Joseph C. Pinckney, and they knew what they were doing. The amateur Unions recruited an unusual number of players who went on to have careers in professional baseball, among them George Wright, Al Martin, and Charlie Pabor. In the late 1860s the Unions built an enclosed ballpark with facilities for spectators, at the present location of Crotona Park in the Bronx. In 1868 they became the national champions of baseball. Crotona Park still has diamonds and a lively baseball scene. Hall of Famer Hank Greenberg played there as a teenager in the 1920s; Manny Ramirez played summer ball there in 1990, as my son did in the 2000s.

To some, suburbs like Morrisania offered not the best of the country and the city, but an unsatisfactory middle ground. In 1851 Nathaniel Parker Willis (the literary man whose girlfriend didn't like him talking to the underdressed Penobscot girl at the Elysian Fields) stepped off the train in Morrisania and found it neither fish nor fowl. "Lawns and park-gates," he wrote, "groves and verandahs, ornamental woods and neat walls, trim hedges and well-placed shrubberies, fine houses and large stables, neat gravel walks and nobody on them—are notes upon one chord, and they certainly seem to me to make a dull tune of Westchester."[61] We will never know if he would have preferred the music of late 20th-century Morrisania, the home of Grandmaster Flash and the birthplace of hip-hop, but Willis was not the only sophisticated New Yorker of the 1850s who was deaf to the charms of lawns and picket fences. Some members of the EUB preferred the lively sociality of the city and wanted

61. Willis, N.P. quoted in Stilgoe, John R. *Borderland: Origins of the American Suburb, 1820-1939*. New Haven: Yale University Press, 1988, p.68

a suburb with the accent on the second syllable—denser and closer to downtown shops, restaurants, and theaters. Within walking distance of the East River ferry, Brooklyn Heights and Cobble Hill in Brooklyn were developed in the 1840s and 1850s as upscale suburbs for them. To imagine how these early New York suburbs looked, think of brownstones, brick rowhouses, and tree-lined streets with flagstone sidewalks, not the lawns, swimming pools, and McMansions that the word suburb calls to mind today. Or simply go to Brooklyn Heights; it hasn't changed much. Brooklyn built so many neighborhoods like this that in the 1890s, when the Brooklyn Dodgers were called the "Superbas," sneering New York City sportswriters called them the "Suburbas." Today, no one thinks of Brooklyn Heights, Park Slope, and Cobble Hill as suburban; not because they have changed, but because our idea of what a suburb is has changed.

Nineteen of these suburban pioneers founded the Excelsiors. Many of them had recently moved from lower Manhattan to the area around Brooklyn Heights. They were the classic

A scene advertising the leafy gentility of Morrisania, an early railroad suburb settled in the 1850s by New Yorkers fleeing the dirty, crowded city for a new kind of life, neither urban nor rural. They brought baseball with them.

EUB mix—physicians, bankers, insurance men, stockbrokers, merchants, and lawyers. The first New York–style baseball club in Brooklyn, the Excelsiors, began as a satellite of the Knickerbockers. The Excelsiors and Knickerbockers were more than friends. They were figuratively and, in a few cases, literally cousins. One founding Excelsior was surgeon Daniel Albert Dodge; another was fellow physician Van Brunt Wyckoff, who made so much money in Brooklyn real estate that he never practiced medicine. Both got their medical degrees from the Columbia-affiliated College of Physicians and Surgeons, or CPS. Dodge's cousin Samuel Kissam lived in Brooklyn a block or two from Carroll Park, where the Excelsiors played before 1860. Although a prominent member of the Knickerbockers, Kissam pops up in two box scores playing for the Excelsiors. Kissam was a stockbroker, but he belonged to a unique medical dynasty; more than two dozen members of his family graduated from the CPS. Several other founding Excelsiors had friends, colleagues, and business partners who belonged to the Knickerbockers. The Knickerbockers advertised their sponsorship of the younger club by playing series with the Excelsiors in both 1858 and 1859. Coverage of an 1858 postgame banquet in *The New York Times* gives an idea of the closeness of the two clubs, as well as the public health reform ideology that they shared.

> Mr. [James Whyte] Davis ... proposed "Health and success to the Excelsior Club," with three times three [i.e., "hip, hip, hooray" three times]. Dr. Jones made a pertinent and witty reply, and proposed three times three for the "Parent of baseball clubs, the Knickerbockers." Dr. Adams ... recommended the practice of the game by Americans, old and young ... Mr. Burtis, of the Excelsior Club ... alluded to an article from the *London Times* in which it was stated that for the want of outdoor athletic exercises and sports,

the youth of America had physically deteriorated and . . . he hailed the game of baseball as the panacea for their loss of physical powers.[62]

The Dr. Jones toasted by James Whyte Davis was Joseph B. Jones. Jones had joined the Excelsiors a year earlier with an un-Knickerbocker-like agenda. We do not have his plan in writing, but its contours are plain from the sequence of events after Jones and his friends took over the club leadership in late 1857. It was to build the Excelsiors into the best club in baseball and take it on the road to popularize the New York version of baseball in other parts of the country. In November 1857 Dr. Jones was elected president in a special election. The Excelsiors normally held officer elections in March, but this time they were held early, presumably in order to have Jones and his allies in place going into the important baseball convention of March 1858. Dr. Jones represented the Excelsiors at the convention, which established the National Association of Base Ball Players, or NABBP, as baseball's governing body. This act marks the beginning, or the beginning of the beginning, of organized baseball. The two key words in the new association's name are "players" and "national." Like contemporary militia units and volunteer fire companies, amateur baseball clubs were controlled by their members. And all of the 25 clubs at the 1858 convention played in or near New York City and Brooklyn; the farthest away was the Liberty club of New Brunswick, New Jersey, 40 miles from Manhattan. The New York game was far from being a national sport. But in 1858 it announced to the world that it intended to be.

PRESIDENT OF THE Excelsior club from late 1857 through 1863, Dr. Jones was elected vice president of the NABBP in 1858, the year of its founding. He became president of both organizations

---

62. *The New York Times*, August 23, 1858, p.5

two years later in 1860. The second step in Jones's plan was to upgrade the Excelsiors' playing talent. This meant pushing the envelope of baseball amateurism. Recruiting players for ability alone was not against the rules in the late 1850s, but it was not openly acknowledged either. Jones found athletes like first baseman and physician Andrew Pearsall, whose superb fielding—this was before the invention of baseball gloves—was attributed to his surgeon's hands. The two met at the CPS, where Jones was Pearsall's personal tutor. The Excelsiors acquired catcher Joseph Leggett, their best player in the B.C. (before Creighton) Era, in a creative way by merging with his club, the Waynes. In 1858 Lem Bergen and John Holder were poached from the Atlantics under shadowy circumstances. Acting as a combination coach and trainer, Leggett pioneered the use of weight training for baseball and put the Excelsiors' top players on a regular workout regimen. Both of these were firsts.

We do not know if Leggett, a Brooklyn volunteer fireman, had any previous connection to Jones or his gymnasium, but it seems likely. The gym was two blocks from Leggett's firehouse and policemen and firemen of the time were particularly active in boxing, gymnastics, and weightlifting. A boxer and gymnast, Jones may well have recruited athletes whom he knew from those worlds. In another innovation, Jones made informal, farm system–like arrangements with Brooklyn junior clubs that provided the Excelsiors with a supply of young talent. The core of the Excelsiors' player development program was their relationship with the junior Star club, which, along with the Niagaras and others, shared their playing field in South Brooklyn. (Brooklyn geography is complicated; today South Brooklyn is in the northern part of Brooklyn. The Eastern District is now called North Brooklyn. But southern Brooklyn is on the south side of the borough. It is probably best to follow Thomas Wolfe and abandon maps altogether.)

The Stars received instruction and organizational support, including access to playing grounds, in exchange for sending their best players to the Excelsiors when they reached 18. Using box scores, you can follow one future Excelsiors player after another as they moved in an orderly progression—usually two per year—from lower junior clubs like the Niagaras to the Stars, a top junior club, and then to the parent club. In one three-year period, Asa Brainard and his brother Harrison, brothers Charles and John Whiting, George Flanley, and James Creighton all joined the Excelsiors after graduating from the Stars. The Excelsior club had its own ladder-like structure. The best players played for the so-called first nine, the top reserves on the second nine, and so on. At the bottom of the ladder was the "muffin nine," who were there to play for laughs and to pay club dues.

THE INNOVATOR JONES

Joseph Jones's name never comes up when historians are making lists of baseball's founding fathers. But it should. A crusading physician, public health activist, and pro-feminist, he advocated physical education for all, including girls and women. He once owned Brooklyn's only gymnasium. Today no one needs to be convinced that staying in shape is good for you, but they did in 1852, when Jones placed a notice in the Brooklyn *Daily Eagle* saying, "Our people do not seem to understand the importance of [gymnastic] exercises, and they are therefore rather neglected. . . . Sedentary men, go and try them!"[63]

After turning to baseball, Dr. Jones used the Excelsiors of Brooklyn to promote the game nationally *as a participant sport*. Club members became his disciples. Not only were the Excelsiors the first to go on the road to popularize the game outside New York

---

63. Brooklyn *Daily Eagle*, October 13, 1852

City and Brooklyn, but individual Excelsiors founded or cofounded baseball clubs in Baltimore, Buffalo, Washington, Richmond, and Alabama.

In 1855 Dr. Jones joined the staff of the Brooklyn City Dispensary, Brooklyn's first public hospital and the antecedent of the present Brooklyn Hospital Center. He was the dispensary's first medical director, a position he held until his death in 1905. As Brooklyn's top health official he directed that city's response to the cholera epidemic of 1866, campaigning for improved sanitation laws, conducting aggressive health inspections, and cleaning up dirty streets, tenements, and vacant lots. We know now that none of this actually prevents cholera, which is spread through water contaminated by bacteria, but Jones's sanitation and public health reforms improved lives all the same.

Practicing what he had always preached about staying in shape, Jones appeared in baseball old timers' games into his 50s. In 1898, when he was 75, he won a citywide bowling tournament. According to a 1931 *Daily Eagle* article about old Brooklyn Heights, "[Dr. Jones's] long white beard and lanky frame were familiar landmarks to everyone in the neighborhood. In his earlier days, Dr. Jones had been a famous sporting character [and] was an accomplished boxer."[64] This sheds light on an item that appeared on the police blotter in 1866. Walking home late one night on Tillary Street, Jones was assaulted by a pair of muggers. One got away; the other he beat so badly that Jones refused to press robbery charges.

I T TOOK ONLY four short years, 1854–1858, for Brooklyn's four top clubs—the Excelsiors, Atlantics, Eckfords, and Putnams—to reach competitive parity with New York's big four—the Knickerbockers, Gothams, Eagles, and Empires—as well as with the Unions of Morrisania. Spectator interest was noticeably on the rise, especially in Brooklyn. The phenomenon of spectators at baseball games, especially matches between two clubs, was not new (remember that in this time the vast majority of baseball games were played intramurally, between members of the same club). What was new was what kind of spectators and how many.

---

64. Brooklyn *Daily Eagle*, June 14, 1931, p. 73

As early as 1855 the *Spirit of the Times* reported that a game at the Red House between the Knickerbockers and Gothams was "crowded." That same year, according to the *New York Atlas*, a "large assemblage" turned out to watch Brooklyn's Atlantics play an intramural married-versus-single members game. In 1857 the *New York Clipper* wrote that an Eagle–Gotham match at the Elysian Fields attracted a "very large assemblage of . . . fashionable spectators."

But there are reasons to take these stories with a generous helping of salt. One is that by the late 1850s journalists had joined the baseball movement and were promoting the sport. As they had done with cricket and thoroughbred horseracing, they exaggerated crowd sizes. There are clues that point in that direction. One is the vagueness of the stories, which use phrases like "a very large assemblage," "very large crowd," and "a large number of spectators," but almost never give a number or even an estimate. Another clue is that almost every game account goes out of its way to mention that there were women, especially "ladies" of the EUB class, at the games. The same can be found in earlier stories about cricket matches and horseraces. There were undoubtedly some real women who attended baseball games in the 1850s, but this is standard Victorian boilerplate. Its purpose was to pique the interest of eligible single men (who can forget the words of Greg Maddux, "chicks dig the long ball"?) and to reassure readers that unlike drinking, gambling, brawling, fire-fighting, and other all-male activities, baseball was respectable. A final reason to be skeptical is that before the Civil War, places like the Red House and the Elysian Fields had no facilities at all for spectators. It is hard to imagine that regular crowds in the four figures would not have changed this.

We start to see real crowds and real numbers in the mid to late 1850s, when the Brooklyn clubs began to play more games with each other and with New York City clubs. In September 1857 the *Clipper* warned that the big Atlantics versus Gothams game would cause traffic problems. In October 1857 the *New York Clipper* reported on an all–New York match at the Elysian Fields between the Empires and Eagles, noting that, "The fraternity and connoisseurs of the game turned out to witness it *en masse.*" But consider what the same paper wrote about a game played five weeks later in the same place: "the Hoboken ferry boats added largely to the number of persons . . . the grounds at the Elysian Fields were densely packed with spectators, barely leaving sufficient room for the prosecution of this beautiful game."[65] That game drew a larger crowd that included the general public, not only baseball insiders. The difference is that it was a Brooklyn versus New York match; the Atlantics were facing the Gothams again. In June 1858 an estimated 1,500–2,000 people came out to see the Excelsiors and Putnams, both of Brooklyn, in Carroll Park. A month later newspapers reported that 3,000 came to Carroll Park to watch Brooklyn's Excelsiors defeat New York's Knickerbockers, 31–13. The crowd was so big that it kept getting in the way of the fielders. "The announcement of a passage at arms between two clubs such as these," the Brooklyn *Daily Eagle* wrote, "is always a rallying cry to hundreds and thousands of the citizens of New York and Brooklyn."[66]

Visitors to Brooklyn in the late 1850s thought that its inhabitants were suffering from a kind of mass baseball insanity. If you look through Brooklyn classified ads of 1857, 1858, or 1859, you will see notice after notice announcing the founding of a new baseball club. The first thing a new club did was to challenge an established club in the next neighborhood. Every vacant lot from Greenpoint to Gravesend became a baseball field. Inter-

65. *New York Clipper*, November 7, 1857, p. 7
66. Brooklyn *Daily Eagle*, July 17, 1858, p.6

club matches built rivalries, and rivalries attracted public interest. This started a virtuous cycle. As baseball clubs came to represent communities, the added drama led to greater public and media attention, which encouraged more young men to take up the game and more people to watch, and so on. But the main event was always the rivalry between the cities of Brooklyn and New York. It had all of the classic ingredients of underdog versus favorite, David versus Goliath, and father versus son. Like a pot-bound plant, baseball needed room to spread its roots and grow. Brooklyn had it and Manhattan did not.

Baseball also needed other kinds of space. In order to evolve, adapt, and progress, baseball needed fertile cultural ground in which it could thrive. As a young city in the process of self-creation, Brooklyn provided that ground. New York was far more socially rigid and fundamentally more conservative. This partly explains the Knickerbockers' ambivalence about baseball competition. The flipside of their self-assertion and concern with respectability was a sense of inferiority to the old-money New York elite and anxiousness about their status in society. It also explains why the Knickerbockers put their aspiration to be seen as gentlemen above competition. But their fastidious brand of amateurism was more a parody than an imitation of the values of the upper classes. The real old money rich had a taste for blood sports, a love of gambling, and few scruples about mixing money and sport. The Knickerbocker Club was a vehicle for expressing its members' class identity and social aspirations as much as it was a sports organization.

In 1858 the Brooklyn clubs initiated baseball's oldest rivalry by challenging their New York counterparts to a best-two-of-three-game all-star series. Unless you count the obscure 1845 series, this would be the first time that a baseball team represented a city. For the modern sports fan, jaded by weekly big games and endless playoffs, it is hard to grasp the excitement this series created. The three-man committee in charge of arrangements, Knickerbocker James Whyte Davis, Thomas Dakin of the Putnams, and Dr. Jones of the Excelsiors (the presence of two Brooklynites and one New Yorker underlines whose idea the series was) originally planned to have the first game at the Elysian Fields. At that time, baseball fields were just that; they had no fences, seats, or other spectator facilities. The baseball fields in Hoboken's Elysian Fields looked like today's Central Park softball diamonds, not Yankee Stadium. If people came to watch, they stood in foul territory or watched from carriages parked in the outfield. But after sensing the growing buzz on both sides of the East River, the committee decided to move the event to a facility with a large wooden grandstand, access to public transportation, refreshment stands, and bathrooms—the Fashion Race Course in Queens, a horseracing track that could seat 10,000 in its grandstand and hold 50,000 total. Named after a legendary racehorse of the 1840s, the Fashion Course was located near National Road and 44th Avenue in Corona, a few blocks from where the New York Mets play today.

Game 1 was the first baseball game that anyone ever paid to see. Admission was 10 cents, plus 20 cents more for parking a one-horse vehicle and 40 cents more for a two-horse vehicle. The announced reason for charging admission was to pay groundskeeping costs. Any profit over expenses was to be donated to the Widows and Orphans Funds of the fire departments of the two cities, which made sense because hundreds of Amateur Era baseball men were firemen or ex-firemen. (After the series, the two funds split $71.10.)

The idea of an intercity all-star match was so new that no one knew exactly how to go about it. Most papers called it the

"Great Base Ball Match;" the classicists at the *New-York Trib-une* went with the "Yankee Olympian games." Some called the teams "All-Brooklyn" and "All-New York," terminology borrowed from cricket. Another entirely new problem was how to decide who should make up the teams and where they should play. Each city appointed a committee to select the players. The committees created teams of candidates that competed against each other in tryout games, more or less the way spring training works now. Oddly, most of the players in the Fashion Course Series changed positions from game to game. Henry Chadwick thought that this was ridiculous, and, as usual, he was right. Today, this happens in Little League, not in professional or even high school baseball, where a manager or coach matches each player with the position that best suits his skills. In 1858 there were no managers or coaches. The lineups themselves testify to baseball's lack of tactical sophistication and inexperience with playing for high stakes. The New York side had Harry Wright, a brilliant baseball mind who would go on to lead Cincinnati's big Red Stockings machine of the late 1860s. Wright may be the reason why the New York lineup for Game 1 reflected a rational plan to score runs—fast and high-percentage hitters at the top of the order, power hitters in the middle. The Brooklyn lineup was more like the proverbial collectively designed horse. Not only were the four principal Brooklyn clubs represented as equally as possible, but the batting order was determined by club affiliation. Excelsiors catcher Joe Leggett led off, followed by fellow Excelsior John Holder. They were followed by two Eckfords, three Atlantics, and finally two Putnams. This may reflect overconfidence or perhaps an attempt to divide up the glory before the fact (the bookmakers made Brooklyn a 100–75 favorite). Stupidity cannot be ruled out.

THE FIRST MAN to come to the plate in the Fashion Course series was New York second baseman Joseph Pinckney. Pinckney
had to wait. At 2:30 p.m., the scheduled start time, there was a
crowd of several thousand at the Fashion Course, but more kept
arriving. According to the *Spirit of the Times*, "The cry was 'still
they come!' up to five o'clock. Every imaginable kind of vehicle
had been enlisted in their service, milk-carts and wagons, beer
wagons, express wagons, stages, and the most stylish private
and public carriages ... the stands were well filled, while the entire homestretch was filled with a triple row of carriages, besides
hundreds, which were upon the field and outside the course."[67]
Final attendance estimates ranged from 4,000–10,000. *The
New York Times* calculated that there were at least 8,000 spectators, including 400–500 women. Whichever number you
believe, it was the largest baseball crowd ever. The *Times* attributed its "decorous conduct" to the fact that nothing stronger
than beer was sold at the track.

There were some glitches. After they got off the train or
horse-drawn omnibus, arriving spectators had to make their
way through an impromptu maze of scams and carnival games.
The most amusing description of the scene comes from the
New-York Tribune:

> At the little railroad station there were a few of the enter-
> prising gentlemen who make fascinating propositions to
> the innocent, whereby the latter can make huge amounts
> of money with the most trifling risks. There were three or
> four cases of benevolent gentlemen with three cards and a
> rather shaky table, whose sole purpose in coming out there
> seemed to be to lose all their heavy rolls of bills to the poor
> people around them.... This seemed to have a tendency
> to throw the money into the hands of a few, and bred the

67. *Spirit of the Times*, July 24, 1858

most unjust suspicion against these gentlemen. . . . There was also the "walk-up-and- try-your-strength machine," the "walk-up-and-try-your weight machine". . . . Indeed, few of the people cared to be weighed, try their strength, or to gamble. They had come to see baseball."[68]

The Brooklyn *Daily Eagle* later reported the arrest of notorious pickpocket "Squibb" Dickson and (the hopefully Gentile) George "Sheeney" Wells for "abstracting $700 from the pocket of a gentleman . . . at the Fashion Race Course, upon the occasion of the late baseball match."

A Brooklyn policeman lost $30 playing Three-card Monte while on duty at the game. He arrested the dealer, got his money back and bought a drink for the *Daily Eagle* reporter who wrote about the incident in exchange for not having his name mentioned. The *Spirit of the Times* gives an account of the postgame traffic jam that will sound all too familiar to the modern sports fan: "Let the reader fancy about nine thousand people simultaneously 'making tracks' for the same gate, with more than three miles of carriages, to take up their precious freight, and go through the same passage, clearing which, the motto is 'everyone for himself, and the devil take the hindmost!'"[69]

When Game 1 finally got started Brooklyn took an early 7–3 lead, but lost 22–18. One thing is clear from the box score: in a game with a lively baseball, no gloves, and no strike zone, pitchers were on the defensive. The New York pitcher, Thomas Van Cott, threw 198 pitches, 55 in a single inning. But he was comparatively economical; Matty O'Brien of the Brooklyn Atlantics threw 264, 69 in one inning. The batting highlight was a home run hit by Brooklyn second baseman John Holder. It was an

---

68. *New-York Tribune*, July 21, 1858, p. 5
69. *Spirit of the Times*, July 24, 1858

inside-the-park homer—before outfield fences, they all were. According to Henry Chadwick, Holder overheard a gambler betting $100 that he would hit a home run in his next trip to the plate. The gambler told Holder that he would pay him $25 if he came through. Holder rested the bat on his shoulder while Van Cott threw dozens of pitches over the plate. Hitters were free to do this in 1858 because baseball had no strike zone. While a new rule allowed umpires to call warning strikes if a batter repeatedly refused to swing at good pitches, it took a couple of seasons of encouragement for them to do so in practice. When Holder finally got his pitch, he smoked it over Harry Wright's head in center field and circled the bases. New York catcher Charles De Bost and Brooklyn's Leggett allowed a total of 18 passed balls. That is unthinkable today; in 2018 the Yankees' Gary Sanchez led the majors with 18 *in an entire season*. But when you consider that these two men had to block 362 pitches without gloves or any protective equipment in a game where 40 runs crossed the plate, 18 passed balls seems like a reasonable number.

Going into Game 2, Brooklyn warmed up with a game of musical chairs, with Pidgeon moving from shortstop to pitcher, Matty O'Brien from pitcher to third, and Dickey Pearce taking over at short. But they evened the series anyway by scoring 29 runs against New York pitcher Thomas Van Cott; a sharp Frank Pidgeon held the New Yorkers to only eight runs. This time 560 total pitches were thrown. Six thousand spectators watched the game in a light rain. When it was announced before Game 3 that Brooklyn's excellent defensive catcher Myron Masten was out with an injury, the betting odds shifted hard toward New York. The bookies had it right. New York pitcher Richard Thorn and his catcher Charles De Bost were dominant and in synch. De Bost allowed a mere three passed balls. Brooklyn starter Frank Pidgeon, the hero of Game 2, didn't have it. In the absence of relief pitching, which had not been invented, Pidgeon labored through a surreal 436 pitches. He threw 87, a game's worth for many starters today, in the first inning alone. New York won the game 29–18 to clinch the series before a crowd of four or five thousand.

Most "connoisseurs of the game" felt that the best team had not won. From 1858 until the mid-1860s, Brooklyn clubs dominated interclub play. During this period to be the best club in Brooklyn was to be the best club in baseball. In 1909 two baseballs from the 1858 series turned up in the possession of Charles De Bost Jr., a Manhattan dry goods wholesaler. As was the custom, the game balls—normally only one was used per game—had been given to the captain of the winning club, De Bost's father Charles De Bost Sr. The balls were inscribed with the dates and scores of the first and third Fashion Course games, and were for a time the oldest known baseballs in existence. After Charles Jr. died, his family donated them to the Hall of Fame. You can see them there today.

THE FASHION COURSE series was a wakeup call to players and clubs that were not keeping up with baseball's quickening competitive pace. The gradual separation of the top-echelon players from the rest of the pack had been underway before the first pitch at the Fashion Course. Putnams pitcher and prominent baseball figure Thomas Dakin dropped out of the Brooklyn lineup in favor of teammate Masten. "Mr. Dakin," *The New York Times* reported, "thinks that his place ... might be filled by a stronger player, and much to his credit gives way."[70] Losing Game 1 spurred the Brooklyn side to cut out more dead wood. This amounted to putting more Atlantics in the lineup. In Game 2 Brooklyn started five Atlantics, three Eckfords, one Putnam,

---

70. *The New York Times*, July 14, 1858

and no Excelsiors. In Game 3, the deciding game of the series, Brooklyn sent out six Atlantics, three Eckfords, and no Putnams or Excelsiors. When a game really mattered, social considerations would no longer trump playing ability. The Putnams were made up of members of the EUB, or, as the *Brooklyn Times* put it, they were "composed of our first citizens." Unlike the Putnams, the Excelsiors thought themselves at the top competitively as well as socially. The Fashion Course series showed them that they were only half right. In the next two years they would add star players A.T. Pearsall, George Flanley, James Creighton, and Asa Brainard. This, they hoped, would bring them up to the level of the Atlantics.

In 1860, only a year and a half after the Fashion Course series, the New York–Brooklyn baseball rivalry fell into a slump. The reason was that the Brooklyn clubs were simply too good. The Gothams, Empires, Eagles, and other old-line New York clubs were outclassed. In 1860 the Knickerbockers played only one match, which they lost to the Excelsiors, 32–9. The former kings of the New York game had fallen permanently behind the competitive curve; they lasted another two decades, but for most of that time as a social club, not a credible baseball organization. The two best clubs in baseball were the Atlantics and the Excelsiors, with the Eckfords a strong third. All were from Brooklyn, whose citizens no longer needed the drama of the intercity rivalry to turn out a big crowd. Any match between top clubs would do. Brooklyn baseball became a world unto itself. By Henry Chadwick's count, in 1859 Brooklyn had at least 70 junior clubs. All of this young talent was a rich resource that gave the top Brooklyn clubs a huge structural advantage. Because the lower-level nines got little press coverage, we cannot be sure how many players the Excelsiors controlled at their peak, but Henry Chadwick said that 91 club members fought in the Civil War.

Baseball's first national star, James Creighton of the Brooklyn Excelsiors invented modern pitching—and it killed him.

The Excelsiors had responded to the humiliation of 1858 with a determined effort to improve. In 1860 the *New York Clipper* listed all the New York City and Brooklyn clubs' grounds and practice days; the Excelsiors were one of only two out of the thirty or so clubs on the list who practiced three days a week rather than the usual two. As the season began, the confident Excelsiors felt ready to "wrest the long-worn laurels from the 'old Atlantics.'"

In the early summer of 1860 both clubs played brilliant baseball before swelling crowds. According to Amateur Era custom, any club that defeated the incumbent champion in a designated championship series (so-called "friendly" matches did not count) became the new champion on the spot. This could be awkward, especially when championship series took months to complete, as they sometimes did. What if Team A beat the champion Team B twice, but Team B lost the championship to Team C in between the two victories? Exactly. But before taking on the Atlantics, Excelsior club president Dr. Joseph B. Jones decided to make a national statement by going on the road to challenge the best clubs in Upstate New York and the Middle Atlantic states and showcase the superior athletes of the New

York game. Philadelphia, Boston, and other places were still playing their own baseball-like games, but the games on this tour would be played by New York rules. The Excelsiors ran the table. Following the Hudson to the Erie Canal and then west— the same route taken by railroads, telegraph lines, and cholera outbreaks—the tour began with a July boat trip up the Hudson River to Albany, where the Excelsiors beat the Champion Club, 24–6. The next day, they defeated a club representing Troy, a city that would soon become a baseball hotbed, 13–7. In Buffalo the Excelsiors scored 24 runs in the fifth inning and won 50–19. In Rochester they won 21–1 and 27–9; they beat Newburgh, 59–14, and returned to Brooklyn on July 12. In September they took the second leg of the tour to Baltimore and Philadelphia. The Baltimore *Daily Exchange* describes the beatdown that the Excelsiors gave their Baltimore namesakes.

> The Baltimore boys picked up the bats very cautiously, while Creighton, the pitcher, stood at his post, carelessly tossing the ball in the air. The first ball thrown to the bat went like a bullet, the stroke of the bat being made simultaneously with the ball entering the catcher's hands. The batter had never struck at such balls, and three misses followed, and he stepped aside. . . . The game closed with the conviction, on the part of the Baltimore club, that the Brooklyn Nine could have made more runs had they desired it.[71]

The final score was 51–6. These tours made pitcher James Creighton a national star. Forged in the crucible of the hyper-competitive New York–area baseball scene, the Excelsiors' thrilling and athletic play inspired hundreds of clubs across the country to switch from their own bat-and-ball games to the game that Creighton and Leggett were playing. In 1860 America

---

71. Baltimore *Daily Exchange*, September 24, 1860

may have been disintegrating politically over slavery and headed for civil war, but amateur athletes across the country were uniting behind the New York game of baseball.

IN MIDSUMMER 1860 the baseball world was full of anticipation for an Excelsiors–Atlantics showdown. But there was something bigger than a championship in the air that nobody saw coming—fans. From the point of view of early 1860, the Fashion Course crowds had never been equaled and seemed to have been a one-off. Crowds in the four figures occasionally appeared at places like the Elysian Fields, Wheat Hill in Williamsburg, or Carroll Park in South Brooklyn, which were home to many baseball clubs. We know that there was little room set aside for spectators at these fields. Accommodating spectators may have been part of the reason why the Excelsiors moved to roomier (and wetter) grounds in Red Hook at the foot of Court Street, below Hamilton Avenue and near the mouth of the Gowanus. But no permanent stands or other facilities for spectators were built there. If you look in the background of the famous New York *Illustrated News* woodcut of the Excelsiors playing the Atlantics there in 1860, you will see groups of people standing in foul territory and others on the roofs of the Brooklyn Yacht Club buildings across the street; spectators were reportedly perched in the rigging of nearby ships. The first game of the Atlantics–Excelsiors series was played at Red Hook on July 19. Some 12,000 fans came to watch—the largest crowd up to that time in baseball history. No admission was charged. With James Creighton in top form, the game was never close. The Excelsiors crushed the champions of baseball, 23–4. Game accounts from 1860 were often critical of boisterous fans and blamed gambling, but this crowd behaved itself. *The New York Times* credited both clubs with having "checked the loud expressions of feeling from outsiders, who were financially interested in the result."[72]

A record 15,000 fans came to the Atlantics' home grounds in the village of Bedford (now the neighborhood of Bedford-Stuyvesant) for Game 2 on August 9. The result would have been nearly identical to that of the first game, except for a seventh-inning, nine-run outburst by the Atlantics, which knocked Creighton out of the box, the only time this happened in Creighton's entire career. Even the Atlantics were surprised; the rally went down in club lore as the "lucky seventh." The Atlantics held off a 9th-inning rally by the Excelsiors to win, 15–14. Excuses were made. Some claimed that Creighton had been ill; others complained that an anonymous fan had yelled out "foul" on a ball hit fair by one of the Excelsiors; the batter did not run and the Atlantics turned a double play. Still, most observers agreed that the outcome had been determined by several magnificent fielding plays. Said the *New-York Tribune*, "a better played game has never been seen."

An amazing 20,000 people came to see the deciding game of the series at the Putnams' grounds, which were on Broadway between Greene and Lafayette Avenues in Brooklyn. An uneasy feeling hung in the air. Observers fretted about the lack of female spectators and the large police presence. Because the game was being played on a neutral open field not controlled by either club, it was difficult to predict what kind of crowd would come and how it might behave. To get an idea of the potential for chaos, imagine what might happen if a National Football League playoff game were played today in Central Park with open admission and no stands or fences. The spectators expected to see one of the two clubs win the championship of 1860, but something unexpected happened.

---

72. *The New York Times*, July 20, 1860, p. 8

IN THE EARLY innings both clubs showed signs of feeling the pressure of playing such an important game in front of so many people. Fearful of making an out and not compelled by the umpire to swing at strikes, batters tired out pitchers by letting dozens of good pitches go by. Henry Chadwick complained that the hitters were playing "'a waiting game,' an objectionable style at best." According to the box score, the Excelsiors' Creighton threw 72 pitches in the first inning, 96 in the second, and 80 in the third, absolutely insane totals by today's standards. With their club down 8–6 in the fifth inning, Atlantics supporters loudly protested the umpire's call on a close play. When the Atlantics made two errors in the top of the sixth, the crowd's mood turned ugly. "Expressions of dissent," wrote Chadwick in the *Daily Eagle*, "became so decided, and symptoms of bad feeling began to manifest itself to such a degree, that the Captain of the Excelsior nine, Mr. Leggett, than whom a fairer, more manly, or more gentlemanly player does not exist, ordered his men to pick up their bats and retire from the field."[73] The attitude of the *Daily Eagle* was typical of the press, which was uniformly sympathetic to the Excelsiors. *The New York Times* wrote:

> The rowdy element which had been excited by a fancied injustice to [the Atlantics'] McMahon in the preceding innings, now became almost insupportable in its violence, and shouts from all parts of the field arose for a new Umpire; the hootings [sic] against the Excelsior Club were perfectly disgraceful. Mr. Leggett was supported by the Atlantic nine in his endeavors to secure order, and by their united exertions a temporary lull was secured, but, although Mr. Leggett distinctly stated that the Excelsiors would withdraw if the tumult was renewed, the hooting was again started with increased vigor, and the Excelsiors

---

73. Brooklyn *Daily Eagle*, August 24, 1860, p.2

immediately left the field, followed by a crowd of roughs, alternately groaning the Excelsiors and cheering the Atlantics. The game is drawn, and, if ever played out, will take place in comparative privacy, on some enclosed ground. The determination shown by the Excelsior Club on this occasion is worthy of great praise, and meets the approval of the vast majority of the respectable portion of the baseball community.[74]

It was unclear if either club had won. Umpire R.H. Thorn confused everyone by ruling that neither club had won the game, but that the Excelsiors had lost by forfeit. The Atlantics claimed victory. The Excelsiors were angry that the Atlantics would accept a victory that they viewed as tainted. A purported game ball was sent anonymously to Atlantics secretary Frederick K. Boughton as an insult. According to the *Daily Eagle*, the Atlantics "have chosen to recognize the ball as the one played with, and have placed it among their other trophies . . . the affair has created some feeling among baseball players." History has repeated and embellished the narrative that a rowdy, uncouth, and—incomprehensibly— predominantly Irish crowd of Atlantics fans, angry that they might lose their bets, were so out of control that the Excelsiors had no choice but to leave the field, and that it was unsportsmanlike of the Atlantics to accept the forfeit. Most baseball histories note, darkly, that the two clubs never played each other again, as if there was such a divergence of culture and values that reconciliation was impossible.

THE FIRST PROBLEM with this version of events is that it is colored by the views of one man, Henry Chadwick. The preeminent baseball writer of the time, Chadwick wrote the accounts

---

74. *The New York Times*, August 24, 1860, p. 8

of the 1860 Excelsiors–Atlantics series read by most contemporary fans and by most historians today. Baseball's chief publicist and promoter, he was not an unbiased reporter. Chadwick had long pushed for the total elimination of gambling in baseball, a campaign that struck many of his contemporaries as extreme and even obsessive. Wanting to market the New York game to the respectable Protestants of the EUB, many of whom disapproved of gambling on moral grounds, Henry Chadwick saw gambling and gamblers as a threat to the game's public image and therefore its acceptance.

1860 was a critical turning point, the season in which the Excelsiors were being used to sell baseball as a national sport. Could it be that what Chadwick painted as rowdy behavior by disappointed gamblers was nothing more than the enthusiasm of excited fans? None of the contemporary accounts of the disputed game alleges a single violent act by a spectator. *The New York Times* used adjectives like "rowdy" and "shameful," but the only specific acts mentioned were "groaning," "shouts," and "hooting." In the *Clipper*'s version, "the crowd began to get uproarious in the extreme, and so insulting were the epithets bestowed on the Excelsiors that Leggett decided to withdraw his forces from the field." From a modern point of view this sounds a little silly. The Excelsiors walked away from a championship game because the opposing team's fans used rough language and booed the umpire? And it may be true that after August 23, 1860 the Atlantics and Excelsiors never played again, but the reason was not lasting bitterness caused by that game. Many individual Excelsiors and Atlantics were friends and remained friends; they socialized and played cricket together both before and after August 23, 1860. Within a week or two of the August 23 game, baseball returned to business as usual. On September 3 Excelsior George Flanley umpired an Atlantics game. On September 22 the American Cricket Club was formed; it included two members of the Excelsiors and three Atlantics. Not having been defeated in a best-of-three series, the Atlantics entered the 1861 season as defending champions once again. Because of the Civil War the Excelsiors did not play at all in 1861 and played only a handful of games in 1862.

IN THE WEEK following the disputed Atlantics–Excelsiors finale of 1860, the Atlantics read one newspaper story after another that took the side of the Excelsiors and blamed the Atlantics and their fans for the debacle. On September 1 they responded.

To the Editor of the New York Daily News:

SIR -- In consequence of . . . all the odium consequent upon the abrupt termination of the game on the Atlantic Club and their friends, we . . . [hope] that a discerning public will . . . give our side of the story a fair hearing.

In the first place, we used every possible effort to have "a clear field and no favor;" and in this . . . we succeeded beyond the possibility of a doubt. What more can any club do? Can we restrain a burst of applause or indignation emanating from an assemblage of more than 15,000 excited spectators, whose feelings are enlisted as the game proceeds?

He who has witnessed the natural excitement which is ever attendant of a vast miscellaneous assemblage . . . knows full well that it is an utter impossibility to prevent the crowd from expressing their sentiments in any manner and as audibly as they please.

Mr. Thorn, the umpire on this occasion, was calm, and expressed himself not at all annoyed by the exclamations of the spectators. The members of the Atlantics nine remarked to him at the most exciting period of the game, that they would sustain him in all of his decisions, and requested and urged the continuance of the play. Then let us ask what caused the abrupt termination? Nothing, in our opinion, judging from the language made use of, but the ungovernable temper of a friend of ours on the other side, who seems to be getting exceedingly nervous of late; and if the nine is to be called off the ground on all occasions where the pressure is rather high, we think that ball playing will soon lose its most essential features ... [and] terminate in the ruin of the game as a national pastime. ...

In conclusion ... we wish the public to remember that the "old Atlantics" are used to these exciting battles; and we would recommend those aspiring to the championship not to be too hasty in leaving the field, as it is a "poor road to travel," and does not lead to that enviable and coveted position.

F. K. BOUGHTON,
Secretary of Atlantic Base Ball Club
Brooklyn, Aug. 31, 1860[75]

Boughton's point of view can be summed up as: "If you can't stand the heat, get out of the kitchen." It needs little interpretation other than to explain that the "friend of ours" was Excelsiors team captain Joe Leggett, who had a history of being rattled by large crowds. The game was stopped because Leggett and the Excelsiors lost their nerve under the psychological pressure of playing the biggest game of their lives in front of the largest crowd they had ever seen. What Boughton and the Atlantics understood, and what the Excelsiors and their supporters in the press seem not to have understood, is that the events of August

75. Brooklyn *Daily Eagle*, September 1, 1860, p.3

[179

23 reflected a new baseball reality. Baseball spectators had become baseball fans and fans were now part of the game. Booing and heckling are the flip side of cheering and applause. As any professional athlete of today can tell you, both come with the territory.

HENRY CHADWICK AND the larger baseball community were slow to grasp the meaning of the massive crowds that turned out for the 1858 Fashion Course series and the 1860 Atlantics–Excelsior series, but Brooklyn's business community was not. After seeing that fans would pay in large numbers to watch baseball, leather merchant William Cammeyer decided to add an enclosed baseball park with locker rooms, a grandstand, and other facilities, to the skating rink and recreation center he was building on Wheat Hill in what is now Williamsburg. Called the Union Grounds, it opened in 1862. Baseball clubs were invited to use it for free—they were the attraction—but fans had to pay their way in. Two years later, entrepreneurs Hamilton Weed and Reuben Decker opened the world's second enclosed ballpark, the Capitoline Grounds, near the Atlantics' original playing field in Bedford. They also charged admission. It did not take long before baseball clubs insisted on a share of the gate receipts. Driven mostly by outsiders—spectators turned fans and non-playing businessmen—this marks the beginning of baseball as an entertainment business.

Whatever their superficial similarities to earlier Amateur Era clubs like the Knickerbockers, Gothams, and Eagles, the Brooklyn clubs were different in spirit. Their desire to beat each other and the big city across the river energized and revolutionized baseball. The rivalry between New York City and Brooklyn is the oldest, longest, and most important of any sports rivalry in American history. It sold the first tickets to a baseball game. It lives on today in the Dodgers–Giants rivalry on the West Coast and in the Mets–Yankees rivalry on the East. It is the watershed event to which we can trace the triumph of the American sports movement and baseball's arrival as a national sport. The first baseball club to go on tour, the first baseball star, and the greatest clubs of the early Amateur Era were all from Brooklyn. It was the home of Henry Chadwick, the most important early baseball writer, and Dr. Joseph B. Jones, the sport's most underrated pioneer. Was Brooklyn the real birthplace of baseball? If by baseball you mean baseball the modern sport, and by birthplace you mean the home of the first fans and the first ballpark, then the answer is yes. It happened in Brooklyn—not the 1947 film with Frank Sinatra and Jimmy Durante, but the beginning of American professional sports.

An 1865 portrayal of baseball as a house divided between New York and Brooklyn. The principal clubs are divided into two categories: Brooklyn (banner on right) and New York City et al. (banner on left). The small full figures along the top and bottom are key members of each of the prominent clubs. The playing field at center is Brooklyn's Union Grounds, the first ballpark. The larger busts on either side are journalist Henry Chadwick and Thomas G. Voorhis, president of the National Association of Base Ball Players. Above and framed in black crepe is the martyred James Creighton, baseball's first national star, who had died three years earlier.

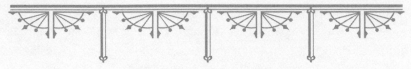

CHAPTER SIX
A Ballplayer's Tale

 AMES CREIGHTON's baseball career was like a nuclear explosion. It didn't last long, but afterward the world was never the same. Pre-Creighton baseball was a hitter's dream. Early baseball rules required pitchers to deliver the ball dead-underhand with no wrist snap. The result was pitches that were slow, straight and easy to hit; pitchers tossed the ball over the plate and ducked. In the 1850s scores in double figures were the norm. Around 1860 Creighton figured out a legal or apparently legal way to throw very hard with movement and command. Widely imitated, his maximum-effort fast pitching changed the game more than a hundred Babe Ruths. The Babe may have hit a lot of home runs, but he did not invent the home run and he did not change the basic structure of the game. Creighton's new style of pitching so upset the balance of power between offense and defense that it led to the creation of the strike zone, which has been the center of the action of a baseball game ever since. Before the strike zone, baseball games were decided by which defense did a better job of controlling balls put in play; ever since, they have been decided by who wins control of the imaginary box hovering over home plate. This is the single biggest

reason that baseball is watchable on TV. It is inexplicable that James Creighton is not in the Baseball Hall of Fame.

As innovative as he was, however, Creighton's story is the oldest and saddest one in the baseball book. He possessed the game's most valuable skill, the ability to get good hitters out. The rare players who can do this are inevitably overworked and abused and have been for 150 years. Every time they take the mound, modern pitchers are doing what James Creighton was the first to do—walk a tightrope between making effective pitches and injuring themselves. Sometimes they fall off the tightrope. Today, it hardly makes news when an exhausted professional pitcher literally rips his elbow ligament into shreds; surgeons simply sew in a new ligament taken from another part of the pitcher's body and 18 months later he is back at work. If that one tears, they do it again. Rest a sore shoulder? Not with championships to win and money on the line. Arm injuries end careers in the majors, the minors, college, and high school every day. But throwing a baseball too hard for too long cost James Creighton more than a career. It killed him.

For historians Creighton is a frustrating and enigmatic figure. We know less about him than we do about his own brother, who was not a famous athlete. One reason why is that he died before he had had a full baseball career or even a full life. He left no colorful quotations. There is one interesting anecdote about Creighton— Jack Chapman's story of how he died—but it is not true. Game accounts and box scores tell us something about how he played, but there is a lot that they don't tell us. How did he throw so much harder than anyone else under the restrictive pitching rules of the time? Did he really throw a curveball? In the absence of action photography, film, or video, we simply do not know. Then there is his personal life. Did his club, the Excelsiors of Brooklyn, pay him to play baseball? What was he really like? What kind of upbringing did he have? A logical place to begin looking for answers to these questions is lot 3384, Section 2 of Green-Wood Cemetery in Brooklyn, New York, where he and the people he lived with—his mother, father, and siblings—are buried.

According to his death certificate James Creighton died on October 18, 1862 from "strangulation of [the] intestine,"[76] a bad way to go. He was 21. The Methodist Reverend Dr. North conducted the funeral services at the home of his father James Creighton Sr. at 307 Henry Street in what is now Cobble Hill, Brooklyn. The next day Creighton was buried. His Excelsiors teammates Joseph Leggett, Henry Polhemus, and George Flanley, and ex-teammate David Kent of the Niagaras carried the coffin. Creighton died too young to tell his own story in letters, memoirs, or post-career interviews. Strangely, his Excelsiors teammates never had much to say about him either, even years later when they were reminiscing about the old days. George Flanley lived until 1915, Leggett until about 1894, and Polhemus until 1895. The prolific baseball journalist Henry Chadwick wrote columns full of stories about the Amateur Era and its great players for the Brooklyn *Daily Eagle*. But Chadwick managed to live until 1908, spilling hundreds of gallons of ink along the way, without telling us one interesting personal detail about Creighton.

JAMES CREIGHTON WAS born in Manhattan in 1841. His father was an Irish Protestant immigrant from County Donegal. In the 1820s he came to New York City, where he married Jane McBrien, an Irish Protestant from County Sligo. In 1829 James Creighton Sr., sometimes spelled "Craton," makes his first appearance in a New York City directory as the manager of a porterhouse, which

---

76. Death Certificate #3586, City of Brooklyn, handwritten by J. Byrne, MD, October 19, 1862

was a tavern featuring ale and hearty food to porters and other working men (this is where both porter ale and the porterhouse steak got their names); later directories list him as the keeper of a porter and cider vault. In the days before refrigeration there were many such vaults in the city, located underground to take advantage of fermentation-friendly low temperatures. His original address was 108 Anthony Street in the impoverished Sixth Ward. Drinking was the Sixth Ward's second favorite vice; one in 60 of its residents made a living providing alcohol to the rest.

James Creighton Jr. grew up in the Sixth Ward. Also known as the Five Points, the area was notorious for crime, free-flowing liquor, and abysmal life expectancy. It was also the only neighborhood in New York—and quite possibly in America—where large numbers of African Americans and whites lived together voluntarily. In the 1840s and 1850s the racial unconventionality of the Five Points attracted a parade of tourists. Guided slumming parties came to experience urban poverty and—even more titillating—interracial drinking and dancing. One such visit shocked even chronicler of London low life Charles Dickens, who overwrote: "Debauchery has made the very houses prematurely old. . . . Here, too are lanes and alleys paved with mud, knee deep . . . underground chambers, where they dance and game . . . hideous tenements which take their name from robbery and murder; all that is loathsome, drooping, and decayed is here."[77] Most of the white residents of the Five Points were Gaelic-speaking and illiterate refugees from the Irish Potato Famine of 1845–1852. One lasting product of the neighborhood's cultural mélange is the art of tapdancing, essentially Irish step dancing as interpreted by African Americans, whose origins can be traced to a particular nightclub on Orange (now Baxter)

77. Dickens, Charles, *American Notes for General Circulation*, London: Chapman and Hall, p. 212

Street. From the Five Points to Harlem to Greenwich Village, the unique cultural interplay between African Americans, immigrants, and native-born whites that began in the neighborhood where James Creighton was born has been a lasting and defining characteristic of New York City.

When James Creighton was still a boy his mother died and the family moved a few blocks west to 48 Anthony Street in the Fifth Ward. This neighborhood was a step up from the Five Points, but in the 1850s it entered a period of decline. As well-to-do residents moved north of 14th Street, their businesses and institutions followed. The prestigious Christ Episcopal Church and New York Hospital, both on Anthony Street, remained, although not for long, alongside the African Methodist and other African American churches. Two blocks away was Ward School No. 10, which Creighton likely attended. If school records of that time were not lost, they would probably tell us that he played cricket or baseball or both on school teams. The 1855 New York State census pages for this part of Anthony Street paint a picture of the squalor of young James Creighton's daily life. About a quarter of the buildings on Anthony Street housed ground floor taverns or shops selling homemade liquor; these were known euphemistically as "groceries." There were honest laborers and artisans, quite a few of them shoemakers born in Ireland or Germany, but judging by the police blotter, drunkenness, violence, and prostitution were rampant.

Looking down one typical page from the Fifth Ward, we find a boarding house inhabited by one Nancy Phillips, 55, born in Connecticut, occupation "prostitution." Next we come to a full-fledged brothel whose inhabitants include Ellen Hughes, 17, born in Ireland; Mary Howell, 25, born in Brooklyn; and New York–born Elizabeth Dusenberry, age 14—all with "prostitution" listed as their occupation.[78] The fact that prostitution, though illegal, is listed as an occupation even for an underage girl speaks to the indifference of pre–Civil War New York to vice and the exploitation of women and children. In February 1858 James Creighton Sr. moved his family across the East River to 307 Henry Street in Brooklyn. This is consistent with the fact that in 1857 James Creighton Sr. appears for the last time in a New York City directory, still living at 48 Worth Street. (Anthony Street had been renamed for a Mexican War hero in order to purge it of unsavory associations with the Five Points.) The Creighton family resurfaces in the 1860 U.S. Census in Brooklyn's Sixth Ward, which is where 307 Henry Street was located.

Why did they move? There are several intriguing possibilities. One is civic unrest. In the 1850s the social fabric of New York City was under strain from explosive growth, economic and political upheaval, and a massive wave of foreign immigrants. Previous Irish immigrants to New York, like James Creighton's parents, had been fewer in number and reassuringly Protestant. Until the 1850s New York's St. Patrick's Day parade was a Protestant affair with marchers dressed in orange rather than green. The cultural strangeness and Catholicism of the new Irish provoked fear bordering on panic. 1857, the year before the Creighton family left New York, was especially tumultuous. A dispute between the Republican state government in Albany and Democratic City Hall over control of the police department led to a breakdown in law enforcement. Criminals and the city's myriad political and armed militias stepped into the resulting power vacuum. Public order reached a low point with the so-called Dead Rabbits Riot, when on July 4th and 5th Irish and nativist gangs battled each other with

---

78. New York State Census 1855, NYC 5th Ward, 1st District

guns, knives, and bricks on barricaded streets a few blocks from the Creighton home. Police factions intervened on both sides. Eight people were killed and one hundred injured. The year ended with the Panic of 1857, an economic recession reminiscent of that of 2008, which began with financial speculation on Wall Street and radiated outward to Europe and much of the world. In New York City the combination of unemployment in excess of 20 percent and rising food prices caused mass demonstrations. In October and November crowds of unemployed workers overwhelmed National Guard units and stormed both the Merchants' Exchange and City Hall.

The Creightons may have left New York because of the political fallout from the chaos of 1857. James Creighton Jr.'s older brother John Creighton was a Tammany Hall operative belonging to the faction led by nativist Isaiah Rynders, boss of the Empire political club. Rynders was one of the instigators of the 1849 Astor Theatre riot. (The Magnolia baseball club, which played at the Elysian Fields before the New York Knickerbockers, was associated with the Empire Club). Later, both Rynders and John Creighton supported Fernando Wood, who served two terms as New York mayor and began the conversion of fractious Tammany Hall into a disciplined political machine. Politics in pre–Civil War New York was a bare-knuckle fight; the Empire Club regarded fraud, voter suppression, and physical intimidation as ordinary election tactics. In the 1830s and 1840s James Creighton Sr. had also been involved in Tammany Hall politics. At a time when taverns served as political headquarters and as polling places, it was common for men in the liquor trade to act as party functionaries. Supportive businessmen were rewarded with licenses, contracts, and patronage jobs for family and friends. In December 1857, however, the machine stalled. The conflict with Albany cost Wood his job as mayor, and Tammany

Hall lost its grip on the New York City government. Perhaps the Creightons moved to Brooklyn because the political changes of 1857 left James Creighton's father and brother without political sponsorship.

Something else happened in the 1850s that may have played into the Creightons' decision to leave New York City: the resurgent national Temperance movement. For a century or so the movement's efforts to persuade government to limit or ban the sale of alcohol had been futile. Fear of Irish immigrants and their supposed innate inability to handle alcohol inspired Temperance activists to try again. Republicans in Albany passed a sweeping Liquor Excise Law requiring all alcohol retailers to provide 30 freeholders (adult men who owned real estate) who would attest to their good moral character, to post a monetary bond, and to close on Sundays and election days. This was setting the bar high in places like the Fifth and Sixth Wards. Anticipating Mayor Wood's refusal to enforce this law, the state government decided to seize control of the New York City police force, which sparked the violent summer of 1857. The new law drove hundreds of groceries and porterhouses out of business. Figures from Anthony Street in New York's Sixth Ward show a drop between 1851 and 1860 in the number of groceries from 17 to seven and in the number of porterhouses from 25 to nine.[79] In later censuses James Creighton Sr. gave his occupation as "retired merchant." He may well have been retired involuntarily by teetotaling, Hibernophobic upstate Republicans.

THERE ARE ALSO positive reasons why the Creightons may have moved to the Sixth Ward of Brooklyn, farmland then being converted into a suburb. Prosperous New Yorkers of the 1850s were

---

79. Bayor and Meagher, eds., *The New York Irish*, Baltimore: Johns Hopkins University Press, p. 119

buying houses in what are now Brooklyn Heights and Cobble Hill for the same reasons that New Yorkers of the 1950s moved to New Jersey and Long Island: space, serenity, and safety. The Creightons, however, do not entirely fit this scenario. They were poorer than most of their neighbors. The 1860 U.S. Census includes the dollar value of dwellings, the occupation and personal worth of heads of households, and names and number of live-in servants. Looking at the 50 households nearest to the Creightons' brick rowhouse gives us an idea of the neighborhood's economic and social character. Common occupations include three "gentleman" (men living on inherited wealth), 13 merchants or commercial merchants, four brokers, two silk importers, three flour dealers, and three physicians. Humbler occupations include one tailor, one teacher, and a pump maker. Housing values vary between $2,500 to $300,000, with most in the $10,000–$20,000 range; personal net worth for a head of household ranges from $1,000–$20,000, with between $5,000 and $10,000 being typical. James Creighton Sr.'s house at 307 Henry Street was valued at $8,000, only a bit below average, but his personal worth is listed as $1,000, one of the lowest figures in the neighborhood.

When it comes to live-in servants the Creightons are even more atypical. The overwhelming majority of the 50 households had one or more servants; about half had two and six had three or more. The Creighton household was one of only six that employed none.[80] Incidentally, baseball histories and references are wrong about where in Brooklyn the Creighton family lived. Because of renumbering, the house where James Creighton Jr. died is now number 461 Henry Street, not the present 307 Henry, which is several blocks to the north. A theme of the Amateur

---

80. U.S. Census 1860, Brooklyn 6th Ward, 3rd District

Era is that membership in a baseball club offered a way to lever-
age athletic talent for higher social and economic status. James
Creighton was far from the only example. His teammate George
Flanley came from humble circumstances. The Excelsiors may
or may not have paid players like these two a literal wage, but
that is not really the point. The Excelsiors found Flanley a government job with the Brooklyn Police Department as a telegrapher in order to have him available to play baseball but also to
integrate him into their community and social class.

THERE IS ONE final possible reason for the Creightons' move to
Brooklyn in 1858: to exploit James Jr.'s athletic talent. 461 Henry
Street stands in an area that was developed by the wealthy Van
Nostrand family. Censuses show that living on the other side of
the same block were three Van Nostrand households and another belonging to a business associate named Henry Suydam. The
Van Nostrand money came from a Manhattan wholesale food
business, but by the 1850s they had followed a path well-worn
by members of the EUB by diversifying into finance, insurance,
and real estate. James Van Nostrand Sr. was president of the
wealthy Merchants Exchange Bank, an antecedent of Citibank.
Living in these houses between 1850 and 1860 we find young
men named Charles C. Suydam, John H. Suydam, and James
Van Nostrand Jr.—three of the principal founders of the Excelsior baseball club. This cannot be a coincidence. Remember
that the Creightons moved to Brooklyn in 1858. That year James
Jr. played for a Brooklyn junior club called the Niagaras. He
switched to another junior organization, the Star club, in 1859.
The Stars functioned as a feeder club for the Excelsiors, sending
their top players to the senior club. The Niagaras seem to have
served a similar function for the Stars, as in effect a lower rung
in the Excelsiors' system.

Pre–Civil War clubs like the Excelsiors competed for players with each other, but because in those days athletes commonly played both sports, they also competed with cricket clubs. Here baseball's amateurism was inconvenient; the cricket clubs of New York and Brooklyn openly paid their best players. When baseball clubs compensated players, they did so indirectly and quietly, so it is not surprising that we have almost no direct evidence. Circumstantial evidence, however, is there to be found. We know that Creighton had been recruited by the Excelsiors no later than 1859 because of the relationship the Stars had with the Excelsiors. The Niagaras had a similar connection to the Excelsiors, which suggests that Creighton was recruited in 1858 or even earlier. This scenario would solve a mystery. In August 1858 James Whyte Davis of the Knickerbockers wrote a parody song for a banquet attended by the principal New York and Brooklyn baseball clubs. Entitled "Ball Days," it contains a stanza or two about each of them. This is one of the stanzas about the Excelsiors:

> They have Leggett for a catcher, and who is always there,
> A gentleman in every sense, whose play is always square;
> Then Russell, Reynolds, Dayton, and also Johnny Holder,
> And the infantile "phenomenon," who'll play when he gets older.[81]

The phrase "infantile phenomenon" comes from Charles Dickens's 1838 novel *Nicholas Nickleby*, in which a child performer is advertised as the "infant phenomenon." It is probably also the origin of "phenom," which is still baseball slang for a promising young player. Is this a winking reference to young James Creighton? It is hard to imagine what else it could be. This would mean that the Excelsiors already "owned" Creighton in a sense in 1858 when he was a member of the

81. Chadwick, Henry. *The Game of Baseball* (reprint), Columbia, S.C.: Camden House, 1983, p. 178

Niagaras. More significantly, all of the other baseball men at the banquet knew it.

It is extremely unlikely that an athlete of Creighton's caliber could have gone unnoticed in New York before 1858, the year he turned 17. Junior baseball clubs of that time included players as young as 15 and New York City schools fielded baseball and cricket teams. The Excelsiors may have recruited Creighton before he moved from New York to Brooklyn and brought Creighton's family to Henry Street as part of that recruitment effort. There is one more connection between the Excelsiors and the Creightons that predates James Creighton's officially joining the Excelsiors in 1860: his older brother John Creighton. John Creighton was not a baseball player, but in 1858 he joined Brooklyn's Montague Hall Democratic Club, where he would have met Excelsiors President Dr. Joseph B. Jones. Jones and John Creighton ran for political office on the same Democratic tickets and were later active in the same chapter of the post-war Soldiers and Sailors Union movement. Of course, these scenarios make more sense if the Excelsiors were actually paying or otherwise compensating James Creighton. James Creighton Sr. may have been helped to buy the house on Henry Street as a form of compensation. But there were contemporary rumors that the Excelsiors were paying James Creighton Jr. an actual salary. The *Troy Daily Whig* of July 3, 1860 stated that the Excelsiors, "pay their pitcher $500 a year."[82] The specificity of the number is certainly intriguing. Then there is the curious fact that Creighton, unlike most ordinary young men, including his own brother, had no apparent occupation between the ages of 16 and 21. Creighton excelled at cricket and was almost certainly paid to play that sport. This is significant because he was playing both sports at the highest level simultaneously. It

---

82. Troy *Daily Whig*, July 3, 1860

is hard to imagine that a gifted athlete with little family money like Creighton played professionally and as an amateur in different sports at the same time.

ALL OF THIS certainly suggests that he was paid, but is there any proof? According to the 1860 census both Creightons, father and son, held jobs in the Customs House. These were highly sought-after patronage plums. In the 1850s about two thirds of all foreign imports to the United States passed through the New York Customs House in lower Manhattan. Opportunities to skim off goods and money, to do favors for well-connected merchants, and for more creative kinds of graft were nearly limitless. Corruption at the Customs House was an ongoing scandal that ended only with modern civil service reforms. In James Creighton's lifetime every change of political administration in Washington meant that Customs House employees would be fired and replaced by men owed favors by incoming politicians. An 1874 Congressional investigation found that it cost the United States about $7 million to collect duties on imports of $642 million, while the port of London spent only $5 million on imports of $1.8 billion.[83] The reason was that many of the clerk, weigher, gauger, and other positions at the New York Customs House were filled by men who did little work or none at all.

It is hard not to suspect that this was the case with the Creightons. Neither had any qualifications for this kind of work. Creighton Sr. was in his late 60s in 1860, an old man for the time, and he had spent most of his working life watching ale ferment. Creighton Jr. was 19 and had no known employment history before or after 1860. There are other reasons to doubt that James Creighton Jr. was a genuine

---

83. Eaton, D.E., *The "Spoils" System and Civil Service Reform in the Custom-House and Post-Office at New York*, New York City, New York: G. P. Putnam's Sons, 1881

public servant. In 1860 he was playing cricket and baseball at least two or three days a week in spring, early summer, and fall, and not in New York City, where the Customs House was located, but in Brooklyn, New Jersey, and Long Island. He was also traveling on the Excelsiors' tours, which totaled several weeks. Most of his teammates on the tours had flexible work schedules because they were self-employed or worked in a family business. The few Excelsiors who held regular jobs did not participate. Did James Creighton and his father have no-show Customs House jobs in 1860 that paid, say, $500 per year? That number is about right for a low-level Customs House position in that time. Did the backers of the Excelsiors have the political juice to arrange such a thing? Absolutely.

THERE IS ONE final bit of circumstantial evidence that James Creighton was paid to play baseball in 1860: the fact that he was not in 1861. In 1861 the Excelsiors shut down because of the Civil War. There is no record of James Creighton or his father working at the Customs House or anywhere else in 1861. We do know that there was a benefit game held in November of that year at the Elysian Fields in Hoboken for James Creighton Jr. and Atlantics shortstop Dickey Pearce.[84] Borrowed from cricket, the benefit game was a fundraiser intended to help a player who was in financial need. A benefit for Atlantics first baseman Joe Start, for example, was justified on the grounds that his father had died and, "like a good son and an affectionate brother he supports a mother and sisters."[85] Late 1861 newspaper articles promoting James Creighton's benefit game mention no health or family problems. His real problem was that the Excelsiors were not paying him, via a no-show Customs House job or any other way. They were not paying him because he was not playing baseball.

84. Brooklyn *Daily Eagle*, November 8, 1861
85. Brooklyn *Daily Eagle*, October 12, 1864, p. 2

FLYING THINGS

Jack Chapman's barehanded circus catches in big games earned him the immortal nickname, "Death to Flying Things." One of his most famous was a walk-off in Philadelphia in 1868. According to one account,

> All eyes were now fixed on Flanly [sic] at the bat, and the entire crowd stood spellbound, until Flanly, getting a ball that suited him, sent it sailing over Pearce's head and down the left field, and which Chapman by a tremendous effort, just managed to secure, after a long run, holding it up over his head in triumph. The crowd gave one terrific yell, and in an instant the entire field was crowded. Thus, by one of the finest catches ever witnessed, was one of the most exciting and closely contested games ever played, terminated.[86]

The Brooklyn-born Chapman played for the Atlantics in the 1860s, where he and teammate Bob Ferguson managed the business side of the club. In 1871 he jumped to the Eckfords for cash and remained a hired gun for the rest of his career. From 1877 until 1892 John Chapman managed, ran, or owned major and minor league clubs across the country. He founded many of them. According to the *Daily Eagle*, "Chapman organized the Louisville club, holding three contracts, for organizer, manager and player."[87] This was the period in which the foundation was laid for today's Organized Baseball. Professional baseball grew from one or two leagues on the East Coast to several dozen from Ohio to Texas to California. Brooklyn was no longer home to the top baseball clubs, but it continued to export baseball men like Chapman to the rest of the country.

John Chapman's finest hour came as manager of the Buffalo Bisons in the late 1880s. Dropping out of the National League after the 1885 season, the Bisons were founding members of the minor International League, which conducted an experiment in racial integration that is little remembered today. Several clubs signed African American

---

86. Philadelphia *Sunday Mercury*, quoted in Brooklyn *Daily Eagle*, August 26, 1868, p. 2
87. Brooklyn *Daily Eagle*, March 15, 1896, p. 4

players. Chapman signed African American second baseman Frank Grant, who in 1886 batted .344 with power. The racist backlash was immediate and powerful. Grant and other African American players endured vile heckling from fans. Toronto fans chanted "Kill the Nigger" at Grant. Opposing players spiked him at second base. The press ranged from sympathetic to hostile, with some papers ridiculing the International League as the "Colored League." "How far," asked the *Sporting Life*, "will this mania for engaging colored players go?" In spring training of 1887 Grant's own teammates refused to sit with him for a team photograph until Chapman forced them. In 1887 the campaign to exclude African Americans escalated, but John Chapman kept putting Grant's name in the lineup. Chapman laughed off the issue of skin color, sometimes calling his second baseman an "Italian."

Finishing second in 1887 and 1888, largely thanks to Grant's heavy hitting, the Buffalo Bisons tried to appease racist IL owners by proposing a limit of two African American players per club. When that was rejected, they suggested a ban on future signings, with current African American players being allowed to stay. In the end the hard-line opponents of racial integration got what they wanted. Grant left the Bisons for the African American Cuban X Giants and the gaps in the color line were closed tight by 1890. Frank Grant remained the only African American player until Jackie Robinson to play three consecutive seasons in Organized Baseball with the same club. In retrospect there were two reasons why this brief episode of racial tolerance happened at all. One was the lack of a baseball commissioner or other authority with the power to prevent it. The other was the personal courage of men like Jack Chapman and Frank Grant.

TODAY FEW VISITORS to the impressive, baseball-themed grave of James Creighton at Green-Wood Cemetery notice the small military veteran's grave marker, sometimes decorated with an American flag, a couple of feet to the north of Creighton's marble monument. This is where John Creighton, Jim's older brother by 14 years, is buried. In 1861, the year of James Creighton's benefit game, John Creighton was off at the war. Many baseball players from the amateur era were also involved in firefighting, militias, politics, and, after 1861, the military. James Creighton Jr. was a full-time athlete. John Creighton was involved in all of the other four. Ironically, he had no known

An 1887 portrait of manager and former Amateur Era great Jack Chapman and his International League Buffalo Bisons, including power-hitting African American second baseman Frank Grant (the only player not being physically touched by a teammate). Despite the opposition of many fans and players, the high-minor International League partially racially integrated for several seasons in the 1880s.

connection to baseball. John was as colorful as James was seemingly featureless. John Creighton's life story is worth telling for its picaresque, even bipolar quality, and because of what it tells us about the Creighton family and the social and historical context of early baseball.

LIKE SO MANY of the earliest amateur baseball players, the young John Creighton was a Bowery B'hoy. Born in 1828 and working in the 1850s as a tin roofer, Creighton was also a volunteer fireman. He was a popular officer in citizen militias. He was active in Tammany Hall politics and a member of Isaiah Rynders's Empire Club. A man of flexible principles but fundamentally a nativist, Rynders was a major player in New York politics in the 1840s. Tammany Hall later lost interest in nativism and began courting support from immigrants. Both Rynders and Tammany Hall stayed faithful to one principle, however—racism. The Broadway Tabernacle, a church directly across the street from the Creightons' first home at 108 Anthony, was the scene of a nasty confrontation in May 1850 between Rynders's thugs and Abolitionists who had come to hear speeches by William Lloyd Garrison and Frederick Douglass. One of Rynders's men rose from his seat and insisted on addressing the meeting. Historian John Jay Chapman describes what followed.

> His thesis was that the blacks were not men, but belonged to the monkey tribe. . . . Nothing daunted, the ex-fugitive from greater terrors [Douglass] began. . . . "The gentleman who has just spoken has undertaken to prove that the blacks are not human beings. . . . I offer myself for your examination. Am I a man?" The audience responded with a thunderous affirmative, which Captain Rynders sought to break by exclaiming: "*You* are not a black man; you are only half a nigger." "Then," replied Mr.

Douglass, turning upon him with the blandest of smiles and an almost affectionate obeisance, "I am half-brother to Captain Rynders!"[88]

Creighton was 22 years old and a Rynders foot soldier; he may have been in the crowd that night. But Tammany Hall was grooming Creighton for greater things than breaking up meetings. John Creighton was an entertaining public speaker who could connect with ordinary people, immigrants included. He was frequently put on the podium at political rallies alongside far more important men. In 1853, at 24 or 25 years old, John Creighton was nominated for the New York State Assembly. In almost any other year this would have guaranteed his election, but in 1853 Tammany Hall was split between the so-called Hard Shells, who opposed slavery, and the Soft Shells, who were sympathetic with the slave-owning South. (Half Shells were in the middle; the metaphorical shells were those of clams, not crabs.) John Creighton was a Soft Shell. The Whigs won in a statewide landslide and Creighton came in third in his Assembly race. For the rest of the 1850s Creighton continued to run for office and continued to lose—the long, hard grind of a political campaign did not fit his erratic personality—but his support of Fernando Wood, a self-made merchant and real estate broker who tamed the Tammany Hall tiger and turned it into a disciplined political machine, paid dividends. The right-hand man of Wood's right-hand man, Alderman William "Billy" Wilson, John Creighton was rewarded with a no-show job in the Customs House.

Fernando Wood was a ruthless demagogue. New York City politics had never been for the squeamish and Wood did not

---

88. Chapman, John Jay, *William Lloyd Garrison*, New York: Moffat, Yard and Co. 1913, pp. 215 ff.

[201

invent target companies, citizen militias, and political gangs, but he was the first to try to transform them into a personal army. Wood opposed Abolitionism, which he blamed for alienating the South and bringing the country to the brink of civil war. Inspired by the annexation of Texas, in the 1850s Wood and Rynders supported illegal efforts by American civilians to seize Cuba, Baja California, and Nicaragua. They contributed money, weapons, and volunteers from New York militias to all three. The contemporary term for these volunteers was "filibusters," which in the mid-19th century meant freelance military adventurers, not attempts to block legislation by talking all night.

The most prominent filibuster of the age was a cold-blooded Tennessean named William Walker. In the mid-1850s Walker led an invasion of Nicaragua, intending to bring it into the United States as a slave state. Walker was financed by New York City transportation magnate Cornelius Vanderbilt, whose interest in Nicaragua was to cement his monopoly of the New York to California shipping, which, before the Panama Canal, involved a passage across Nicaragua. Many of Walker's soldiers were militiamen from New Orleans and New York City. As commander of a company of New York militiamen, Captain John Creighton played a significant role in the Nicaraguan affair. Creighton's political ally, William Wilson, went to Nicaragua too, but to speculate in real estate, not to fight. Also along for the ride with Walker's Nicaraguan excursion was journalist, railroad advocate, political operative, and baseball booster George Wilkes.

IN NEW YORK City on December 26, 1855, federal officials seized the *Northern Light*, a ship carrying supplies and men to Walker in Nicaragua. Among the arrested were Addison Farnsworth, George B. Hall (son of the Mayor of Brooklyn), and John

Creighton.[89] All were New York City militia officers, customs house employees, and members of the Empire political club; all would later serve as officers in New York units in the Civil War. Creighton and Farnsworth spent the night in the Eldridge Street jail, where they enjoyed cigars, brandy, and female company courtesy of Isaiah Rynders. Released on bail, Creighton made his way in March 1856 to Nicaragua, arriving just in time for the Battle of Santa Rosa. When Walker's troops came under surprise attack, the filibusters' commanding officer, a bumbling Hungarian mercenary named Colonel Schlessinger, became incapacitated by fear. Chaos ensued. According to the New York *Weekly Herald*, Captain Creighton was the only commander who managed to rally his troops and return fire.[90] After the battle, an exasperated Creighton put a loaded pistol to Schlessinger's head. John Creighton quit and returned to New York, where the charges against him were dropped and he went to work for the successful presidential campaign of James Buchanan.

In the spring of 1857 Democratic Mayor and Tammany leader Fernando Wood attempted to organize the city's volunteer militias under the command of William Wilson and John Creighton, ostensibly to protect New York City from the hated "black Republicans." Creighton and others within Tammany Hall initially expressed qualms about creating a Praetorian Guard answerable only to the mayor, but after Albany passed a law dissolving the New York City police and replacing it with a state-run department, hotter heads prevailed. Wood refused to obey the law, after which New York City was caught between mutually hostile police forces for several months. In June 1857, at the height of the conflict, William Walker sailed to New York. Among those meeting Walker at Pier 1 on the Hudson River was

89. New York *Daily Times*, December 27, 1855, p. 1
90. New York *Weekly Herald*, May 10, 1856, p. 1

John Creighton, who, according to Horace Greeley's *New-York Tribune*, put "himself in a melodramatic attitude, [and] pointed out Walker to the admiring crowd assembled, to the tune of 'See the Conquering Hero Comes,' performed by a band on the pier." Tammany Hall attempted to give Walker a hero's welcome in City Hall Park, but a steady rain ruined the event. The dismal weather served as an omen for Walker, Wood, and Rynders. The Dead Rabbits Riot of July 1857 spelled the emergence of Irish American political power and the end of Rynders's control of the Sixth Ward. Fernando Wood was forced to disband his municipal police and leave office. Walker returned to Nicaragua but was abandoned by Vanderbilt after Walker double-crossed him. In September 1860 Walker was executed by Honduran authorities under mysterious circumstances.

IN JANUARY 1858 the 29-year-old John Creighton made a fresh start in Brooklyn. On October 12 he married the daughter of John Phipard, a cabinetmaker who was active in an anti-alcohol organization called the Sons of Temperance. Creighton, who battled a lifelong drinking problem, held various offices in the Sons of Temperance and gave lectures on alcoholism and abstinence. When the Civil War began in 1861, New Yorkers had to take sides. Wilson and Creighton chose to defend the Union. In doing so, they broke with their patron Fernando Wood. Reelected mayor in 1860, Wood continued to oppose the Union cause. He refused to cooperate with the military draft and even threatened to secede and reconstitute the New York metropolitan area as an independent nation. On April 15, 1861 President Abraham Lincoln publicly asked for 75,000 volunteer soldiers. According to the Brooklyn *Daily Eagle* of June 27, 1861, "Mr. John Creighton, who was the first man to open a recruiting office in this city, and who, we believe, raised two full companies for the war, is now, we are informed, the Lieutenant-Colonel in Billy Wilson's Zouaves."[91] Officially known as the 6th NY Regiment, the unit was nicknamed after the North African–style Zouave uniform favored by many New York units. John Creighton filled the regiment with the kind of men he knew from his career as a ward heeler: militiamen, firemen, and Tammany Hall loyalists, many of them poor Irish or German immigrants. The New York newspapers had as much fun with the prospect of sending these rough urbanites to fight the Confederate Army as today's media might with a plan to send gangsters from Brooklyn to fight ISIS.

In the late summer of 1861, Wilson's Zouaves were dispatched to Florida, where John Creighton's military career came to an abrupt end, ironically at an engagement with the same name as the main event of Creighton's campaign in Nicaragua. The regiment was stationed on a barrier island near Pensacola called Santa Rosa, when it came under attack by Confederate troops. This Battle of Santa Rosa was also a fiasco. Both sides overestimated the numbers of their opponent, panicked, and ran. The 6th New York's shaky performance raised existing tensions between the undisciplined volunteers and regular Army officers, whose attitude was expressed by West Point graduate General Orville E. Babcock: "Oh, but Billy Wilson's men are the very flower of the Dead Rabbits, the *creme de la creme* of Bowery society. I only want a decent excuse to shoot one or two." Colonel Harvey Brown, a crusty veteran of the War of 1812, and John Creighton took a particular dislike to each other. Creighton made things worse by choosing this moment to fall off the wagon. He was court-martialed for being drunk on duty. The transcript of John Creighton's court martial is a page turner. Private James Degan

---

91. Brooklyn *Daily Eagle*, June 27, 1861, p. 1

testified that at 1:00 a.m. on July 13 Creighton appeared at his sentinel post and grabbed Degan's musket. "Breathing whiskey fumes into the night air, and lurching left and right in an attempt to keep his balance, Creighton raised the musket to his shoulder and took a shot at the Federal guard boat that was visible just offshore." In his defense, Creighton testified, "What I did was perfectly justifiable and I am only sorry . . . that Colonel Brown was not in the boat, where I might have shot him."[92] Creighton showed some legal talent by successfully challenging his court-martial on procedural grounds; embarrassed, the Army allowed him to resign with an honorable discharge. Two years later, Brown himself resigned under a cloud after using excessive force against New York and Brooklyn civilians during the 1863 Draft Riots.

JOHN CREIGHTON'S LIFE continued to follow a strange trajectory. In 1864 he tried to get back into the military by recruiting an African American regiment in Brooklyn. He worked as a law clerk for the politically connected Court Street attorney Thomas Pearsall, who represented Abolitionist newspaper editor Theodore Tilton in the case that sparked Rev. Henry Ward Beecher's 1874 sex scandal. Pearsall became a mentor to John Creighton and helped him pass the bar. On May 9, 1873, John Creighton was in Topeka, Kansas, on a business trip. According to the Ft. Scott, Kansas, *Daily Monitor*, "[Creighton] committed suicide at the McMeekin House, in [Topeka] to-day, by shooting himself through the heart, in the presence of his son, a mere boy. Creighton . . . is a brother of the celebrated baseball pitcher of that name. He came here from Brooklyn, NY about three weeks ago. No direct cause is known for the commission

---

92. Lowry, Thomas P., *Tarnished Eagles*, Mechanicsburg, Penn.: Stackpole Books, p. 81

of the rash act, except that he was without money and has been dissipating [drinking] for about two weeks."[93]

Curiously, the Kansas newspaper stories about John Creighton's death are the only places we know of where the two Creighton brothers are linked in print. No doubt, John Creighton had been using his connection to his famous late brother to promote whatever hopeless business venture he was pursuing in Topeka. But why did neither Henry Chadwick nor any other sports journalist ever mention that the star pitcher James Creighton and John Creighton, Tammany Hall politician, high-ranking militia officer, Nicaragua filibuster, and Lt. Colonel in Billy Wilson's celebrated Zouaves were brothers? The answer is that to guardians of baseball's respectability like Chadwick, a connection to the world of John Creighton was the last thing that the sport needed.

WHEN JOHN CREIGHTON died, James Creighton Sr. was in his 80s and partially paralyzed from a stroke; he died three years later. For the last few years of his life he was taken care of by his widowed daughter Mary Ann Parkes, who lived next door. In 1871 she had married a stockbroker named Charles Parkes, who died of a heart attack while she was eight months pregnant with a child that she named James Creighton Parkes. James Creighton Parkes grew up to become a real estate broker and was living in suburban New Jersey when in 1937 he saw an article in the Brooklyn *Daily Eagle* about the recently established Baseball Hall of Fame. He was annoyed to read that Candy Cummings, who pitched for the Excelsiors in the late 1860s, was credited with inventing the curveball. Parkes sent a letter to the editor saying, "an uncle of mine, James Creighton

---

93. Fort Scott *Daily Monitor*, May 10, 1873, p. 1

. . . discovered the first curved ball, although at that time they didn't know just what it was."[94] Parkes had a grandson, born in 1935, also named James Creighton Parkes, who I ran across a few years ago while looking for descendants of James Creighton. I thought that this man might be the living relative I was looking for and tried to find him. What I found instead was a 1999 obituary in *The New York Times*. Reading it, I realized that I knew who he was. Better known as Jim Parkes, he was a prominent New York City orthopedic surgeon and, interestingly, an early advocate of weight training in sports. He played college football at Dartmouth, as well as tennis and golf. By complete coincidence, in the 1980s he treated my father for a

JAMES CREIGHTON,

Pitcher of the EXCELSIOR BASE BALL CLUB of Brooklyn, N. '

The 19th-century photographic *carte de visite*, originally a social calling card, evolved into the modern post card and the collectible, sports-themed tobacco card. Sold after his death, this *carte de visite* of pitcher James Creighton can be considered the first baseball card.

94. Brooklyn *Daily Eagle*, June 14, 1937, p. 17

knee injury. Baseball fans might remember him better as the New York Mets' team doctor in the 1970s and 1980s, and as president of the MLB Physicians Association. Until recently, his daughter was Chief Marketing Officer for MLB, a fitting job for the great, great, great niece of the man who invented modern pitching—and made it pay.

Is there any chance that the first James Creighton Parkes was correct about his uncle inventing the curveball? One of the difficulties with answering this question is that Creighton threw a lemon-peel baseball, which had completely different stitching from today's ball. Stitching makes a huge difference in how a pitcher grips the ball, and in how much and what kind of spin and break he can create. The fact is that we do not know what Amateur Era pitchers could do with a lemon-peel ball and we will never know. Another problem is that baseball terminology invariably lags behind innovations in playing techniques. Before the curveball became common, there was no language to describe it. Atlantics star Pete O'Brien, who faced Creighton, described Creighton's pitching as "something entirely new, a low, swift delivery, the ball rising from the ground past the shoulder of the catcher."[95] Does this mean that he delivered the ball from a lower point than other pitchers, or that his pitches had a four-seam-type hop to them, or that he was throwing an underhand breaking pitch of some kind? Eyewitnesses all agreed that Creighton threw extremely hard, but they also talked of his use of "twist." What they meant by that is unclear. It seems that Creighton was able to achieve a break or some other kind of deceptive movement on his pitches. If he really did throw a curve, perhaps his nephew was right that, "at that time they didn't know just what it was."

95. Anon. Biographical note on contemporary photo quoted in Thorn, John, *Baseball in the Garden of Eden*, New York: Simon and Schuster, 2011, p. 123

James Creighton was accused of cheating. According to the rules of 1862, a pitcher had to deliver the ball with a motion similar to that used in pitching horseshoes. It is hard to imagine how Creighton could have generated his legendary velocity using this kind of delivery. Creighton's contemporaries had trouble imagining it, too, which is why some complained that Creighton was "throwing," or using a disguised wrist snap. Throwing was cheating. In support of the cheating hypothesis, some baseball historians cite a remark by English cricketer John Lillywhite in the *New York Clipper* of August 5, 1911. Lillywhite told the *Clipper* of seeing Creighton during a visit to New York fifty years earlier. "Why," he remembered saying, "that man is not bowling, he is throwing under-hand, it is the best disguised under-hand throwing I ever saw, and might readily be taken for a fair delivery."[96] Unfortunately, as not every writer who cites this quotation seems to have noticed, Lillywhite is referring to watching Creighton bowl in a cricket match, not pitching in a baseball game. Even if Creighton was cheating at cricket, of course, this does not mean that he was cheating at baseball. Second, in the 19th century both baseball pitching and cricket bowling were undergoing a gradual evolution to higher arm angles, and players in both sports were blurring the line between pitching (i.e., delivering the ball without breaking the wrist) and throwing (what we call "pitching"). Lillywhite himself was accused of doing just that. Finally, the most credible eyewitnesses to Creighton's new style of pitching believed that it was within the rules. This included the Atlantics' Pete O'Brien and 19th-century baseball's most respected rules authority, Henry Chadwick. They could have

---

96. *New York Clipper*, August 5, 1911, p. 12

been wrong, but the fact that O'Brien was captain of the Excelsiors' archrival Atlantics suggests that he sincerely believed that Creighton's pitching delivery was within the rules as they were then applied.

Based on Pete O'Brien's description of Creighton's delivery, some of Creighton's perceived velocity may actually have been the result of a deceptive release point. Before radar guns, it was not easy to distinguish between pitches that were difficult to pick up visually and pitches that were simply traveling very fast. Contemporaries of Creighton also said that he did not run up to the pitching line, as other pitchers of the time did, but took a single stride like a modern pitcher. The few images we have of Creighton's delivery show him twisting his lower body in a strange way. Both would be consistent with Creighton using a lot of hip torque, which would create a whipping action and increased arm speed. They are also consistent with throwing a curveball, which is almost impossible to do while on the run.

We may not know exactly what kind of pitches James Creighton threw or how he threw them, but we do know that they had a devastating effect on opposing batters. In the early days of baseball, pitchers were little more than human pitching machines. James Creighton changed all that. He transformed the pitcher into the most important defensive position. Creighton and the generation of fast pitchers who emulated him drove the game's evolution from a high-scoring batting contest into a fair fight between pitchers and batters. Because batters tried to tire out Creighton and his imitators by leaving the bat on their shoulders and taking dozens of pitches, umpires began calling warning strikes to counteract this tactic. It took a few years, but called strikes eventually became part of the game. This was followed by called balls and, ultimately, the establishment of the modern strike zone. The strike zone that we use today is a response to Creighton's revolutionary new way of pitching.

DURING AN OCTOBER 14, 1862 game against the Unions, the 21-year-old Creighton became ill. He died in agony four days later. The press and public understandably assumed that the cause was a traumatic injury sustained during the October 14 baseball game. Because Creighton was also playing cricket in the fall of 1862, the cricket community encouraged the idea that Creighton's death was baseball's fault. The September 16, 1865 Brooklyn *Daily Eagle* gives the following account: "... in making a third attempt at the ball [Creighton] struck with great force and immediately fell down. After a while he felt no more uneasiness, and played the balance of the game. But alas! He had ruptured some of the internal organs, and in a few days the baseball fraternity were startled with the announcement: 'Creighton is dead.'"[97] Like an expensive Bordeaux, the story of Creighton's death improved with age. In his 1910 book *The National Game*, Alfred Spink published the following account by former Atlantics outfielder John C. Chapman: "I was present at the game between the Excelsiors and the Unions of Morrisania at which Jim Creighton injured himself. He did it in hitting out a home run. When he had crossed the rubber [i.e. home plate] he turned to George Flanley and said, 'I must have snapped my belt'.... It turned out that he had suffered a fatal injury."[98]

Both of these stories are inconsistent with Creighton's actual cause of death, a strangulated intestine. That is what

97. Brooklyn *Daily Eagle*, September 16, 1865, p. 2
98. Spink, Alfred H, *The National Game*, St. Louis, MO: National Game Pub. Co. 1910, p. 128

Creighton's doctor wrote on his death certificate; a contemporary record in the archives of Green-Wood Cemetery corroborates it. A strangulated intestine is normally caused by an inguinal hernia, which is an inherited weakness or gap in the inguinal canal, behind the groin area, through which contents of the abdomen sometimes protrude. If a section of intestine becomes caught, its blood supply can be cut off, which would lead to a gangrene infection. Today, an inguinal hernia can be easily diagnosed and repaired with surgery, and a strangulated intestine is quite treatable. But in the 1860s there were no surgical options or antibiotics, so reaching the gangrene stage meant certain death.

There are two problems with the idea that Creighton fatally injured himself swinging a bat one day in 1862. One is that an inguinal hernia is a chronic condition and is not caused by a single event. The hernia would have worsened over a long period, probably years. The other problem is that the inguinal hernia was a well understood medical problem in the mid-19th century. Creighton would have been treated for it and would have worn a truss. And the Excelsiors club was full of doctors. At least two of them, team president Joseph B. Jones and first baseman A.T. Pearsall, knew Creighton intimately. They would have known that inguinal hernias are exacerbated by long-term physical stress, for instance from repeated violent twisting or weightlifting, and they would have known of the risk of a strangulated intestine.

PITCHERS IN CREIGHTON'S time threw a lot of pitches in a game. Creighton threw more than most because of the waiting tactics used against him by overmatched batters. It was not unusual for Creighton to record pitch counts in the 200s or even the 300s, numbers that are unthinkable today. His unusual pitching delivery may have added additional strain. We know that he lifted weights. Add the fact that he was also playing cricket. Game accounts suggest that in 1862 Creighton was, in fact, breaking down physically. In the 1850s and 1860s, the pitcher was an everyday player who was expected to pitch one complete game after another; instead of a rotation, teams had one pitcher and a rarely used backup who usually played second base or right field. James Creighton, however, left an unusual number of games early and occasionally missed a pitching start entirely—the October 14, 1862 game, for example—without explanation.

Did the Excelsiors knowingly risk Creighton's health by overworking him? Consider the club's reaction to newspaper stories that blamed baseball for the death of the country's finest young athlete. After weeks of silence, the following item appeared in a December 12, 1862 *New York Times* story about the proceedings of the annual NABBP convention: "Mr. JONES touchingly alluded to the death of JAMES CREIGHTON, and desired to correct a misstatement which had been promulgated, that he died from the injuries received in a ball match between the Union and Excelsior Clubs, which was not the case, as his death was caused by an injury sustained in a cricket match."[99] "Mr. Jones" is Excelsiors President and medical doctor Dr. Joseph B. Jones, who knew that James Creighton's death had absolutely nothing to do with "an injury sustained" in a particular baseball game or a particular cricket match. As for why he would issue this statement, it is hard to think of any reason other than a guilty conscience or a desire to protect baseball's public image, or both.

---

99. *The New York Times*, December 12, 1862

THE LOSS OF Creighton at 21 years old hung heavily over baseball for years. A posthumous *carte de visite* with a photograph of Creighton that was sold to the public has been called the first baseball card. In 1865, three years after Creighton's death, *Frank Leslie's Illustrated Newspaper* carried a two-page spread depicting the baseball world and its principal clubs and figures. At the top is a larger than life James Creighton, shrouded in black crepe, looking down as if from the next world. Creighton's death cast a particular pall over the Excelsiors. Even though the club continued to play through the 1860s, the club never returned to the heights of 1860. Around 1870, like its parent the Knickerbockers, the Excelsior club began a gradual decline from a competitive baseball organization to a social club. Grief and guilt over Creighton's untimely death may have played a role in this. These emotions may also explain why Creighton's teammates had so little to say about him in later years.

Well into the professional era, baseball clubs made pilgrimages to Creighton's grave monument in Brooklyn's Green-Wood cemetery—a form of tribute that has no parallel. In 1866 the Washington Nationals traveled to Brooklyn to play the Excelsiors. Before sitting down for oysters and quail at Van Brunt Wyckoff's mansion on 17th Street, the Nationals stopped at Green-Wood to pay their respects to Creighton. The Brooklyn *Daily Eagle* reporter covering the event called Creighton's grave "the Mecca of ball players, the sole relic of the noblest and manliest exponent that the national game has ever had."[100] When historians ask why the New York Game beat out the Boston and Philadelphia bat-and-ball games, as well as cricket, to become America's national pastime, one answer may be another question—who was their Creighton?

---

100. Brooklyn *Daily Eagle*, July 6, 1866, p. 1

A SUNDOWN PERAMBULATION

As it has since it opened in 1838, Brooklyn's Green-Wood Cemetery welcomes the living, inviting us to stroll along its landscaped ridges and walk among its monuments. But it is more than just a pretty place. Historian Garry Wills wrote that the idea behind this kind of cemetery is that "the place of the dead must be made a school for the living." One of the lessons that Green-Wood can teach us is the life stories of the amateurs who gave us baseball. An astounding number of them are buried there.

If you walk up Spruce Avenue along the southern edge of the cemetery and turn left onto Orchard Avenue, you will find yourself on Tulip Hill. This is the site of James Creighton's marble, baseball-themed monument, restored in 2014 thanks to the generosity of broadcaster Keith Olbermann. You may notice that the graves around Creighton's have something in common. It is firefighting, amateur baseball's first cousin. On the left is a plot belonging to Manhattan volunteer fire company Engine #6, also known as "Americus." Located on the Lower East Side, this company was the political power base of Tammany Hall politician and fireman Boss Tweed. Across Orchard Avenue from Creighton is the grave of fire chief Harry Howard, the man who thought of having firemen bunk overnight in the firehouse. He served as foreman of Atlantic Hose #14, a Bowery B'hoy company that joined in the street riots of July 1857. A few yards to the north of Creighton's grave is the 1848 Firemen's Memorial, which bears the names of firemen who died on the job between 1811 and 1860. A tourist attraction in the 19th century, it has a tapered marble column upon which stands the figure of a fireman, trumpet in hand, carrying a small child to safety. Boss Tweed himself is buried a few yards away.

In 1866 the Washington Nationals paid a visit to Brooklyn to play the Excelsiors. The two clubs had a close relationship; former Excelsiors player Frank Jones was an early leader of the Nationals. After the Excelsiors took them on a carriage ride along Upper New York Bay, the Nationals stopped at Green-Wood and walked up to Tulip

Hill to pay "silent but eloquent tribute to the memory of the greatest ball player ever known, some culling green mementos from his grave." You can do the same today, although you can also visit the many baseball graves that have been added since 1866, including those of journalist Henry Chadwick; Jack Chapman, Asa Brainard, Joseph Jones, and dozens of other Knickerbockers, Gothams, Eagles, Excelsiors, and Atlantics.

In order to realize its ambition to become America's first national sport, amateur baseball focused its marketing efforts on the economically comfortable, moralistic white Protestant urban bourgeoisie -- a class with the time, money and inclination for recreation.

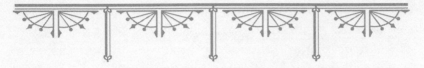

CHAPTER SEVEN
Philadelphia Stories

 OU MIGHT WONDER what the upstate hamlet of Piermont is doing on the list of the earliest baseball clubs outside of New York City.[101] Little Piermont—1856 population about 1,500—was home to Rockland County's first known baseball club. It was not an important place from any point of view except one; it was the eastern terminus of the Erie Railroad, which ran from Dunkirk, New York, near Buffalo through the southern tier counties of New York State. Until the Erie Railroad was extended to Jersey City, passengers and freight were ferried between Duane Street in Manhattan and a pier at Piermont. For a brief and shining moment, Piermont was an important node in the vast New York City metropolitan area transportation network. And during that moment railroad engineer Henry Belding, who had come to Piermont to work for the Erie Railroad, founded the Belding baseball club.

Every city and town in the United States has its own story of how and when the sport of baseball got there. But there are two themes that you will find in almost all of them—new transportation technology and New Yorkers. Baseball did not emanate

---

101. protoball.org/NY

from New York City like the concentric ripples made by a stone thrown into a pond. It followed new shipping routes, canals, and railroad lines—with all of their turns, quirks, and gaps. Chronological maps of mid-19th-century America's rolling transportation revolution and a map showing the spread of the sport of baseball would be strikingly similar.

Like the 19th century itself, which Mark Twain called "raging, tearing, booming," baseball was in a hurry. From Buffalo to Cincinnati to Detroit to San Francisco, it went where it could go as soon as it could go there. The most famous example is the Cincinnati Red Stockings' 1869 undefeated touring season. The club won the first game of the season on May 4, 1869. Six days later, Leland Stanford of the Central Pacific Railroad drove home the railroad spike that made it possible to take an uninterrupted train trip across the United States from the Atlantic to the Pacific. The 1869 Cincinnati Red Stockings crisscrossed the country, won 57 games, lost none, and became the first baseball club to play on both coasts in the same year. For the movement to make baseball a national sport, the 1869 Red Stockings' tour was a victory lap.

WHEN IT WAS young, baseball traveled on foot or in a horse-drawn carriage. When it left Manhattan Island, it took a ferry to New Jersey, Brooklyn, and Queens. After New York City was connected to Albany and the Hudson River ports in between by riverboat service, baseball steamed up the Hudson. In 1857, a baseball club was founded near Newburgh, New York, 70 miles north of New York City, by Charles Havemeyer, brother-in-law of Knickerbocker baseball club member Louis Belloni. After the Erie Canal and the New York Central Railroad, which paralleled the canal, connected the Hudson River to western New York and Lake Erie, the new sport of baseball turned left at Albany and headed west. In 1857 members of the Brooklyn Excelsiors who had moved from Buffalo to Brooklyn for school or business returned home to found a baseball club. Between 1856 and 1858 cities near the Erie Canal like Albany, Rochester, and Syracuse formed their own New York City–style baseball clubs. Because they were so close to the Elysian Fields, where baseball was played in the 1840s, the first known New Jersey baseball clubs sprang up in nearby Jersey City, Orange, Irvington, and Newark.

One of the first New Jersey baseball clubs outside of the Elysian Fields sphere of influence was the Liberty Club, founded in New Brunswick in 1857. But baseball in New Brunswick goes back further than that, at least in some form. An 1857 story in the *New York Clipper* tells of a pickup game there that called itself the "Old Fogies" and that had been playing "old fashioned baseball," whatever that was, for years.[102] In order to play against another club, they were getting up to speed on the latest New York rules. In 1858 the Liberty Club became the first New Jersey club to send delegates to a New York baseball convention. It was also one of the places where Thomas Fitzgerald, the future Philadelphia baseball pioneer, lived as a young man. New Brunswick stands at the intersection of the two main pre-railroad routes from New York City to Philadelphia, the colonial-era King's Highway and the Delaware and Raritan Canal. The canal fed industrial growth in New York and northern New Jersey by cutting the cost of shipping eastern Pennsylvania coal; it is also the likely reason that baseball arrived so early in New Brunswick, Princeton, and Trenton, all cities that were connected by the canal.

In the 1850s packet ships ran between New York City and New Orleans, Savannah, and Charleston. New York and New Orleans were knit close together by the cotton trade. This is the

---

102. *New York Clipper*, October 10, 1857

reason that the earliest baseball clubs in the deep South were founded in New Orleans well before the Civil War. The first Savannah club, the Pioneers, was founded in 1865 by two expatriate New Yorkers—Edward G. Saltzman, a member of the Gotham club of New York, and James Wilson of the Greenpoint Eckfords. A watchmaker who left New York after losing everything in an 1855 fire, Saltzman had earlier founded the first baseball club in Boston, the Tri-Mountains.

Above all, however, the spread of baseball in the 1850s and 1860s is a railroad story. The first railroad lines were local; they were designed *not* to connect to other lines in other places. American bat-and-ball games also began as local, unconnected subcultures, peculiar to their own cities or regions. But both were systematized, standardized, and organized into instruments of national unification. The New York and Harlem Railroad brought New Yorkers to the new suburbs of Yorkville, Harlem, Morrisania, and Westchester County; early baseball clubs appeared in all of these places. Significantly, baseball sometimes followed expanding railroad lines instead of heading straight to large population centers. The small Vermont towns of Irasburg, Brandon, and Pawlet all formed baseball clubs before the state's largest cities because they were on advancing railroad lines. If you draw a line on a map connecting Hamilton, Burlington, St. Thomas, London, Ingersoll, Guelph, and Toronto—southern Ontario cities where some of Canada's first baseball clubs appeared between 1856 and 1860—you will be tracing the lines of the Great Western Railway, which linked Niagara Falls, near Buffalo, to Windsor, near Detroit, in 1854. Baseball took the train to metropolises like Philadelphia and Boston, too, but those cities presented an added challenge. When the baseball movement arrived in the late 1850s, both Philadelphia and Boston were already playing bat-and-ball games of their own.

IF YOU TOOK a Sunday stroll through Germantown or Camden in 1855, you might encounter a group of men from Philadelphia playing a game that looked like wiffle ball in a funhouse mirror. Called town ball, it had been played by Philadelphians for decades. But if you came back to the same place 10 years later, they would be playing baseball. By the end of the Civil War, town ball was as dead as yesterday's cheesesteak. Who killed town ball? Baseball is a likely suspect; it had means, motive, and opportunity. But the railroad is chargeable as an accomplice. In 1834 the Camden and Amboy Railroad seriously shortened the distance between New York City and Philadelphia using 75 miles of iron tracks and the "John Bull," an imported British locomotive. A one-way trip took under five hours. This replaced a combination steamship and stagecoach trip that took 9.5 hours. Before that, travelling by sailboat or horse-drawn carriage took twice that or even longer. Philadelphia-bound passengers on the Camden and Amboy would take a short boat trip from lower Manhattan to South Amboy, New Jersey, then board a train for Camden, New Jersey, where they would change to a ferry to cross the Delaware River to Philadelphia. The Camden and Amboy was the first American railroad powered by steam instead of horses, and the first built primarily to carry passengers. The early railroads were dangerous—in 1833 future rail magnate Cornelius Vanderbilt vowed never to ride the train again after he broke a leg in an accident on the Camden and Amboy—but the technology swiftly improved. Twenty years later, the Pennsylvania Railroad ran a parallel line from Jersey City to Philadelphia along the west bank of the Delaware. The economic benefits of shrinking the cost and time of travel between America's two largest cities were massive and mutual. The railroad also brought the two cities closer culturally. When baseball started to expand, it was a matter of time before it collided with Philadelphia town ball.

Like pre–Civil War New York City, Philadelphia had volunteer firefighting, militias, and most of baseball's other cultural antecedents. It participated in the national sports movement. It had reforming doctors and nativism, as well as similar kinds of class, racial, and religious conflict. Philadelphia's 1844 riots—in which two Catholic churches were burned down and the state militia had to be called in to stop nativist mobs from burning more—were arguably worse than the Astor Theatre Riot. Graduates of the city's famous medical schools urged Philadelphians to exercise in order to ward off disease; in the 1820s and 1830s, boxing and gymnastics achieved limited popularity. Philadelphia had pleasure gardens along the Schuylkill River, west of Broad St. and on the northern periphery, some of which accommodated sports, but the open spaces most convenient to downtown Philadelphia were on the other side of the Delaware in Camden.

When it comes to early bat-and-ball sports, the parallels between the two cities are eerie. Just as New Yorkers took the ferry to Hoboken to play baseball, Philadelphians took the ferry to Camden to play town ball. Both ferries had the same owner, the Stevens family, which also ran the Camden and Amboy Railroad. Both cities had thriving cricket clubs with members who crossed over and played the local bat-and-ball game. The matrix of modern baseball was the nameless 1830s pickup game that spawned the Gotham, New York, and Washington clubs. Town ball had the Olympic club, which also dated to the early 1830s, and which absorbed several other clubs. Both games had historical connections to student culture, one at New York's Columbia College and the other at Philadelphia's Central High School. Philadelphia's answer to the Brooklyn Excelsiors was the Athletic club, which was organized by members of Philadelphia's EUB in 1859. The ambitious, aggressive Athletics focused on interclub competition, recruited and developed players, and

224]

quickly became Philadelphia's best club. But there was one big difference. After one season of playing town ball the Athletics switched to baseball.

The oddest thing about the odd game of town ball is how much we don't know about it. In 2007, baseball historian Richard Hershberger heroically reconstructed town ball from the surviving box scores, game accounts, and descriptions.[103] It was usually, but not always, played by two teams of 11. There was a pitcher and a catcher, but no position players. Instead of four bases, five stakes were driven into the ground to form a circle small enough to fit inside a modern Little League infield. The batter hit the ball and ran around the circle. If he made it all the way around, he scored a run; if he didn't, he was out. Everybody in the lineup batted once in each inning. Game scores were high, sometimes reaching triple figures. Box scores differentiate between "regular circuits" and "grannies," which might be useful if we knew what those terms meant. We also do not know what the bat looked like, how the pitchers pitched, or how the game ended. There are two things that we do know. One is that town ball players picked up New York–style baseball fairly easily, so the fundamental skills required by the two games could not have been drastically different. The other is that Philadelphians gave up on their homegrown game with surprisingly little resistance. In 1860, wrote sportswriter Charles Peverelly, the members of the old Olympic town ball club "set aside their time-honored play, endeared by the memories of thirty years, to press on in the race of progress. . . . Three hundred and sixty feet, compared with the old Town Ball circle of eighty feet, was enlarging their sphere of action with a vengeance."[104]

103. Hershberger, Richard in *Base Ball*, Vol. 1, No. 2, p. 28
104. Freyer and Rucker, eds. *Peverelly's National Game*, Charleston, S.C.: Arcadia 2005, p. 101

Did the Olympics convert to New York baseball because they thought it was a better game? Who knows? A better question might be who cares. Town ball had spread west with settlers from Pennsylvania to places like Kentucky and Ohio, but it never reached the point of creating standard rules or a governing body. It did not proselytize and had no need of an origin story (much less two). In 1860 town ball was going nowhere, while baseball was, in Peverelly's word, "progress," the coming thing. This is not historical determinism. Baseball was a movement with a serious purpose and explicit national ambitions; town ball was just a game. Plenty of New Yorkers went to Philadelphia during the 1850s and 1860s and plenty of Philadelphians went to New York. But no one ever tried to organize a town ball club in New York City or Brooklyn. If the Olympics and other clubs from Philadelphia wanted to compete on a national level, they realized that they would have to learn baseball. The murder of town ball was an act of euthanasia.

BASEBALL HISTORIES OFTEN tell us that Philadelphia adopted the New York game after being shocked and awed by James Creighton and the visiting Excelsiors. In late September 1860 the Excelsiors took the train down from Brooklyn and defeated a team made up of the best ballplayers in Philadelphia by a score of 15–4. This was a worse loss for Philadelphia than it looks. To score only four runs in a baseball game in 1860 was a rare embarrassment. (Two weeks earlier, a 7–4 defeat of the Unions by the Excelsiors made headlines as "one of the smallest scores on record.")[105] For the time, the Excelsiors' 15 runs are nothing to brag about either, but the Excelsiors were not facing a local novice. The opposing pitcher was Richard F. Stevens, a veteran

---

105. *Wilkes' Spirit of the Times*, September 15, 1860

of the New York baseball scene who had played against them in a Knickerbocker uniform less than two years earlier. Stevens was capable of holding down the Excelsiors' offense—if God dropped everything else—but it is also possible that with a safe lead the Excelsiors went easy on their old friend. The Excelsiors had another reason not to humiliate their hosts; the Philadelphians were paying for their stay at the luxurious new Continental Hotel, including meals and entertainment.

Watching Creighton, Leggett, et al. play in person may have sealed the deal, but the Excelsiors' visit did not directly cause Philadelphia to switch from town ball to baseball. The excitement of New York's baseball scene was felt across the country through the press before it arrived in person. The Minerva club, the Penn Tigers, and the Pennsylvania, Hamilton, Nonpareil, Equity, and Continental clubs had all begun playing baseball before the Excelsiors' visit. Both the Olympics and Athletics began as town ball clubs, but they too started playing the New York game before the Excelsiors came to town. The season of 1860 was year one of the Philadelphia baseball era. In 1859 town ball seemed to be thriving; in 1861 it was clearly on the route to extinction. Once again, the reason why lies in the who, not in the what. If we look at the kinds of Philadelphians who embraced the New York game, we see patterns that repeat themselves everywhere amateur baseball went. Some of the first to join team baseball were students. Some were upwardly mobile clerks and tradesmen. Others worked in cutting-edge transportation and communications technologies, including printing, engraving, and photography. Early Knickerbocker Henry T. Anthony was a pioneering photographer and associate of Samuel Morse and Mathew Brady; John Lowell, the patron of baseball in Boston, was an engraver; Atlantic club cofounder William Babcock was a printer and engraver spe-

[227

cializing in currency (during the Civil War, his brother defected to the South and made Confederate money before joining the Confederate army). Newspaper men and railroad employees were among the earliest baseball players in Detroit, Camden, New Orleans, Philadelphia, and Boston. The Camden and Amboy, the Michigan Central, and many other railroads fielded their own teams. In 1867 J.B. Sutherland of the Michigan Central Railroad—and its baseball club—designed the first refrigerated railroad car, making it possible to ship fresh meat and produce long distances. Because of their white color and similar shape, marijuana cigarettes borrowed the nickname of Sutherland's invention, "reefer."

There was one other kind of baseball pioneer. If you dig deep enough into the first known baseball players and clubs in Philadelphia—or almost anywhere else—you will turn up transplanted New Yorkers and others with roots in baseball country. Many of them were ex-members of the Knickerbockers, Eagles, Gothams, Empires, Excelsiors, Atlantics, Eckfords, and other early New York clubs. There are too many examples to list in one place. Hundreds of baseball-playing New Yorkers went to California in the Gold Rush of 1848 and afterward. Men who had played with the original New York City Eagles founded the Eagle club of San Francisco in 1859. The Cyclones, the first baseball club in St. Louis, was founded by Merrit Griswold, who almost singlehandedly convinced local clubs to switch from cricket and town ball to baseball. Born in New York in 1835, Griswold had played in Brooklyn in the late 1850s with the Putnams and Hiawathas. Through business relationships, members of the Brooklyn Excelsiors helped found the first baseball club in Baltimore, also called Excelsior. A member of the Brooklyn Atlantics founded the first baseball club in Richmond, Virginia; former Brooklyn Excelsiors helped established baseball in Washington and in Alabama. What united all of these different kinds of baseball pioneers was their ambition to participate in the future of the wider America beyond their neighborhood, town, or city. They believed in sports as an important social good and shared a vision of baseball as an instrument of progress.

BASEBALL DADS

These thirteen men have been called the "Father of Baseball" in print at least once.

Robert Ferguson[106]	Billy McMahon[107]
John Joyce[108]	H Chadwick[109] +
A Doubleday	A Cartwright +
Doc Adams[110]	Duncan Curry +
Harry Wright[111] +	T G Van Cott[112]
William Wheaton[113]	Albert Spalding[114]
Louis Wadsworth[115]	

+ = "Father of Baseball" inscribed on grave or plaque

106. Lincoln, Neb., *Evening Call*, July 21, 1888, p. 3
107. Los Angeles *Daily Herald*, September 21, 1887, p. 8
108. Chicago *Tribune*, August 19, 1877, p. 7
109. Brooklyn *Daily Eagle*, April 21, 1908, p. 22
110. Montpelier *Argus and Patriot*, August 28, 1895, p. 3
111. Wilkes-Barre *Times*, May 29, 1897, p. 3
112. Elmira *Star-Gazette*, December 19, 1894, p. 1
113. *The New York Times*, March 12, 2011
114. Port Huron *Times Herald*, September 10, 1915, p. 1
115. *The New York Times*, March 12, 2011

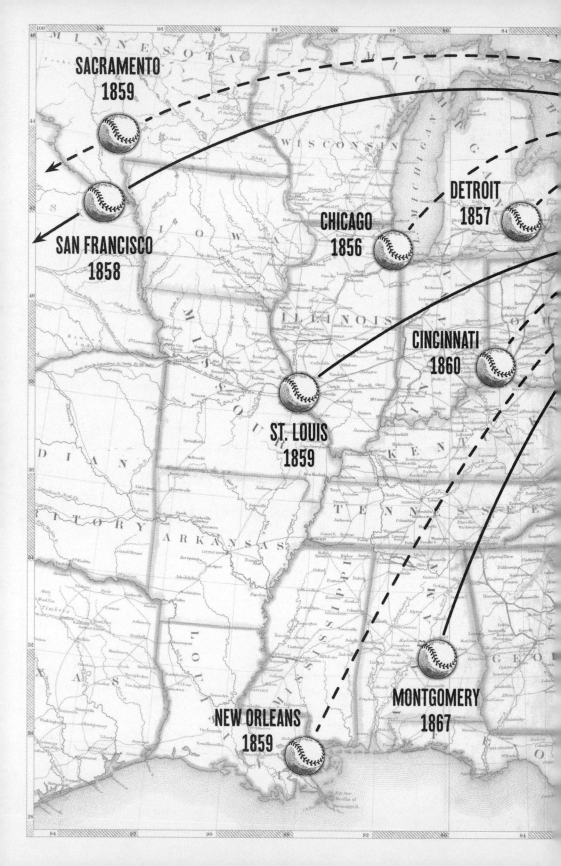

HAMILTON, ONTARIO 1854

BUFFALO 1858

ALBANY 1856

PORTLAND 1858

BOSTON 1857

NEW YORK

PHILADELPHIA 1858

BALTIMORE 1858

WASHINGTON 1859

RICHMOND 1866

SAVANNAH 1867

HOW BASEBALL EXPANDED

SIGNIFICANT EARLY CLUBS

Selected as important examples; not a complete list.

1857 — BOSTON — *Tri-Mountain*
1858 — PORTLAND, MAINE — *Portlands*
1859 — WASHINGTON, DC — *National*
1858 — BALTIMORE — *Excelsior*
1867 — SAVANNAH — *Pioneer*
1859 — NEW ORLEANS — *Louisianas*
1859 — ST. LOUIS — *Cyclone*
1859 — SACRAMENTO — *Sacramentos*
1856 — CHICAGO — *Union*
1857 — DETROIT — *Franklin*
1867 — MONTGOMERY — *Pelham*
1866 — RICHMOND — *Pastime*
1858 — BUFFALO — *Niagara*
1860 — CINCINNATI — *Buckeye*
1858 — PHILADELPHIA — *Penn Tigers*
1854 — HAMILTON, ONTARIO — *Young Canada*

KEY

EARLY CLUB WITH A DIRECT LINK TO A PARTICULAR NEW YORK CITY OR BROOKLYN CLUB

- - - - EARLY CLUB FOUNDED BY OR MADE UP LARGELY OF NEW YORKERS

{ NO LINE } FIRST-KNOWN OR IMPORTANT EARLY CLUB

SATELLITE CLUBS

Early clubs & the New York City or Brooklyn club they grew out of.

BOSTON'S TRI-MOUNTAINS . . . . GOTHAM (New York City)
BUFFALO'S NIAGARAS . . . . EXCELSIOR (Brooklyn)
BALTIMORE'S EXCELSIORS . . . . EXCELSIOR (Brooklyn)
WASHINGTON'S NATIONALS . . . . EXCELSIOR (Brooklyn)
ST. LOUIS'S CYCLONES . . . . PUTNAM (Brooklyn) & HIAWATHA (Brooklyn)
SAN FRANCISCO'S EAGLES . . . . EAGLE (New York City)
RICHMOND'S PASTIMES . . . . ATLANTIC (Brooklyn)
MONTGOMERY'S PELHAMS . . . . EXCELSIOR (Brooklyn)
SAVANNAH'S PIONEER . . . . GOTHAM (New York City) & ECKFORD (Brooklyn)

IN HIS 1866 book *American Pastimes* Peverelly says that the first Philadelphia club to adopt the New York game was the Minerva club, which was organized in 1857.[116] Named after the Roman goddess of learning, wisdom, and commerce, this was a junior club made up of students at the prestigious Central High School, today the second-oldest continuously operating public high school in the United States. Its graduates were well represented among Philadelphia's EUB. From its founding in 1836 Central High School encouraged athletics, including cricket and town ball. Early members of the Olympic town ball club were alumni. (Typically, sports clubs in pre–Civil War America with names like Minerva, Olympic, and Sons of Diagoras, were founded by students showing off their Latin and Greek.) In 1863 Central High School students formed the Active baseball club, which produced John "Count" Sensenderfer, who later played for both the amateur and professional Philadelphia Athletics. The Minerva club's founding president was Theodore Wiedersheim, who was born in 1846 and lied about his age in order to fight in the Civil War. He saw action in the Cumberland Valley campaign, rose to the rank of Captain in the 1st Pennsylvania National Guard, and later became a successful stockbroker and banker. Founded by graduates of the Harrison Grammar School, many of whom also went to Central High, the Harrison Literary Institute formed a baseball club in 1859 (and a militia unit in the war fever of 1861).

---

116. Freyer and Rucker, eds. *Peverelly's National Game*, Charleston, S.C.: Arcadia 2005, p. 102

The Penn Tigers were founded in September 1858; later renamed the Winona club, this was the first known adult baseball club in Philadelphia. They took their original name from Penn Township, a northern district that was absorbed by Philadelphia in 1854. (Winona was a Native American chief's daughter who, in American folklore, leaps from a cliff to her death rather than marry a man she did not love.) The Tigers were ambitious mechanics and tradesmen who were making the transition to the EUB, with a few wealthier men mixed in. They played not far from the Ridge Avenue railway depot near 24th Street and Columbia Avenue (renamed in the 20th century after the unforgettable Philadelphia NAACP leader Cecil B. Moore, who explained his civil rights activism by saying, "After nine years in the Marine Corps, I don't intend to take another order from any son of a bitch that walks."). Used by many Philadelphia clubs, this playing field was replaced in the late 1860s by a more formal baseball park with clubhouses and stands. The reason was the arrival of two of the latest sporting trends from Brooklyn: fans and paid admission. In the 1880s it became the site of Recreation Park, where Camden's Walt Whitman went to see Harry Wright, his old friend from the 1850s New York baseball scene, manage the National League club that would later be called the Phillies.

The Tigers included a manufacturer of coal gas meters, gas works clerks and engineers, a machinist, and a brass finisher. The club's founding president was a man named Joseph P. Alden. Alden is forgotten today, but *Wilkes' Spirit of the Times* called him the man "to whose untiring exertions we are greatly indebted for the introduction of the noble game in the Keystone State."[117] We might know more about Joseph Alden if he had not died in his early 30s, but clearly, he was busy proselytizing on behalf of the

---

117. *Wilkes' Spirit of the Times*, March 30, 1861

New York game of baseball. There is a clue to why in his family background. Alden was a machinist and the son of a well-to-do inventor and engineer named Manoah Alden (a descendant of John Alden of the *Mayflower*), who came from a small town near Pittsfield, Massachusetts. Less than 50 miles from Albany, Pittsfield lies on the west side of an ancient boundary dividing the culture of the Hudson River valley from that of eastern New England. Before 1860, it was also more or less the line between the New York game—which had been played in the Pittsfield area as far back as we can trace—and the so-called Massachusetts game, which Bostonians played. Today, that line is roughly the same as the boundary separating Red Sox fan territory from that of the Yankees and Mets, and the rhoticity line, which is not a counseling service for fantasy baseball addicts; it divides people who pronounce final "r's" from people who don't.[118]

Founded in 1859, the Continentals were central Philadelphia clerks, bookkeepers, and other "quills," who may also have been members of the Continental Guard militia unit. The Pennsylvania club, which played in Camden, was made up of printers, compositors, typographers, and at least one publisher. The Hamiltons were engineers, lawyers, and bankers who lived in the upscale West Philadelphia streetcar suburb of Hamilton Village. The members of the Mercantile club were also solid members of the EUB, "some of [Philadelphia's] best citizens," according to the *New York Clipper*, including commission merchants, cloth wholesalers and importers, and an executive of the Pennsylvania Railroad. The Equity club included the best players from Camden, among them Richard F. Stevens, who was working in Camden for his uncle Robert L. Stevens, president of the Camden and Amboy Railroad.

---

118. *The New York Times*, April 24, 2014

In 1859 and 1860 Philadelphians were in a hurry to catch up in baseball and the New York and Brooklyn clubs were glad to help. In December 1859 the *New York Clipper* observed that "the game of baseball appears to be growing in favor in Philadelphia." A month later, the Winona club called for a general meeting of Philadelphia baseball clubs. In March 1860 the *Clipper* reported that there were five clubs playing the New York game; in July the *Clipper* updated that to 12 and noted that George Phelps, president of the Brooklyn Atlantics, had paid a visit to see the Equity club defeat the Winonas, 59–39.[119] In September NABBP vice president Thomas Dakin, the most important member of Brooklyn's Putnams, umpired a game in Philadelphia. Prominent Brooklyn baseball men were not traveling to Philadelphia to see the Liberty Bell; they were there to promote the game and build a local baseball infrastructure. In December 1860 the first Philadelphia clubs attended the national baseball convention in New York City.

THE ATHLETICS' MOST important member was not a frontline player. He was a newspaper publisher, frequent libel suit defendant, and keen baseball mind named Thomas Fitzgerald. Fitzgerald was charming and combative, the kind of person that people in the 19th century called "whole-souled." A cofounder of the club, Fitzgerald served as the Athletics' president from 1861 to 1866, the period when they became one of the best clubs in the country. Along with DeWitt Clinton Moore, Fitzgerald was the club's leader until his ugly divorce from the Athletics in 1866. Named after the man who built the Erie Canal, Moore came from Ewing in central New Jersey, next door to Trenton, where one of the state's first baseball clubs was founded. He may well have brought some baseball expertise with him to Philadelphia.

119. *New York Clipper*, July 14, 1860

A previously unpublished Thomas Sully oil portrait of publisher Thomas Fitzgerald c. 30 years old. Fitzgerald is remembered as amateur baseball's chief ally in Philadelphia; it is less well remembered that he was born and raised in New York City.

Six years younger than Thomas Fitzgerald, Moore played for the Athletics' first nine and captained the club on the field.

Fitzgerald and Moore loved baseball and baseball loved them back. An ambitious literary man who had married a woman descended from two cultured Philadelphia families, the Riters and the Leverings, Thomas Fitzgerald was the kind of influential member of the EUB that baseball was looking for in order to sell the game in Philadelphia. The New York City–area baseball world welcomed the Athletics' delegates to the 1860 NABBP convention. "The Athletics are fortunate," wrote *Wilkes' Spirit of the Times*, "in having a prominent gentleman of Philadelphia attached to their organization—we allude to Colonel D. W. C. Moore—[who] places a proper estimate and value upon all ennobling and health-bestowing outdoor pastimes ... the lovers of baseball in Philadelphia ought to feel grateful to him for the zeal which he has exhibited in pushing on the baseball column in that city."[120] Moore was elected NABBP vice president by the first convention he or any Philadelphian attended.

---

120. *Wilkes' Spirit of the Times*, February 9, 1861

In late 1862 Thomas Fitzgerald was elected president of the NABBP, baseball's *soi-disant* national governing body. A former town ball player living well outside the New York metropolitan area might seem a strange pick for baseball's top job at that early date. But it is doubtful that Fitzgerald was either a baseball novice or a stranger to the New York baseball scene. Colonel Fitzgerald's career with the Athletics is punctuated by hints of baseball connections dating from his New York City upbringing and pre-existing personal relationships with members of the Brooklyn and New York baseball clubs. Like so many other early New York ballplayers, Fitzgerald served in a militia unit; he probably also belonged to a volunteer fire company. On a trip to Washington in the 1860s, he mentioned that he had visited that city years earlier as a member of a New York City militia. In Philadelphia in 1859, although he held no public office in the fire department or anywhere else, he was one of the dignitaries who personally welcomed members of the "Constitution" Engine Company No. 7, who were visiting from Brooklyn. The likeliest explanation is that he knew them. During the early 1860s Fitzgerald was the middleman who arranged for New Jersey and New York baseball clubs to exchange visits with Philadelphia clubs in order to spread and teach the game.

The *New York Clipper*'s coverage of an 1862 visit to Philadelphia by the Eckfords of Greenpoint conveys the warm relations that Fitzgerald had with clubs from Brooklyn, in particular those in the so-called Eastern District, now the location of the Brooklyn neighborhoods Williamsburg and Greenpoint.

> On Tuesday morning the Eckfords and their friends were escorted to the Navy Yard by the Philadelphians. . . . At night they accepted the invitation of Mrs. John Drew [actress Drew Barrymore's great-great-grandmother] to visit

the Arch Street Theatre, where seats were reserved for them. On Wednesday they were taken to the Exhibition of Fine Arts, and in the evening went to the Walnut Street Theatre . . . the performances of Miss Charlotte Thompson especially pleasing the Eckfords. On Thursday morning the party went out to Girard College, and in the evening were hospitably entertained at the residence of Col. Fitzgerald. After supper at the hotel that evening, they marched round to the colonel's residence, where he was awaiting them, and after enjoying some delightful piano playing at the hands of Mr. [Riter] Fitzgerald [Thomas Fitzgerald's son].[121]

This is not the kind of fun that today's professional baseball players are looking for on a road trip. Stories like this remind us how culturally different Amateur Era baseball was from modern professional baseball. They also help us understand the weirdest thing about the Athletic club, that it grew out of a classical music organization, Philadelphia's Haydn and Handel Musical Society.[122] Many founding and early members of the club were involved in music, singing, or the theater. This included De-Witt Clinton Moore, who was superintendent of Philadelphia's Sunday schools and a church choir director; and Hicks Hayhurst and Joseph Megary, amateur actors who belonged to the Boothenian Dramatic Association, which was named after John Wilkes Booth's pro-Union older brother Edwin Booth. Publisher Thomas Fitzgerald was an amateur vocalist, a drama critic, and a frequent lecturer on classical music.

After the Athletics dropped town ball in 1860, much of its membership resigned and the young club had to patch together a credible baseball team. Their best players were Moore, outfielder Hicks Hayhurst, and Nate Berkenstock, a slugging first baseman.

---

121. *New York Clipper*, November 8, 1862
122. *New York Clipper*, October 5, 1861

They filled out the roster with cricketers like Charles Vernou (an ancestor of Jacqueline Kennedy Onassis) and F. W. Mudie, who had come to America with the touring English cricket eleven of 1859 and decided to stay. Some of them belonged to the St. George Cricket Club (no relation to the St. George club that played in the Elysian Fields), landlord of the Athletics' grounds in Camac's Woods at 13th St. and Montgomery Avenue, the present site of Temple University. The cricketers were a stopgap; none of them stuck with the Athletics as a starting player. The club had another problem: an aging core. In 1861 Moore was 36, Hayhurst was in his early to mid-30s, and Berkenstock was 30.

LIKE DR. JOSEPH Jones's Brooklyn Excelsiors of the late 1850s, Fitzgerald's Athletics methodically improved themselves with mergers, by bringing in established players from other clubs, and by casting a wide net for young talent. An 1861 merger with the United club brought 19-year-old infielder Isaac Wilkins, a graduate of Central High School. The Athletics had already recruited Hicks Hayhurst from the Winonas, and between 1861 and 1864 they added 17-year-old pitcher Dick McBride, 20-year-old Fergy Malone, 17-year-old Tom Pratt, and the Gaskill brothers, Charles and Edwin, who were in their early 20s. Malone was an Irish-born convert from cricket; the Gaskills were from New Jersey. Pratt was born near Boston, grew up in Philadelphia, and had two different stints with the great Atlantics of Brooklyn as their primary pitcher. (His family business had branches in all three cities.) The final phase of the Athletics' crash development plan was to play as many games as possible against New York and Brooklyn clubs. In midsummer of 1862 Colonel Moore—both Moore and Fitzgerald were honorary colonels in the state militia—issued a challenge to the baseball clubs of Newark, New York City, and Brooklyn: "if not to win the ball," said the demure

Moore, then "merely to learn their way of 'doing the thing.'"[123] Thomas Fitzgerald's idea, this was the first-ever multi-club intercity tournament. In front of large crowds, a composite team representing Philadelphia surprised no one by losing to Newark, Brooklyn's Eastern District, and Brooklyn's Western District, but it upset a New York team made up of Gothams (including Harry Wright), Eagles, Empires, and Knickerbockers, 46–23.

I used to know a professional gambler (my father-in-law) who told me to bet against any visiting baseball team that was playing a Saturday day game in a major city. The idea was that red-blooded athletes would not fail to exhaust the possibilities of a Friday night in New York or Chicago. In 1862 the Philadelphia clubs had won some credibility, but nobody would have bet on any of them against a good Brooklyn club with a good night's sleep. In June players from four Brooklyn clubs (Atlantic, Enterprise, Star, and Exercise) made a return trip to Philadelphia and got hustled. Both cities were asked to divide their players into an "A" team and a "B" team. The Brooklynites assumed that they were supposed to put their best players on the "A" team. The four teams then played a four-game round robin. Henry Chadwick explained what happened.

> The Brooklyn players left New York on Monday, June 30th, at 2 P.M., and arrived at Philadelphia at 6:30, where they were met by a numerous delegation of the Philadelphia players, and duly escorted to the Washington House, Chestnut Street, a first class hotel . . . On their arrival, they were taken into the parlor, where two splendid bowls of claret [red Bordeaux wine] punch were placed, and as fast as they were emptied by the thirsty travelers, they were replenished. . . . The players of the Brooklyn party should have retired early after their trip, in view of the work they

---

123. Brooklyn *Daily Eagle*, June 3, 1862, p. 2

had before them, but their friends in the city of Philadelphia would not think of such a thing, so parties were made up for rambles around the town, and they did not get "home until morning:" the consequence was that the majority were totally unfit to play. . . ."[124]

Beside getting them drunk, the Philadelphians hoodwinked the Brooklynites by putting some of their best players on the "B" team. So, after the Philadelphia "A" team beat a hungover Brooklyn "A" team 16–10, Philadelphia "B" easily defeated Brooklyn "B," 22–9. In the end, Brooklyn won only one of the four games in the tournament, by a score of 18–15. As the *New York Clipper* tells it, there were no hard feelings at the post-tournament dinner, which ended awash in brandy and wartime patriotism. Colonel Thomas Fitzgerald raised a glass to,

> "the baseball players of Brooklyn," which was received with all the honors. From this time to the close, a delightful social time was had, songs, sentiments and speeches ruling the hour for the time being, in which Col.s Fitzgerald and Moore . . . took a prominent part. . . . At 12 o'clock the party broke up, the last song being the *Star Spangled Banner*, which was given with a will.[125]

With the Athletics of 1865, Colonel Fitzgerald had a contender for baseball's national championship. The finishing touch was bringing in 25-year-old slugging second baseman Al Reach, who was playing for his hometown Greenpoint Eckfords. The 1865 Athletics went 15–3, winning two from the solid Unions of Morrisania and losing two to baseball's champion Brooklyn Atlantics. The 1866 club was even better, going 23–2. That Athletics club defeated the Unions, the Washington Nationals, and

---

124. *New York Clipper*, July 12, 1862
125. *New York Clipper*, July 12, 1862

the Atlantics; their two losses came against the Unions and Atlantics. The *Clipper* called Colonel Fitzgerald "the prime mover of everything calculated to advance the interests or extend the popularity of baseball in [Philadelphia]."[126] Fitzgerald took the field with the Athletics only once that we know of, in an intramural game, but he knew too much about baseball not to have grown up playing the game. Because he was born in 1819, however, Fitzgerald's playing days—his teens and 20s—came during baseball's Dark Ages. We know that baseball was played in the 1830s, but we have almost no names, box scores, or game accounts. Of course, in order to have played baseball at that time, Thomas Fitzgerald would also have to have lived in or near New York City. Fitzgerald was close-mouthed about his life before he came to Philadelphia as a 22-year-old in 1842, but he was in fact a New Yorker, born and raised.

YOU MAY HAVE met people who, when asked about their childhood, recite the same impersonal facts, things like the exact time or date of their birth, and little more. Usually there is a reason. Sometimes it is trauma or unhappiness that they want to forget; sometimes they were orphaned or adopted and that is all they know. When Colonel Thomas Fitzgerald was asked about his childhood, he said that he was born in New York City on December 22, 1819, on the spot where the Harper Brothers publishing house later had a printing plant. He sometimes added that he was working as a printer at a young age, when other children were in school.[127] Other than allowing people to believe that he was related to Irish nobility, the titled Hiberno–Norman Fitzgerald dynasty known as the Geraldines, that was the whole story.

---

126. New York *Herald*, August 30, 1865, p. 1
127. Reading *Times*, June 26, 1891, p. 1

Family was important to Thomas Fitzgerald when he was an adult. After he became wealthy, he made annual summer visits to Ireland, where he did in fact hobnob with aristocratic Fitzgeralds like the Duke of Leinster and the Marquis of Kildare. He was close to his daughter and his five sons, who helped him run his newspaper, the *City Item*. All five Fitzgerald boys played for Philadelphia baseball clubs, including the Minervas, the *City Item*'s own team, and a junior club named after the Eckfords of Greenpoint. This makes it particularly strange that Thomas Fitzgerald never, as far as we know, uttered a single word about his mother, father, or siblings, not even their names. Searching for Fitzgerald's origins, I could not locate a birth or baptismal record, which given the date is not surprising. But the specificity of Fitzgerald's statement that he was born on the site of a printing plant owned by the Harper Brothers is a clue that leads to a particular part of lower Manhattan. In the 19th century the Harper Brothers publishing house was on Franklin Square in the Fourth Ward, a district that in the early 19th century was shared by printers, sailors, poor Irish immigrants, African Americans, and New York's earliest Chinese community. No one was living at that exact address in 1819. But to the east of the Harper Brothers buildings was tiny Hague Street, which intersected Franklin Square. Hague Street is no longer there; it was obliterated to construct an off-ramp for the Brooklyn Bridge. Around 1820 a publisher named William Colyer had a printing plant at number 5 Hague Street.[128] Colyer was a cousin and business partner of the Harper Brothers.

Longworth's New York City directories for the early decades of the 19th century contain only a handful of people named Fitzgerald. Many of them lived in the Fourth Ward of Manhattan,

---

128. New York *Evening Post*, August 25, 1843, p. 2; and July 3, 1845, p. 4

particularly in several households on tiny Hague Street and nearby Oak Street. These families were most likely related. The 1827 directory contains only 11 people named Fitzgerald; one is listed as "Fitzgerald, widow of Edmund, grocer." She lived at 8 Hague. Born in Ireland in 1774, her name was Ellen Fitzgerald. Her husband Edmund Fitzgerald, also born in Ireland, had died in 1823, leaving no money or possessions. Censuses from 1840 and earlier list only heads of households by name; for everyone else it gives only numbers broken down by sex, race, age range, and, for African Americans, if they were free or slaves. Comparing all the Fitzgerald families in New York City listed in the 1820 and 1830 censuses, there are two who fit most of what Thomas Fitzgerald said about his early background, and who had a male child born around 1819 who could have been Thomas Fitzgerald.

One is the family of Edmund and Ellen Fitzgerald. They lived within literal spitting distance of a printing house owned by a member of the Harper family. They emigrated to the U.S. in 1799. The date suggests that Edmund and Ellen Fitzgerald were among New York's many refugees from the Irish Rebellion of 1798. Perhaps Thomas Fitzgerald inherited his parents' Irish Republicanism; as an adult, he was active in organizations that both supported Irish independence and opposed American slavery. New York City in 1823 was a rough place for a widowed unskilled immigrant. Some in Ellen Fitzgerald's position abandoned their children or resorted to prostitution. She had three children: Edmund Jr. who was 15 or 16 years old; Ellen, who was 7 or 8; and a younger son, presumably three-year-old Thomas. We do not know how Mrs. Fitzgerald survived the next six or seven years. According to a city directory, in 1827 Edmund Jr. was working as a grocer, as his father had. But it would have been difficult for an unskilled laborer in his teens to support an entire family. The likelihood is that they were desperately poor.

The other candidates for Thomas Fitzgerald's parents are Garrit Fitzgerald and his wife Catherine Fitzgerald, who lived on Oak Street in the Fourth Ward and who may well have been related to Edmund and Ellen. Their story is even bleaker. Catherine Fitzgerald died in childbirth in 1826 and a Garrit Fitzgerald of Oak Street died in the cholera epidemic of 1832, when Thomas Fitzgerald would have been between 11 and 13 years old. A couple named Garrit and Catherine Fitzgerald baptized a son named Thomas at St. Peter's Roman Catholic Church in New York City in late December 1818, which is tantalizing because it is almost one year earlier to the day than the date of birth given by the adult Thomas Fitzgerald. Could Thomas Fitzgerald actually have been born not on December 22, 1819 but on December 22, 1818? Perhaps, but it is hard to imagine how, throughout his life, Thomas Fitzgerald could have consistently thought that he was exactly one year younger than his actual age. One of the less far-fetched possible explanations would be that he was cared for by an orphanage or other strangers in infancy and that they mis-recorded or misunderstood his birth year. Another is that two different Thomas Fitzgeralds were born about a year apart. Given names, of course, run in families; some or all of the 4th Ward Fitzgerald families may have been related and Thomas is not an uncommon name.

WHICHEVER OF THESE families Thomas Fitzgerald was born into, his childhood was in all likelihood Dickensian. Widowers in 1826 did not normally raise children. If he was the son of Garrit Fitzgerald, Thomas would have been sent to relatives, an orphanage, into an apprenticeship—or first one of these and then another. According to Thomas Fitzgerald himself, he worked as a printer at a very young age. If he was the son of Ellen Fitzgerald, she might have decided to apprentice her youngest son to a printer as soon as he was old enough in order to have one fewer mouth to feed. Irish immigrant families of the time were known to sacrifice one child's education for the sake of the others. (Apprenticeships normally lasted for four to seven years and were legally binding; apprentices worked for little or nothing except for room and board). We do not know how young Thomas Fitzgerald was when he was in effect given into temporary slavery. Eleven or younger was unusual but not unheard of. Apprentices often lived at their employer's home or shop. Many were exploited by their employers and hazed by older apprentices. We can only wonder what kind of misery lies behind Thomas Fitzgerald's statement that he was working "at an age when other children were in school."

The printer that Thomas Fitzgerald went to work for may well have been the family's neighbor on Hague Street, Harper Brothers cousin William Colyer. Colyer worked in Manhattan but he lived across the East River in Williamsburg, where in 1840 he hired fresh-off-the-boat European political radical Thomas Ainge Devyr to edit a Democratic Party newspaper that he was launching in Brooklyn. In his eccentric and entertaining autobiography Devyr says that Colyer paid him through an associate named Fitzgerald. Devyr's son Thomas Devyr Jr., born in Brooklyn in 1844, was an outstanding athlete who played baseball for the Marions, Eckfords, and Mutuals. He was caught up in baseball's first game-fixing scandal in 1865 and banned from the sport, but he was reinstated after one year thanks to lobbying by Henry Chadwick, a fellow Brooklynite who also had a father who had left England as a political refugee. The Devyrs and Chadwicks probably knew each other—it would be surprising if they didn't—but there is no question that Tom Devyr the ballplayer knew Thomas Fitzgerald. In 1896, after Thomas Devyr Jr. died at 51, a reporter visited his bare Greenpoint apartment and reflected on the former baseball star's faded glory. "Of all the many prizes he received," he wrote, "none remained in his possession at the time of his death, save a book of poems, bestowed on him by Colonel Thomas Fitzgerald, president of the Athletic Club of Philadelphia." This raises the possibility that Thomas Fitzgerald knew the Devyrs before he moved to Philadelphia. All we know about Fitzgerald's life immediately before his arrival in Philadelphia in the mid-1840s are the names of the newspapers he worked for, as he moved up from printer to journalist to editor. Beside the New York *Commercial Advertiser*, the list includes the New Brunswick, New Jersey, *Fredonian*, the Philadelphia *Bulletin*, and the Tallahassee *Floridian*. He had no known family in any of these places. In his teens and early 20s Thomas Fitzgerald seems to have been, like Walt Whitman, a rootless printer and journalist, single, and living alone. Did he resent being apprenticed as a boy? Did he simply want to put an unhappy childhood behind him? Whatever the reason, Fitzgerald moved to Philadelphia in the mid-1840s and decided to become someone else.

THOMAS FITZGERALD COFOUNDED the *City Item* as a weekly in 1847. He had three partners, friends from his days as a printer and journalist in New York; one of them was George G. Foster, who had invented the "City Items" column for the *New-York Tribune*. The original "City Items" was a potpourri of gossip items, comments on musical concerts or plays, politics, crime, and city life, all delivered with Foster's urbane wit. "His special contribution," writes historian George Rogers Taylor, ". . . arises from his focusing his attention so largely on common people, not only beggars and prostitutes but on the great numbers of working men and women, the dandies and the bill posters, the b'hoys and g'hals, the women arriving by carriage to shop at Stewart's [the elegant New York department store] and the seamstresses working in garrets. . . . Foster described in realistic detail those whom Walt Whitman sketched poetically in the 15th section of 'Song of Myself.'"[129] The idea of Fitzgerald and his partners was to turn this journalistic innovation from New York into a business plan for an entire newspaper in Philadelphia. It succeeded. In the 1850s Fitzgerald bought out Foster and the others, eventually making the *Item* a daily newspaper. He married Sarah Levering Riter of Germantown in 1844. She was an educated woman from a well-to-do family who taught music to private pupils. We do not know what his wife and family knew about his early life but the face that Thomas Fitzgerald showed to Philadelphia and the world after he became a successful publisher was largely a work of fiction. Fitzgerald lectured on Mozart and wrote about opera, classical instrumental music, and the theater. He published articles and poetry for the Philadelphia-based *Graham's Magazine* and *Godey's Ladies Book*, and composed songs. An eloquent public speaker, he entered local Democratic politics (the only kind there was in Philadelphia), was appointed to a city school board, and advocated successfully for musical education in the public schools. He had several plays produced, his greatest success being the 1868 *Light at Last*, starring Louisa Lane Drew.

In the 1860s Thomas Fitzgerald switched to the Republican Party. A fervent Abolitionist, he had campaigned across Pennsylvania for Abraham Lincoln as a War Democrat; they became friends. Another part of Fitzgerald's self-reinvention was changing religions. In 1870 Fitzgerald and three of his sons were confirmed in the Episcopal Church; church records note that only Thomas Fitzgerald had been baptized Roman Catholic.[130]

---

129. Taylor, George Rogers, *New York History* Vol. 58, No. 3 (July 1977), pp. 297–298
130. St. Paul's Episcopal Church Philadelphia Confirmation Record, 1870, p. 221

Finally, in the 1880s and 1890s he began making regular trips to Europe, where he visited Carton House in Ireland, the home of the Duke of Leinster, whose surname was Fitzgerald. American newspapers carried stories about Thomas Fitzgerald's visits to his illustrious relatives in the old country. In 1888, however, New York's *Irish American Weekly* pointed out that Catholic-born Thomas Fitzgerald of Philadelphia could not have been related to the Duke of Leinster or anyone else in the family in the 1880s.

> The New York *Herald* must have been betrayed into a curious historical jumble, when . . . it referred to Colonel Thomas Fitzgerald of Philadelphia as a possible Presidential candidate in the following terms: "Fitzgerald . . . has been put in nomination as the lineal descendant of a dynasty of Irish kings and the oldest American representative of the Duke of Leinster's family." [It is] absurd . . . to connect the present Duke of Leinster with the Geraldines. He is neither a Geraldine nor an Irishman; and every true Fitzgerald repudiates him and his claims.[131]

Not to detour into the thickets of a murky aristocratic succession controversy, Thomas Fitzgerald was probably no more closely related to the Duke of Leinster or the original Geraldines than F. Scott, Ella, or any other of the thousands of people in the world named Fitzgerald. Perhaps the Duke of Leinster socialized with Thomas Fitzgerald because he enjoyed the company of a gregarious American millionaire. He would not have been the first European aristocrat to do so.

What explains Thomas Fitzgerald's transformation from unschooled apprentice printer from the slums into erudite man of the world? His wife had a good education. But Fitzgerald most likely educated himself. In the early 19th century a well-traveled

---

131. New York *Irish American Weekly*, April 7, 1888, p. 4

path led from apprentice to printer to journalist to writer; printers' and typographers' unions offered free night classes, access to libraries, and other forms of education. Many 19th-century American literary men rose from equally humble origins. This includes members of Fitzgerald's New York social and professional milieu, such as Rufus Griswold (Edgar Allan Poe's literary executor, or executioner), George Wilkes, and George G. Foster. Rumored to have been illegitimate and raised in a brothel, George Wilkes did not have an expensive education but he published a scholarly work on the plays of Shakespeare and the national sports weekly, *Wilkes' Spirit of the Times*. The child of a Vermont shoemaker, Griswold left home at 15 and educated himself while working as printer; he became a published poet and literary critic. Fellow Vermonter Foster was another self-made man of letters. Thomas Fitzgerald's writing style itself tells us where he came from. It is well seasoned with Bowery B'hoy self-assertion and the joy in puncturing smugness and hypocrisy that characterizes Mike Walsh or the George Wilkes of his youthful *Subterranean* and *National Police Gazette* days.

Meanwhile, back in New York's Fourth Ward, Edmund Fitzgerald Jr.—our leading candidate for Thomas Fitzgerald's older brother—was moving up the Tammany Hall food chain. In 1841 he appeared on a Democratic committee with publisher William Colyer. In 1845 he was a poll inspector and member of the party ward committee. Later that year he was named police captain of the Fourth Ward; he and his mother Ellen moved into an apartment above the police station at 9 Oak Street, less than half a block from Hague Street. In 1847 Edmund Fitzgerald ran successfully for New York City Alderman, a lucrative position. The Fitzgerald family fortunes were looking up, but in 1852 the unmarried and childless Edmund died, leaving his entire estate to his mother Ellen. She died five years later at the age of 83.

Ellen Fitzgerald is buried in the crypt under old St. Patrick's Cathedral on New York City's Mulberry Street. The inelegant inscription on the vault's marble door—"Ellen Fitzgerald's Family Vault 1852"—conveys the vanity of a simple woman who, after a long and hard life, managed to afford an expensive exit. According to a former custodian of the crypt, future President John F. Kennedy once paid Ellen Fitzgerald a visit, believing that he was related to her through his grandfather, Boston mayor John "Honey Fitz" Fitzgerald.

It is easy to see why Thomas Fitzgerald never discussed his early life. He lost one or both parents as a boy. He was sent to work instead of school. Even if he had no hard feelings toward the rest of his family, the sophisticated and successful pillar of Philadelphia society that he became did not need or want any connection to the Fitzgeralds of the Fourth Ward.

THOMAS FITZGERALD THE socially prominent Philadelphian was a shrewd baseball man who was determined to build the Athletics into a top club. He was aggressive in building the Athletics into a winner, but there were some things that he was not willing to do to win baseball games. Several times during the 1860s, disputes within the Athletics would cause Fitzgerald to put his foot down and resign as club president. Each time the dispute was settled and the club asked him to come back. We do not know what these disputes were about, but a good guess would be violations of the amateur ethic. The 1866 version was so bitter that Fitzgerald's resignation was accepted. It is clear from the public relations war that broke out afterward that Fitzgerald had resigned over the club paying players illegally and lowering their admission standards in order to improve the club on the field. Because amateurism was essentially a form of social exclusion, these two issues overlapped.

In early March 1866 the Athletics had unanimously re-elected Fitzgerald as president for the fifth time. The club was at a high point, with the largest membership in the country—over 400 members who paid dues of $20 per year—a fat bank account, and one of the nation's best baseball teams. The Athletics were in fact about to come within one unplayed game of becoming the first club from outside baseball's Holy Land, the New York City metropolitan area, to win a national baseball championship.

In May newspapers reported the shocking news that Fitzgerald had resigned to take over as president of the Equity club (which immediately began to improve). Fitzgerald's *City Item* ran a series of stories accusing DeWitt Clinton Moore and Hicks Hayhurst of the Athletics of using "hired men," mercenaries who were paid $20 a week, in violation of NABBP rules on amateurism.[132] The *Item* gave Fitzgerald's successor as club president, choir director DeWitt Clinton Moore, the derisive nickname of "the psalm-singing hypocrite"—"P.S.H." for short. That had to hurt.[133] The paper asked, "Now in the case of a close game—a game, say, between the Atlantics, Excelsiors, Mutuals and Eurekas—would you trust some of these 'hired men' should they receive liberal offers from the outside betting fraternity? Don't you think an offer of $500 would have its effect? Can you trust a fellow who sells his services to the highest bidder?"[134] In July the *City Item* reprinted the following want ad from the *New York Clipper*, with commentary added by Fitzgerald.

WANTED — A FIRST-CLASS BASE BALL PITCHER, for a series of match games to come off this season. By addressing to A. Sneider, P. O. Box 141, Sunbury, [PA], you can learn particulars.

132. Philadelphia *City Item*, August 18, 1866
133. Philadelphia *City Item*, July 21, 1866
134. Philadelphia *City Item*, August 25, 1866

We call the attention of pitchers, who desire to hire themselves out by the day, week, month, or year, to the above advertisement.... How much can Sneider give? Can he pay
$20 per week? What security does he offer? Has he any
poor relations? Will cold victuals be thrown in?[135]

Fitzgerald's *jihad* against professionalism on his old club made
enemies; some of them retaliated by falsely accusing him of offering cash to entice players to join his new club, the Equity. Fitzgerald was publicly expelled from the Athletics, the club that he had
cofounded. But many in baseball took his side. When Fitzgerald
ran a comic caricature of one of the "hired men," saying of them,
"They generally come from New York, with only one or two exceptions [hint, hint], and are about the hardest set we ever saw," he
got a fan letter from Brooklyn. "Dear Sir," it read, "Will you have
the kindness to mail me three or four copies of your paper containing the portrait of the 'Hired Man?' I called at the 'Excelsior' Club
Room the other evening, and was much amused, *as were many
others*, by hearing Dr. Jones read several extracts from last week's
paper. Hoping 'Our National Game' may continue to prosper as it
has done, and that the 'Hired Men' may soon become extinct...."[136]

Fitzgerald's paper specified that the Athletics had four players who were paid directly or "constructively." He did not name
names—he didn't need another lawsuit—but he offered enough
information, including publishing a list of starting Athletics
players who were *not* paid, that we can identify the filthy four
with some confidence. Three of the players are Patsy Dockney
from Hoboken; Lipman Pike from Brooklyn; and Al Reach, also
from Brooklyn. The other one is almost certainly star pitcher
Dick McBride, a native Philadelphian.

---

135. Philadelphia *City Item*, July 21, 1866
136. Philadelphia *City Item*, September 1, 1866

Dockney and Pike are a good fit for the category of "the hardest set we ever saw." Both were far more at home in a saloon than a concert hall. As Fitzgerald wrote, "The officers of the Athletic Club have done much to bring the game into contempt by employing men to play in their nine who have been repeatedly arrested and confined in the station house . . . on the charge of drunkenness and rioting. There was a time when a player would have been expelled from the club for drunkenness and rioting, but that day seems to have passed." Dockney's brilliant career as a catcher was derailed by a barroom brawl in which his chest was sliced open by a meat cleaver; he later sold fish in the Washington Market and served a prison stretch for theft.

A speedy left-handed power hitter who once won a race around the bases against a thoroughbred horse (he passed the horse rounding third), Pike had a long career in amateur and pro baseball. Baseball historians like to portray Pike, baseball's first Jewish star, as a victim of persistent anti-Semitism, but the evidence for this is nonexistent. Amateur Era baseball and mid-19th-century America, particularly New York City, were refreshingly free of anti-Semitism. In 1881 Lipman Pike was put on a temporary blacklist by the National League for being "dissipated [i.e., drunk] and insubordinate [i.e., he annoyed a club owner]." If there was an ulterior reason, we do not know it; none of the other eight players on the list was Jewish. Al Reach was no lowlife but rumor had it that in 1866 the Athletics paid him by giving him a house. Both Dockney and Pike left Philadelphia after the *City Item* stories, in late 1866.

Many baseball histories claim that in 1865 Reach was given $25 per week by Fitzgerald and the Athletics to leave the Eckfords and play for Philadelphia, and that this makes Thomas Fitzgerald a hypocrite. Today, Reach and James Creighton are at the top of most modern lists of Amateur Era secret professionals, players who were paid "under the table." But this misreads the times and the baseball world in which Reach and Creighton lived.

Until the 1869 season the letter of the NABBP rules prohibited clubs from paying or compensating players in any form, but as with many rules, baseball and otherwise, as applied the prohibition was more subtle. As far as we know, no one in baseball in 1865 considered Reach's relationship with his club to be improper. The fact that we are confused today about the distinction between amateurism and professionalism in 1860s baseball—or that the NABBP did not want to police it—does not mean that the distinction did not exist. Two things are clear. Some forms of player compensation were generally regarded as honest and others were not; and this depended on the player's relationship with his club. Virtually all of the outrage about so-called professionalism in the Amateur Era was about players jumping, or "revolving" from one club to another. The central issue in these cases was loyalty, not payment per se. The same Excelsiors who applauded Thomas Fitzgerald's campaign against "hired men" had helped James Creighton and his father buy a house and obtain no-show patronage posts in the New York City Customs House. They also secured star second baseman and police telegrapher George Flanley, who came from a poor family, a better job in the Brooklyn Police Department. These were not seen in their time as violations of the amateur ethic but as mutual assistance by club members. The moralistic Henry Chadwick himself drew a distinction between "hired men" and "those whose loss of time and necessary expenses are very properly paid." "All clubs," he wrote, "who have first class players in their nines whose positions in life are not surrounded with pecuniary advantages, or who are not, in fact, well off in the world, of course take care that their players are not sufferers from sacrificing their time to sustain the playing reputation of the club of which they are prominent players. But this style of thing is . . . very different from 'hiring men,' or paying them so much a week for their services, just as 'professional' cricketers are paid."[137]

The Excelsiors may have aided James Creighton financially in order to allow him to play but the Excelsiors did not lie about it and they did not need to. Interestingly, they did finesse the issue of when Creighton had come to Brooklyn, saying that he had moved there as a young boy, instead of in 1858 when he was 17 years old. Baseball references today repeat this falsehood. The reason they did so was to suggest that Creighton legitimately belonged to the community that had produced his teammates. In any case, he remained with the Excelsiors for the rest of his (albeit brief) life. Creighton was no mercenary.

Neither was Al Reach. In 1865 Reach was playing for the Athletics but still living in Brooklyn, while he considered moving his entire family—father, brothers, and fiancée—to Philadelphia. A likely explanation for the $25 per week the club gave him is that it was reimbursement for expenses: the two or three round trips a week that he had to make by train between New York and Philadelphia during the summer and fall of 1865 in order to play with the Athletics. The amount is about right. After Reach did bring his family to Philadelphia in 1866, Thomas Fitzgerald helped him and his brother establish a cigar shop, but this was already Reach's brother's business. The important fact is that in the 1860s no one saw Reach as in any sense a mercenary; he came to Philadelphia intending to put down roots and he did. It is revealing that in 1866 Fitzgerald's baseball enemies did not attack him for having paid Al Reach; instead they used made-up charges that he had dangled money in front of other players to get them to jump to his Equity club. Reach played the rest of

---

137. Philadelphia *City Item*, August 18, 1866

his career in Philadelphia, where he started the sporting goods business that made him rich and where in 1883 he cofounded the National League Philadelphia Phillies. Dick McBride also played virtually his entire amateur and professional career in Philadelphia, his hometown. Like Reach, McBride was one of the Athletics' most valuable players.

There are two possible reasons why both might have been paid by the club in 1866. One is fairness; equal or lesser players brought from outside were getting paid. The other is that in the late 1860s baseball clubs throughout the country were raiding each other's rosters in a kind of feeding frenzy; the Athletics may have paid Reach and McBride so they would not be tempted to leave. One look at their careers, on the other hand, will tell you that Patsy Dockney and Lipman Pike were out and out mercenaries. Dockney played for the Gothams in 1864 and 1865; the Athletics in 1866; the Eurekas of Newark in 1867; and both the Cincinnati Buckeyes and the New York Mutuals in 1868. Lipman Pike came up through Brooklyn junior clubs under the control of the Atlantics, where he was playing when he jumped to the Philadelphia Athletics for the 1866 season. He went on to play in New York, Baltimore, Hartford, St. Louis, Cincinnati, and Providence.

THE CONTROVERSY OVER Fitzgerald and the four "hired men" blew over without anybody being disciplined or suspended. It was just one more bit of unpleasantness in a chaotic and quarrelsome baseball season. In 1866 baseball was caught between two eras. Home clubs still treated visiting clubs to banquets and outings as if they were personal guests but when it came to money issues like scheduling championship games or divvying up gate receipts, clubs played hardball. In 1866 a war-weary America embraced baseball as entertainment. The money was pouring in. Not all of the men who ran the top clubs, however, were up to handling the change. As with other Amateur Era traditions, baseball was outgrowing the traditional way of determining a national champion, a three-game series negotiated by the interested parties themselves. A scheduling disagreement marred the championship series between the Athletics and the Atlantics in 1865. There were leftover hard feelings but the Athletics were looking forward to another shot at the Atlantics in the three-game championship series they hoped to play in 1866. They would be disappointed again.

Game 1 was scheduled for October 1, 1866 at Camac's Woods in Philadelphia. With the police struggling to hold back a crowd of 25,000 and growing, the Athletics took a 2–0 lead in the first. When fans spilled out onto the field, the badly outnumbered Philadelphia police lost control. "A man was dragged by the police from the crowd with his head covered in blood," wrote the *Boston Post*, "which caused additional excitement, and it was impossible to continue the game."[138] The newspapers blamed gamblers, of course, but most of the spectators were fans—ordinary people rooting for their boys to beat Brooklyn. It was Colonel DeWitt Clinton Moore and the Athletics who were responsible for the fiasco; they had sold too many 25-cent tickets and botched the security arrangements. The game was rescheduled for Brooklyn's Capitoline Grounds on October 15.

The greatest dynasty of the Amateur Era, the Atlantics were baseball's champions in 1857, 1858, 1859, 1860, 1861, 1864, and 1865. The club had transcended its origins as a pickup game of traders from Brooklyn's Atlantic Market to become the city's unofficial hometown baseball club. Like the Excelsiors, the Atlantics were built on a broad base of young homegrown talent.

---

138. Boston *Post*, October 4, 1866

They had relationships with the Enterprise and other junior clubs playing in Bedford, where the Atlantics' grounds and later the Capitoline Grounds were located. The Atlantics were also backed by Hugh McLaughlin's Democratic party machine and the city government, many of whose functionaries played for the laid-back Pastime club. Pastime members such as City Registrar of Deeds William Barre, Alderman and Street Commissioner Robert Furey, and other baseball-friendly politicians helped out the Atlantics with jobs for players and other favors. It is a little too easy to paint the Atlantics as a kind of anti-Excelsiors—uncouth, Irish, in bed with gambling and machine politics. The Excelsiors may have been favored by Brooklyn's EUB and the Atlantics may have had a seamy side, but they both had members with political and gambling connections, and the Atlantics were not the only club with a member that had a criminal record. Certainly, there was no great gulf between the two clubs on a personal level. William Barre and Excelsiors centerfielder (and rich cotton dealer) Harry Polhemus belonged to the same fancy men's clubs and were best friends. Atlantics club officer Alexander R. Samuels, a rare Jewish Civil War cavalry officer as well as a philanderer, caterer, theater manager, and convicted wiretapper—he was caught intercepting telegraphed horserace results *a la* the 1973 film *The Sting*—was a regular billiards partner of Excelsiors club president Dr. Joseph B. Jones. The morally upright Henry Chadwick had plenty of good friends among the Excelsiors, Atlantics, and Pastimes.

In Brooklyn on October 15 the walls of the Capitoline Grounds and Police Superintendent Folk's 150 policemen kept perfect order among the crowd of 15,000–20,000. The Atlantics led 12–11 after six innings but they scored eight in the seventh and won 27–17. The Athletics, according to the *New York Clipper*, "[bore] their defeat gracefully"—their fans, not so much. In the city that would become infamous in the 20th century for proverbially booing the crack in the Liberty Bell and literally booing the great Mike Schmidt, "insinuations [were] openly made that treachery lost the Athletics the match, that certain of the players in the Philadelphia nine purposely made 'wild throws,' 'muffed balls,' etc., in order that the Brooklyn club might gain the victory, and thus secure for their friends the large sums of money wagered."[139] Incredibly, the same Philadelphia papers that had defended the Athletics' use of accused "hired men" Patsy Dockney, Al Reach, and Lip Pike, now accused these men of betraying the club for money.

The Athletics and Atlantics returned to Philadelphia for Game 2 on October 22. Following the sensible suggestion of Henry Chadwick, in order to avoid a repeat of October 1 the Athletics quadrupled the admission charge and limited the crowd to 4,000. They also promised to give the Atlantics half of the gate receipts to make up for the cost and inconvenience of their wasted first trip to Philadelphia. A small crowd of well-mannered people who could afford dollar baseball tickets watched the Athletics win 31–12 and even up the series. But after the game an argument broke out over what the meaning of is was. To the Atlantics, half of the gate receipts meant half of the gross; the Athletics, who had spent $1,200 on new perimeter fencing, angered them by offering half of the receipts net of expenses. Game 3 was never played and the Atlantics remained champions.

HOWEVER RELUCTANTLY, EVERY 19th-century American institution had to take a stand on race. Amateur baseball's time came in the fall of 1867, when an African American club, the Pythians of Philadelphia, applied for admission to the NABBP via its subsidiary, the Pennsylvania state baseball association.

139. *New York Clipper*, October 27, 1866

This touched off another baseball controversy with national repercussions that Thomas Fitzgerald jumped into with both feet. The difference this time was that the "hired men" controversy had cost Fitzgerald his position as president of the Athletics, the most important baseball club in Philadelphia. In 1867, when baseball urgently needed an effective advocate for racial inclusion, Fitzgerald's influence in the sport was at a low point. Of course, he still had one weapon—the barrels of ink he purchased to print his popular newspaper, the *City Item*.

To understand the story of the Pythians and organized baseball, a little background is necessary. It is difficult to say which 19th-century American city had the worst race relations. Philadelphia was certainly a contender. The city had bloody race riots—that is, white people rioting—in 1834, 1838, and 1842. Instead of segregating its streetcars, until 1867 Philadelphia banned African Americans entirely. No exceptions were made for African American wives and children who, late in the war, were visiting hospitalized Civil War veterans. Frederick Douglass, whose son Frederick Douglass Jr. played baseball for the African American Alert club in Washington DC, called Philadelphia the "up-South."

But thanks to racially liberal Quakers and the Underground Railroad, the city also had a large African American community anchored by institutions like the Institute for Colored Youth. A school for higher education founded in 1837 by a wealthy Quaker and originally located at 7th and Lombard Streets, the Institute moved in 1902 to Delaware County, where it continues today under the name Cheyney University. Like other Philadelphians, African Americans in Philadelphia had long played cricket and town ball. In 1866 a group of African American business and professional men founded a baseball club. They named it the Pythians. Their on-field leader was Octavius Catto, a teacher at the Institute for Colored Youth and a civil rights activist who led campaigns for African Americans to fight in the Civil War and to use the Philadelphia streetcar system.

DRAWING THE LINE

Wall Street stockbroker James Whyte Davis had two nicknames: "The Fiend" because of his intensity, and "Too Late" because he had an annoying habit of showing up in the middle of the first inning. Like other early Knickerbockers, Davis belonged to volunteer fire company Oceana Hose No. 36. Elected several times to the Knickerbocker club presidency, he served on the three-man committee that put on the 1858 Fashion Course series between New York and Brooklyn. He was also a good enough outfielder at age 32 to play centerfield in the second game of the series. Confirming the eternal truth of modern hitting coach Rick Down's mantra, "If you can't dance, you can't hit," Davis won the dance contest at the New York Stock Exchange Christmas Party in 1880, the year that he retired from baseball at the age of 54.

James Whyte Davis was a participant in baseball's first official act of racial exclusion. We do not know enough to assess Davis's exact degree of responsibility, but it probably lies somewhere between main actor and guilty bystander. In the fall of 1867 the Pythian club of Philadelphia, made up of teachers, professionals, and other African American members of the EUB, caused much seat shifting and throat clearing when it applied to join the Pennsylvania state baseball association. Acceptance would have made the Pythians members of the all-white NABBP. The Pythians were talked into withdrawing their application before anyone had to vote on the record, but later in the year the NABBP convention, meeting in Philadelphia, decided to make sure that this didn't become a trend. Historians would later call early baseball's color line a "gentlemen's agreement," but both of those words are inapt. In 1867 the NABBP wrote it down in black and white. The delegates passed a rule barring from membership any club "composed of persons of color, or any portion of them."[140] This grammatically clumsy resolution was written by the Nominating Committee, which had three members. One was William E. Sinn, owner of Philadelphia's New Chestnut Street Theater and president of its employee baseball

140. Philadelphia *Sunday Mercury*, December 15, 1867

club. Sinn had been arrested in 1861 for trying to join the Confederate army and may well have held racist views, but the reason he was on the committee was because he let the convention use his theater. Sinn had zero influence in baseball. The other two members were prominent veteran baseball men Dr. William H. Bell, former member of the NABBP Rules Committee and cofounder of the Eckfords and several other clubs; and James Whyte Davis, one of the two Knickerbocker delegates to the 1867 convention.

The Knickerbockers were orthodox amateurs who dissented from the creeping professionalism of the late Amateur Era. They refused to accept a penny from any ticket sales to their games. Ironically, some of them later asserted parental rights over professional baseball. In 1893 James Whyte Davis asked Edward Talcott, one of the owners of the New York Giants, to launch a fund to pay for Davis's grave monument, which he wanted inscribed as follows: "Wrapped in the original flag of the Knickerbocker Base Ball Club of N.Y., here lies the body of James Whyte Davis, a member for thirty years. He was not 'Too Late,' reaching the 'Home Plate.'" Davis thought that this should be paid for by the National League players, who, in Davis's mind, owed their livelihood to him and the Knickerbockers. Neither the fund nor the monument materialized. It is doubtful that anyone then playing major league baseball had ever heard of him. When he died in 1899, James Whyte Davis was dressed in his old uniform, wrapped in the club flag he had designed in 1855, and buried in Brooklyn's Green-Wood Cemetery in an unmarked grave. 117 years later, the Society for American Baseball Research raised the funds to give Davis his gravestone, inscribed as he had asked.

1870 AND 1871 WERE RACIALLY TROUBLED years in America. In February, Congress passed the 15th Amendment to the Constitution, which guaranteed American men voting rights "regardless of race, color, or previous servitude." In Philadelphia, the entrenched Democratic Party reacted with a campaign of intimidation and threats aimed at stopping African Americans, who overwhelmingly supported Republicans, from voting. On Election Day 1871 African Americans in the city's public places were harassed, assaulted, and fired upon by roving gangs deployed by Democratic politicians. Octavius Catto was near the intersection of South Street and 9th, on his way home, when a Moyamensing volunteer fireman and part-time Democratic Party goon named Frank Kelly shot him dead. (Historians often call Kelly "Irish" based on nothing more than his surname; to imply that Kelly's presumed Irish or Irish American identity is somehow relevant to his racism is particularly offensive in telling the story of a man who was murdered for what, not who he was.) Catto was given full military honors and Philadelphia's largest funeral since the ceremonies for Abraham Lincoln in 1865. It took the Philadelphia police six years to find and arrest Kelly but a jury acquitted him of murder. No one in Philadelphia was surprised. In 2017 a statue of Octavius Catto with his arms out and palms turned up in a questioning gesture, as eyewitnesses said they were when he died, was dedicated outside Philadelphia City Hall.

In 1867, their first full season, Octavius Catto's Pythians defeated local African American rivals the Excelsiors and L'Ouvertures and established themselves as the consensus African American champions of Philadelphia. They went to Washington, where they beat the African American Alerts and Mutuals. The Pythians' success inspired civic pride in some quarters of the mainstream press. When the Philadelphia Excelsiors defeated an African American club from New York in October 1867, the Philadelphia *Sunday Mercury* wrote: "[The New York papers] apply the title of Champions to the Excelsiors, and then abuse and ridicule them, after the fashion of New York. The Pythians, also of this city, are the recognized champions among colored organizations, and should they ever conclude to visit New York, an opportunity will be afforded Philadelphia defamers to see a well-behaved set of gentlemen."[141]

141. Philadelphia *Sunday Mercury*, October 6, 1867

Amateur baseball was always looking for a few "well behaved gentlemen." So far all of them had been white but the NABBP had no actual policy banning African Americans. None of the African American clubs in New York City or Brooklyn had ever tried to join. In October 1867 the clubs of the Pennsylvania State baseball association were holding their annual convention in Harrisburg. The president of the association happened to be Philadelphia Athletics delegate Hicks Hayhurst, a Quaker and racial liberal who had umpired Pythian games. The Pythians were a credible African American baseball club equal or superior to many NABBP clubs in education and social class. Culturally, socially, and economically they belonged to the EUB. They decided that the time was right to test amateur baseball's principles. They sent Raymond Burr, the son of Abolitionist newspaper editor John Pierre Burr (who was rumored to be the unacknowledged child of U.S. Vice President Aaron Burr and a Haitian servant) to Harrisburg to apply for admission to the association. Burr was politely treated but after voting to approve 265 out of 266 applications for membership, the nominations committee postponed consideration of the Pythians until the following day. That night, no doubt trying to head off a divisive conflict, Hayhurst convinced Burr to withdraw the Pythians' application by telling him that it had no chance of winning in a public vote.[142]

The nightmare of white discomfort was averted but men of influence in baseball decided to make sure the issue never came up again. At the NABBP national convention, held soon after in Philadelphia, a committee made up of Knickerbocker James Whyte Davis, Greenpoint Eckfords cofounder Dr. William H. Bell, and another man authored a resolution that barred any club with one or more African American members. When it passed, baseball's first color line was drawn.

---

142. Casway, J., *Octavius Catto and the Pythians of Philadelphia*, Pennsylvania Legacies, May 2007, p. 5

In 1868 the Pythians returned to playing other African American clubs, but they still had friends in white baseball. Colonel Thomas Fitzgerald was one of them, but after the bridges he had burned in his nasty breakup with the Athletics, all he could do was complain in the pages of his newspaper. He criticized the state convention for rejecting the Pythians in 1867. In 1869, seeing that the Pythians had improved to the point that they could hold their own against a mid-level white club, Fitzgerald started to beat the drum for a kind of baseball integration. His tactic was to encourage or, if necessary, embarrass prominent white clubs into playing against the Pythians. Thomas Fitzgerald's racial attitudes seem shockingly out of their time but the fact that he published them in a newspaper with a large circulation suggests that there were more people with views like his than we might think. Fitzgerald despised blackface entertainment, calling it low and vulgar. He mocked DeWitt Clinton Moore for telling racist jokes in a lame African American accent. In May Fitzgerald trolled racists with a news item that read, "There are two baseball clubs in Wilmington, North Carolina [in 1898 the site of an infamous anti–African American pogrom], composed of colored men, but they allow white men to play with them occasionally." In July he wrote, "The Pythians Club (colored) have beaten all the colored clubs, and would like to play a match with some of their white brethren. What say you, Athletics, Olympics, Keystones, Intrepids, etc." This was followed by, "Why is it that the Athletics will not play the colored baseball club the Pythians? Are they afraid of them? As I hear the Pythians are very strong, I think it quite possible that *apprehension of being beaten by them* is the real cause."[143]

Calling the white clubs out got results, although not from the Athletics. In September 1869 Philadelphia's venerable white

143. Philadelphia *City Item*, July 31, 1869

266]

Olympic club took the field against the Pythians, with Thomas Fitzgerald umpiring. The Olympics won the first baseball game ever played between a NABBP club and an African American club, 44–23. After this game, the door opened a crack. Isolated interracial games were played in 1869 in Boston and Washington. The Pythians found other white opponents, including the *City Item* employees' team, with three of Fitzgerald's sons in the lineup. The Pythians won that game, 27–17, in front of a large crowd. "The *City Item*," wrote the Philadelphia *Morning Post*, "is especially to be commended for having the manliness to grapple with our great social question in a practical way. So far from losing anything by this defeat, the *City Item* must gain immensely in the estimation of all people whose opinion is worth the having. The moral effect of these interchanges of good feeling between the classes must be great, and the evidences of it upon the ground were unmistakable."[144] On this note of hope the story of the Pythians ends. After Catto's assassination, the Pythians announced that "in the death of Octavius V. Catto our organization has lost its most active and valued member."[145] They promised that they would carry on his struggle for "truth, justice and equality." But they would not do it through baseball.

LIKE PHILADELPHIA, THE city of Boston had a homegrown bat-and-ball game that wasn't baseball. Called baseball, round ball, or the Massachusetts game, it was a bit like town ball. One difference was that it had fast, overhand pitching—fifty years before baseball did. Another is that it was based, oddly enough, in the suburbs. In 1860 the Massachusetts game's annual convention was attended by clubs from Ashland, South Dedham,

---

144. Philadelphia *Morning Post* quoted in Philadelphia *City Item*, September 25, 1869
145. *New National Era*, October 19, 1871

East Douglas, Mansfield, Charlestown, Westboro, Upton, East Cambridge, North Brookfield, Sharon, Waltham, Walpole Centre, Weymouth, Haverhill, South Walpole, North Weymouth, Marlboro, Medway, Bolton, Roxbury, Randolph, Natick, Holliston, and Milford. Boston proper was represented by the Olympics, the Bay States, and the Pythians. People liked watching the Massachusetts game; interclub games drew crowds as large as several thousand in the late 1850s.

The Massachusetts game made an attempt at becoming an organized sport but it never quite got there. Not every game becomes a sport. Like Peter Pan, both town ball and the Massachusetts game were having fun and did not want to grow up. Reflecting the game's general lack of coherence, the rules of the Massachusetts game were vague, even to the point of being negotiable from game to game. In 1857 the Union club of Medway needed a face-saving way to back out of a challenge from the stronger Massapoag club of Sharon. The Unions accepted, but on the conditions that "the number of bases . . . be *five*, instead of *four*; the fifth base or home base being the batters' stand, which shall be 40 feet (instead of 12 feet) from the first base; the distance from the fourth to the fifth or home base to be also 40 feet."[146] The Massapoags passed. In 1858, the same year that the NABBP was founded in New York City, the Boston-area clubs held their first convention. Not everyone got the memo about why they were meeting. After a set of rules and regulations were voted on, according to the *New York Clipper*, "A warm [i.e., angry] discussion of about two hours followed the report, some parts of which not being in conformity with the views entertained by different delegates. Mr. B. F. Guild, President of the Tri-Mountain Club, of Boston, [stated that their club] would be obliged to withdraw

---

146. Boston *Herald* October 9, 1857

from the Association, as the rules ... could not be accepted by their Club, as they preferred to play the New York game."[147]

Another problem for the Massachusetts game was that the New York game had it surrounded before the battle even started. Even worse, by the time of the first Massachusetts club convention in 1858 the New York invader was already inside the walls in the person of the Tri-Mountains club. Despite its name the Massachusetts game was not played much west of Worcester. Places like Westfield, Springfield, Pittsfield, and North Adams had long played the New York game and formed baseball clubs in the 1850s. The New York game was also the people's choice in Portland, Maine, 112 miles north-northeast of Boston, which seems strange until you look at it from an economic and transportation point of view. A shipbuilding and lumber center, Portland did business directly with New York City and Brooklyn. When Boston was expanding its rail network in the 1830s, 1840s, and 1850s, Portland was determined not to be swallowed up by the larger Boston economy. It made sure that its railroads did not link with those in eastern Massachusetts. Commercially, it also looked north, in the early 1850s connecting to the Montreal-based Grand Trunk Railway, which bypassed Boston and opened a route to eastern Canada, the Great Lakes, and the American upper Midwest.

Boston had an early lead over other American cities in building railroads, which made possible the suburbs where most of the clubs playing the Massachusetts game were located. Because of the railroad lines' radial layout, these clubs commonly met to play matches on the neutral ground of the Boston Common. Built in 1634, the 50-acre Common is America's oldest big-city park. But Boston as a whole lacked space for outdoor team sports, something that stunted the growth of baseball in the 1850s and

---

147. *New York Clipper*, May 29, 1858

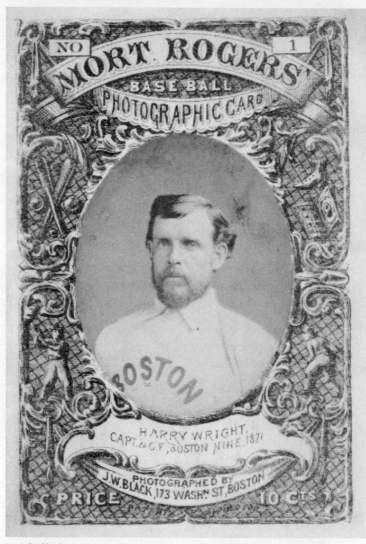

Baseball player-turned entrepreneur Mort Rogers moved from Brooklyn to Boston in the 1860s. There he published the first national baseball weekly and invented collectible photographic scorecards, like this Harry Wright example, which he sold at games.

1860s. Today the Boston Common contains exactly one baseball field. The Tri-Mountains, Boston's first baseball club, was founded by New Yorker Edward G. Saltzman, who had played with the Gotham club, and two business partners from New York and Brooklyn. In June 1857 the *New York Clipper* erroneously reported that "Mr. F. Guild [sic], the treasurer of the [Tri-Mountains], is now in New York, and has put himself under the instructions of the gentlemen of the Knickerbocker, who no doubt will give him all the instruction necessary in reference to the New York system." This was followed a week later by a correction, apparently after the *Clipper* got an earful from a certain non-Knickerbocker. "[The Tri-Mountains] are indebted for their instruction in the game," it reads, " . . . to the directions of Mr. E. G. Saltzman, their President, who is a member of the Gotham Club of your city . . . the only *instructions* [Mr. Guild] received while in N.Y. were what he gathered during an hour very pleasantly spent as a spectator of the excellent play of the Empire Club." The descendant of an old Boston family, Benjamin Franklin Guild was the editor and publisher of Boston's *Commercial Bulletin* newspaper.

The Tri-Mountains had no local opponent—remember, the vast majority of Amateur Era baseball games were intramural—until 1858, when they played the Portlands of Maine on the Boston Common. We have an eyewitness account of this game from James D'Wolfe Lovett, a 17-year-old native Bostonian who had grown up playing the Massachusetts game and cricket.

The Portlands won by the score of 47 to 42. This match was attended by many ball players, local and otherwise, who were curious to see what the new thing was like, and who looked on with a dignified toleration befitting those who "guessed" that the old game was good enough for them. But some who came to scoff remained to pray. It was evident that this new type was "catching" and that many present were in that condition when they are said to "take things." There were points about the new game which appealed to them. The pitching, instead of swift throwing, looked easy to hit, and the pitcher stood off so far, and then there was no danger of getting plugged with the ball while running bases; and the ball was so lively and could be batted so far! Yes, decidedly, there were points about this new game which pleased many who had never played ball before, and who thought that they would like to try it. . . .[148]

It is hard to believe that baseball defeated the Massachusetts game because its lively ball or anything else made it a better game to play. The same has been said a thousand times about baseball and cricket; obviously, Americans played both cricket and the Massachusetts game (and town ball and wicket and other games) and enjoyed them all. Baseball's supposed superiority is another example of the human brain's tendency to create reasons after the fact why what happened had to happen. Baseball's national ambition and the fact that it was played by New Yorkers were its real main selling points. As in Philadelphia, baseball conquered Boston by appealing to socially influential members of the EUB and to others who were particularly connected to and interested in what was happening in the wider world: students, entrepreneurs, and expatriates from New York and other parts of baseball country.

The early Amateur Era baseball scene in Boston was smaller than that of New York City, Brooklyn, or Philadelphia and it never caught up. When the Professional Era started in 1871, the Mutuals, Athletics, and other amateur clubs in New York, Brooklyn, Philadelphia and elsewhere went pro and joined the National Association. Boston went a different route. Without a

---

148. Lovett, James D'Wolfe. *Old Boston Boys and the Games They Played*. Boston, Mass.: Privately Printed, 1906, pp. 210 ff.

broad base of amateur talent to build on, a group of Boston businessmen in effect bought the Red Stockings' name, their manager, and most of their key players from Cincinnati. Between the late 1850s and the mid-1860s the dominant clubs in the Boston area were the Tri-Mountains, the Bowdoins, the Lowells, and the Harvard College clubs. The Bowdoins and the Lowells, who eventually merged, were founded and sponsored by wealthy engraver John Lowell, a native of baseball-playing Portland, Maine. The Tri-Mountains were founded by transplanted New Yorkers. In 1860 the Bowdoins paid a visit to New York City and invited the Excelsiors to play them in Boston, an invitation the Excelsiors were able to accept in 1862. Young Jim Lovett, who now played baseball for the Lowell club, was there, too.

On July 10 the Excelsiors of New York arrived in Boston. They were in their prime at this time, and, being the first New York club to visit Boston, created much excitement. Their nine consisted of Young, Russell, Pearsall, Polhemus, Brainard, Flanley, Creighton, Cook, and Leggett. Ball players from all parts of New England came to see them play, and our eyes were opened to many things. They beat the Bowdoins 41 to 15. Much good natured chaff was passed back and forth between John Lowell and Joe Leggett in this game, which made fun for everybody. Once when the latter was at the bat, he motioned to John, who was then playing center field, to go back a little further; John backed off about ten feet, upon which Leggett sung out, "A little further, still, John," and the latter, laughing, backed away another ten feet, whereupon Leggett struck a ball and sent it flying over John's head for a home run, amidst shouts of laughter from the crowd.[149]

---

149. Lovett, James D'Wolfe. *Old Boston Boys and the Games They Played*. Boston, Mass.: Privately Printed, 1906, p. 150

In the 19th century, as in the 21st, you couldn't swing a bat in Boston without hitting a student. High school, prep school, and college students were in the thick of the sports and baseball movements. Schools helped spread baseball for several reasons. Students tend to be forward-looking. Schools encourage physical education and sponsor sports clubs. Naturally, the first schools and colleges to play baseball were in New York City. As we know, Columbia College and baseball go way back. Founded by Townsend Harris in 1847 as the Free Academy, City College had student baseball clubs well before the Civil War. The Catholic St. John's College in the Bronx—now Fordham—had baseball clubs in the late 1850s. In 1866 two Cuban Fordham varsity players, Esteban Bellan and a teammate named Cristodoro, were recruited by the national champion Unions of Morrisania; Bellan later played for the Unions of Lansingburgh, also called the Troy Haymakers, along with another Cuban Fordham graduate, Rafael de la Rua. These sons of the Cuban bourgeoisie were the earliest Latinos to play baseball at a high level. Bellan played a couple of seasons of professional baseball before returning in 1874 to Cuba, where he played and managed in the first baseball leagues and where he is remembered today as a founding father of Cuban baseball.

The New York schools were followed by prep schools and colleges throughout the Northeast where prosperous New Yorkers sent their sons. Yale had informal baseball clubs in the late 1850s. In Boston, baseball and higher education were particularly intimate. In the 1860s the Boston equivalent of Brooklyn versus New York City was the town and gown rivalry between the Lowells and Harvard. This rivalry was so intense that when Lowells star Gerrit Miller went to Harvard as a student, he refused to play against his old club. In 1864 John Lowell offered a trophy silver ball to be competed for on a challenge basis by the

Boston clubs. In 1867 it was retired and melted down because clubs were trying too hard to win it. The Lowells once won the ball on a forfeit by challenging Harvard when the students were home on an academic break. The final score was the Lowells eight silver balls, Harvard four, and the Tri-Mountains three. In head to head silver ball games with the Lowells, Harvard won, 4–3. Most members of the Lowells had grown up in the West End. The Boston Common and the not yet landscaped Public Garden were their childhood playgrounds. Some of the Lowells went on to study at Harvard, but when they were founded in 1861 they were a junior club made up of younger students from Phelps, Dixwell's, Boston Latin, and other Boston secondary schools. Two of the Lowells' most important players were Mort Rogers and Gerrit Miller. Both were New Yorkers.

BORN IN BROOKLYN around 1845, Mortimer Rogers was playing for the Resolutes in 1865 when he struck up a friendship with some of the Lowells who were visiting New York. Later that year, he moved to Boston and joined the club. Although a good hitter and reputedly the best centerfielder in New England, Rogers looked at amateur baseball and saw a business opportunity. Over the next five years he served as vice president, secretary, and treasurer of the NABBP. In 1868 he started the first baseball-centered weekly, the *New England Base Ballist*. At the 1869 NABBP convention, which was held in Boston to promote the game there, Rogers's paper, now called the *National Chronicle*, was named the official newspaper of the NABBP. In 1871 Rogers began selling his new invention, "baseball photographic cards," at ballparks across the country. Printed scorecards that featured numbered photographic portraits of baseball players, these were, depending on whom you ask, the forerunners of the modern collectible baseball card.

Gerrit Smith Miller was a 16-year-old student at Dixwell's Private Latin School when he joined the Lowell club in 1861, its first season. Dixwell's school was near the present location of Emerson College at 20 Boylston Place. Dixwell's was about twenty steps from the Boston Common, where prep and high school boys got black eyes and muddy clothes playing various informal rugby-like games. While still at Dixwell's, Miller organized a club called the Oneidas, which played its own brand of football. The Oneidas' game is widely considered to be the direct ancestor of the game played by today's NFL, which means that the father of American football was a teenage baseball player. Tracing Gerrit Smith Miller's family background takes us to other interesting places, including Upstate New York when it was a laboratory for social change and radical politics. Born in Peterboro, New York, near Syracuse, Miller was named after his grandfather Gerrit Smith, a 19th-century land reformer, station master on the Underground Railroad, Temperance activist, and supporter of the vote for women. The phrase anti-slavery activist is too mild for Smith. He was a co-conspirator in John Brown's 1859 raid on Harper's Ferry, after which then-Senator Jefferson Davis demanded that Smith be hanged. African American Abolitionist minister Henry Highland Garnet once said, "There are two places where slaveholders cannot come, Heaven and Peterboro."

Gerrit Smith was also a friend and sometime ally of ex-Chartist land reformer Thomas Ainge Devyr, the father of Brooklyn baseball star Tom Devyr. Smith's daughter, and Gerrit Smith Miller's mother, Elizabeth Miller, invented bloomers, the baggy pants worn as a political statement by 19th-century feminists, and cofounded the National Woman Suffrage Association with her cousin Elizabeth Cady Stanton and Susan B. Anthony. In the 19th century, many feminists supported the American public health reform and sports movements. Stanton believed in physical education and athletics for women. So did Emma Willard, Mary Lyon, and other founders of 19th-century women's seminaries that became women's colleges and encouraged sports and exercise. As Dr. Joseph B. Jones of the Brooklyn Excelsiors discovered, advocating exercise for women and girls could be politically risky but all-female Vassar College had baseball clubs in the 1860s, as did Smith College in the 1870s. The first organized sport at Mt. Holyoke, the world's oldest continuously operating women's college, was baseball. In August 1868 Thomas Fitzgerald's Philadelphia *City Item* ran the following story.

> At Peterboro, writes Mrs. [Elizabeth] Cady Stanton, there is a baseball club of girls. Nannie Miller, a grand-daughter of Gerrit Smith, is the captain, and handles the bat with a grace and strength worthy of notice. It was a pretty sight to see the girls with their white dresses and blue ribbons flying, in full possession of the public square, while the boys were quiet spectators of the scene.[150]

Nannie Miller, who grew up to be the well-known feminist Anne Fitzhugh Miller, was Gerrit Miller's sister.

IN 1862 THE Lowells helped a group of students from the class of 1866 of Harvard, their future archrivals, lay out a baseball diamond near the Washington Elm on Cambridge Common and organize a baseball club. The roots of the Harvard club were in Phillips Exeter, a New Hampshire prep school attended by Harvard '66 students George Flagg and Frank Wright. As Wright recalled, during Latin class a classmate passed him a note suggesting they start a baseball club. "A majority of the fellows wished to form a club to play Massachusetts baseball ... but

---

150. Philadelphia *City Item*, August 15, 1868

a few of us who hailed from New York State carried the meeting in favor of the new game, then called the 'Brooklyn' game."[151] Harvard had a head start on other American colleges but a big reason why it dominated college baseball through the 1860s was its captain and star player from 1867–1871, Archie Bush. Bush's life story hits most of the big themes of late Amateur Era baseball—New York, the Civil War, student culture, and the railroad. Born Archibald McClure Bush in 1846 in Albany, he joined the army at 17 and served two years in the Civil War before entering the prep school Phillips Andover in 1864. After graduating from Harvard in 1871 he joined his father in the family business, manufacturing railroad cars at Troy, New York's Gilbert, Bush and Co. car works. When he was a freshman at Andover, Bush, his cousin James McClure (who had played in the army), and James Wells (a member of Brooklyn's Active club) organized the school's first baseball club. Four players from the club went on to play for Yale and two for Harvard. Yale and Princeton formed varsity baseball clubs and other colleges followed, among them Williams, Amherst, Brown, and Wesleyan.

Colleges took baseball seriously in the Amateur Era and it did not take them long to become competitive; they toured the East Coast and played top clubs like the Athletics, Atlantics, and Excelsiors. (Many of them employed ringers, players who were not undergrads.) In 1866 Williams was mocked in collegiate circles for hiring a baseball coach from New York City. But they were setting a trend. Hamilton College in Upstate New York brought in Excelsiors second baseman George Flanley to consult on its baseball program; Harry Wright helped Harvard in 1871. Amazingly, the 1869 NABBP convention elected Archie Bush president while he was still a college undergraduate.

---

151. Lovett, James D'Wolfe. *Old Boston Boys and the Games They Played*. Boston, Mass.: Privately Printed, 1906, p. 156

Colleges and prep schools were fertile ground for baseball because, like the army during the Civil War, they mixed together young men who came from baseball-playing parts of the country with young men who didn't. But they also spread the sport by sending their graduates back home or out into the world. The first great collegiate team, the Harvard Class of 1866 club, was the talk of Cambridge and Boston from 1863 to 1866. In July 1866 a dozen or so young Cincinnatians, four of them 1866 graduates of Harvard Law School and one a member of Harvard College Class of 1867, decided to form a baseball club. This is how the Cincinnati Red Stockings began.

UNION PRISONERS AT SALISBURY, N.C.

This print of a July 4, 1862 baseball game played by Union officers in the Confederate prison camp at Salisbury, North Carolina, was based on a drawing from life by one of the POWs, Prussian army veteran and professional artist Captain Otto Boetticher of the 68th New York Volunteers. Many, if not all, of the figures are portraits of actual individuals, including the Irish American hero Colonel Michael Corcoran, who is seated farthest to the right.

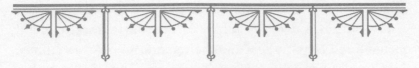

CHAPTER EIGHT
Amateur Hour

HE CIVIL WAR caused about 1.5 million casualties. One of them was cricket. Once taken seriously as a potential national sport for Americans, cricket fell behind baseball in popularity during the war years and never recovered. Yet baseball came home from the war without a scratch. We do not know why the war affected cricket and baseball differently, but we do know the reason why we don't know the reason—the chaos of war.

We can see the small picture of baseball in the wartime military: There are anecdotes, game accounts, and box scores of particular games. We can also see the big picture, that the war mixed soldiers from baseball-playing areas with soldiers from other areas on a grand scale. The mystery lies in the middle. We do not know the names of 95 percent of the baseball players who enlisted; we have only a general idea of what units they served in and how those units interacted with other units. Trying to understand how the Civil War affected the growth and spread of baseball is like trying to understand a forest from satellite photos and slides of root tissue without being able to see the trees.

A total of 2.8 million men fought on the Union side. About four hundred thousand of them were male New Yorkers in their

20s, a category that included most contemporary American baseball players. This meant that in practice soldiers from baseball wildernesses like Wisconsin or Missouri almost certainly encountered New Yorkers and their game. To take one influential club as an example, Henry Chadwick said that 91 members of Brooklyn's Excelsiors served. Back home in Brooklyn, the decimated Excelsior club played no games at all against other clubs in 1861, the first year of the war, and only a handful in 1862 and 1863. The Excelsiors had been particularly active in spreading the game of baseball in the pre-war years, so it is no surprise that individual members of the club—among them Frank Jones, a pioneer of baseball in Washington, and A.T. Pearsall, who co-founded early clubs in Virginia and Alabama—continued to do so while serving in the military. Civil War soldiers had plenty of leisure time for baseball and other sports. War is hell, but a significant part of that hell is boredom. Like all wars the Civil War had long periods when the main job of soldiers and sailors was, as they say in the military, to hurry up and wait.

Despite the general lull in interclub competition on the home front, especially in the early years of the war, Albert Spalding claimed that the Civil War helped baseball realize its destiny to unify the nation. According to his influential 1911 history, *America's National Game*, playing the game in the post-war years—and even before that, during breaks in the hostilities—helped heal the wounds of war. "When true patriots of all sections were striving to forget that there had been a time of black and dismal war," he wrote, "[baseball] was a beacon, lighting their paths to a future of perpetual peace ... before the decade of the sixties had died the game of baseball helped all of us to 'know no North, no South' [the phrase belongs to John Minor Botts, the Virginia politician and Henry Chadwick's uncle by marriage], only remembering a reunited Nation, whose game it was henceforth to be forever."[152]

That makes you want to stand up and salute, but there are few real facts to back it up. In December 1866, a year and a half after the war ended, the NABBP held its first post-war national baseball convention. One hundred-ninety-nine clubs from Union states attended. Only three came from Confederate states. There is circumstantial evidence that the demographic mixing that took place during the war consolidated baseball's popularity in the Northeast and accelerated baseball's spread westward, but for the wartime South all we have is a smattering of unreliable stories about Confederate troops playing among themselves, or sometimes—even more unreliably—against the enemy under a flag of truce. It is cause for skepticism that these stories tend to appear in soldiers' reminiscences written many decades after the fact, when hearts and minds had softened.

In the years immediately following the war the northern baseball establishment publicly hoped that the game might play a role in national reunification. New baseball clubs were formed in the South but that did not mean that their members shared this hope. Many looked upon the northern-based NABBP as the baseball equivalent of carpetbagger governments. "We are not, or do we expect to be members of the National Baseball Convention," wrote the president of the Richmond baseball club in 1866. "Our reason: We are Southerners."[153] The hostility was mutual. In 1866 the Philadelphia *Sunday Mercury* wrote, "A club bearing the name of 'Mosby' has been organized in Richmond, Va. They should make a reconnaissance in this latitude."[154]

---

152. Spalding, Albert G. *Baseball: America's National Game.* New York: American Sports, 1911, p. 93
153. Swanson, Ryan A. *When Baseball Went White.* Lincoln: University of Nebraska Press, 2014, p. 21
154. Philadelphia *Sunday Mercury*, July 15, 1866

Ironically, the infamous Confederate cavalry unit Mosby's Rangers included a former member of the Brooklyn Atlantics. Baseball spread in the postwar South the same way that the custom of celebrating Thanksgiving did—slowly and grudgingly. Neither was fully embraced in Dixie until its association with the Union cause had been forgotten.

Another contributing factor to baseball's slow growth in the South was that the war gutted the region's economy and left its railroad system a twisted, smoking ruin. To look at it another way, from a talent perspective, baseball is like a pyramid. The broader the development of the sport in a particular place—the base of the pyramid—the better the players and clubs will be at the top. The former Confederate states produce a bonanza of baseball talent today, but during the Amateur Era they fielded no clubs at the top competitive level. When the 1869 Cincinnati Red Stockings travelled to New Orleans, a southern baseball hotbed, they made the best clubs there look like Little League teams. There were no southern clubs in the National Association, the first professional league, or in the first 86 years of the National League. The Confederacy's first major league franchise was the 1962 Houston Colt 45s, now known as the Astros.

There are two first-hand sources of information about baseball during the Civil War. One is individual soldiers' personal stories, told in letters, diaries and memoirs. We know quite a bit about the lives and military careers of dozens of amateur baseball players. Later on, I will tell a few of these stories because they shed light on the war as experienced on the ground and the war's effect on baseball. The other source is contemporary newspaper accounts of individual games played by servicemen. Most of these stories and accounts involve New York units. This is no surprise because so many of the journalists who covered the war were New Yorkers. But this kind of information is by nature haphazard and anecdotal. In peacetime, newspapers were trying to cover the sport in a systematic way. In wartime, for obvious reasons, sports news became a low priority; baseball news was often treated as filler. The formerly baseball-centric national sports weekly *Wilkes' Spirit of the Times* ran pages of war coverage. Its publisher, George Wilkes, personally covered the war; he witnessed the first Battle of Bull Run. Later in the war Wilkes campaigned successfully to have Ulysses S. Grant put in command of the Union Army. Even Henry Chadwick did some war reporting and in 1865 he took a sabbatical from sportswriting to edit a book on the origins of Secessionism written by John Minor Botts.

Baseball in the military during the war years experienced a kind of second childhood, a return to the early Amateur Era. Without club rivalries or fans there was little at stake beyond the occasional bet and there were no championships to be won. Add to this that most of the baseball players who fought in the Civil War were not stars from the first nines of famous clubs like the Atlantics, Excelsiors, Athletics, and Mutuals. They were anonymous as athletes and as soldiers. The journalists who reported on the war had a geographic bias; the nation's most influential newspapers were published in New York City, as were the national sports weeklies. But they also had a class bias. Because both the volunteer and militia units of the time were self-constituted, there were stark ethnic and class differences between them. For example, in the 1860s the 7th New York National Guard, called the 7th New York State Militia in wartime, was drawn from the same EUB demographic as the baseball clubs that played at the Elysian Fields. By comparison, there were other New York regiments made up, say, of Irish or German immigrants, or upstate farm boys. Newspapers printed far more baseball stories about units like the 7th NYSM. Was this because these kinds of units had more baseball players, because they had more friends in journalism, or simply because the New York papers were more interested in them for class reasons?

A final problem is our frame of reference for war itself. All modern wars are foreign wars. Civil wars, of course, are fought at home. When our grandfathers served in World War II they typically traveled thousands of miles and were absent for years at a time. The average length of service in WWII was 33 months; 73 percent of all U.S. servicemen left the country for at least 16 months. Sixty percent of them were draftees. Almost no one fought in the Civil War against their will. 94 percent of Civil War servicemen were volunteers. When the war started, it was expected to be brief. Volunteers typically enlisted for 90 days. National Guard units could be called up for even shorter periods. This explains news items like this one, from the *Wilkes' Spirit of the Times* of June 5, 1861, less than two months after the war started: "The ball grounds at the Elysian Fields, Hoboken, begin to wear a very lively look. The members of the Empire, Eagle, Gotham, St. Nicholas, Mutual, Alpine and Jefferson clubs are mustering in full force on practice days.... Several important matches are nearly arranged.... The return of the Seventh National Guard added a reinforcement of some forty members to our prominent baseball clubs."[155]

EVEN AFTER IT sunk in that the war might not end in a few months and regular army enlistments were lengthened, for many servicemen home was only a day or two away by train or boat. Men who already belonged to state militias, as did countless baseball players, could be activated for no more than nine months. Even baseball players on active duty sometimes

---

155. *Wilkes' Spirit of the Times*, June 5, 1861

traveled home on leave and played for their old clubs. In 1862 Joe Sprague of the Eckfords had only six days after the end of his three-month enlistment with the 13th NYSM to prepare for the deciding game of the championship series with the Brooklyn Atlantics, which Sprague pitched and won.

The Brooklyn-based 13th NYSM was full of men with baseball connections, including two brothers of Walt Whitman, and Morgan Bulkeley, the future first president of the National League (and member of the Mills Commission that named Abner Doubleday the inventor of baseball). When the Civil War started, the United States Army had fewer than 20,000 men. Twenty percent of them, mostly officers, immediately resigned to join the Confederate Army. By the end of the war four years later, the U.S. armed forces had added almost 3 million recruits. Like Nelson Shaurman of the Charter Oak baseball club of Brooklyn, some had marched in a few parades as militiamen, but when it came to real warfare they were complete amateurs. Born in Greene County, New York, in 1820, Shaurman went to Brooklyn as a young man and worked as a builder. Like many early New York Republicans he was a former member of the nativist Know Nothing Party and an Abolitionist. After Albany Republicans disbanded the New York and Brooklyn municipal police departments in 1857 and replaced them with state-controlled departments, Nelson Shaurman was appointed captain of Brooklyn's Third Precinct. In 1858 the Brooklyn *Daily Eagle*, which supported the Democratic Party, made fun of him for arresting boys for breaking local Blue Laws by playing baseball on Sunday. The paper mercifully left out the fact that Shaurman himself played baseball, although on Mondays and Thursdays—the Charter Oaks' practice days.

The Charter Oaks played their first known interclub game in 1858, when they defeated the Esculapians, 37–22. The game was played on a long, narrow lot bounded by Smith, Hoyt, Degraw, and Sackett Streets, just to the east of the Excelsiors' grounds, today called Carroll Park. The former site of Bergen Hill, which in 1846 was leveled shovelful by shovelful by Irish immigrant laborers and used to fill in the wetlands between Kane Street and Hamilton Avenue, the grounds were also home to the Independents, Niagaras, Stars, Olympics, and Marions. As their name suggests, the Esculapians were physicians and medical students; in the lineup that day were future Excelsior A.T. Pearsall and Andrew Otterson. Both had close personal and professional connections to Excelsiors president Joseph B. Jones. Otterson and Jones, both of whom would later serve terms as Brooklyn Health Officer, were two of the five founding officers of the Brooklyn Medical Society in 1856; another was John Byrne, the man who in 1862 treated James Creighton's fatal infection and signed his death certificate. In 1858 and 1859 the Charter Oaks tried to develop talent in the same way as Brooklyn's top clubs, by recruiting players from junior clubs, but the well-connected Atlantics and the well-heeled Excelsiors took the cream of the crop. Instead of James Creighton, the Charter Oaks got John Shields; instead of the Whiting brothers, they got the Patchen brothers. Oddly enough, on the baseball diamond the humble Charter Oaks had the mighty Excelsiors' number. In early 1859, with Shaurman at shortstop, they beat the Excelsiors, 18–17. The Charter Oaks' finest hour was an April 1860 upset win over James Creighton by a score of 12–11. Admittedly, the Charter Oaks won these games by the slimmest of margins, but on paper they did not belong on the same field as the Excelsiors.

Nine days after the Confederate attack on Fort Sumter, Shaurman enlisted as a private in the 13th New York State Militia, Joe Sprague's unit. The 13th NYSM also had Ebenezer Ebbets, cousin of Charles Ebbets, the future owner of the Brooklyn Dodgers;

Knickerbocker, Excelsior, and future governor of the New York Stock Exchange Samuel H. Kissam; Excelsior captain and future embezzler Joseph Leggett; Excelsior John B. Woodward, who later commanded the regiment; Excelsior and future Wall Street millionaire John C. Whiting; and Charter Oak member and stockbroker Samuel Patchen. The 13th NYSM did police duty, seizing arms caches and suppressing Secessionist violence in Annapolis and Baltimore before coming home on July 30, 1861. Arriving at the Brooklyn ferry landing, they marched to City Hall and then to Fort Greene Park. Artillery salutes boomed from the rooftops and red, white and blue bunting hung from upper-story windows. Shaurman and his fellow militiamen were accompanied by a parade of police, militia, and military units, with bands and drum corps. Following these were fire companies Pacific Engine No. 14, Water Witch Hose No. 8, and others whose membership overlapped that of the 13th. As if to underline the unity of the three elements of traditional urban male culture—militias, firefighting, and baseball—the line also included members of 13 Brooklyn baseball clubs, among them the Atlantic, Exercise, Excelsior, Enterprise, Niagara, Pastime, and Star. Each ballplayer wore a badge with the motto, "Base-Ball Fraternity."[156]

WITH MORE WAR to be fought, Nelson Shaurman did not stay home for long. He and Joseph S. Morgan, a former captain of Brooklyn's socially exclusive City Guard, got to work raising a new regiment called the 90th New York Volunteers. According to the Brooklyn *Daily Eagle*, "Already one company is nearly raised by Capt. Nelson Shaurman, and have gone into camp at East New York. Capt. Shaurman is well and favorably known, and if anybody can raise a company of good men, he can do it."

---

156. Brooklyn *Daily Eagle*, July 30, 1861

As usual, a successful recruiter was rewarded with an officer's commission. This meant, in the early years of the war at least, that the officer corps of the Union Army was made up of men with wide social influence and connections. Some were political bosses and ward healers; others were popular officers in volunteer fire companies and citizen militias. And quite a few were, like Nelson Shaurman, prominent baseball men.

Shaurman's military career could not happen in today's highly professional armed forces, but in the Civil War there was a surprising number of stories like his. With experienced leadership in short supply, a fast learner could shoot up through the ranks with dizzying speed. A private in 1861, made captain of the 90th New York's Company G in early 1862, and promoted to major in July of that year, Nelson Shaurman became a Lieutenant Colonel in August 1863, and a full colonel in June 1864. He was mustered out of the 90th New York in 1866 with the brevet rank of brigadier-general.

In January 1862, when the 90th New York Volunteers were sent to occupy Key West, Florida, Colonel Morgan's abhorrence of slavery got him into trouble. He freed the local slaves on his own, in advance of the Emancipation Proclamation. In 1863, angered by accounts of the abuse and enslavement of African American Union POWs, Morgan ordered his men to evict most of the civilian population of Key West from their homes and deport them to the war zone. Shocked by Morgan's order, the 90th NY's junior officers published a letter of protest in their hometown paper, the Brooklyn *Daily Eagle*. Colonel Morgan was relieved of his command and replaced by Nelson Shaurman. Other Union commanders must have acted similarly; in April President Lincoln signed the Lieber Code, which outlawed inhumane treatment of non-combatants and ultimately served as the basis for both the Hague and Geneva Conventions on the laws of war.

In 1864 the 90th New York suffered heavy casualties at the Battle of Cedar Creek in Virginia. The *Daily Eagle* wrote that Colonel Shaurman had lost an arm in the fighting. A few days later it issued a correction. "[We] received a visit from the Colonel," it read, "who brought both arms with him, and we are happy to say, that they are still attached to his body in the natural way. . . . A twenty-pound shot, in the course of its travels, grazed his breast and left arm, leaving its mark, which is still painfully visible across the Colonel's body." In 1879, when Nelson Shaurman was 59, Henry Chadwick wrote that some of the politicos from the old Pastime club, including Frank Quevedo, Robert Furey, and William Barre, were planning to reunite baseball veterans from 1859 for an old timers' game in Prospect Park. "Major Shaurman," Chadwick added, was ready to "take bat in hand and show how fields were won."[157]

BENJAMIN K. KIMBERLEY was a native of Batavia, New York, a city between Buffalo and Rochester, who moved to Brooklyn in the late 1850s, worked in a bank and joined the Excelsiors. He was a baseball proselytizer, helping nurture the early Buffalo clubs and travelling to Boston and Philadelphia, where he appears in early baseball box scores as a scorer or umpire. He continued to help promote the game while serving in the Civil War with the 44th NY and the 13th NYSM. According to a regimental history, while camped at Culpepper, Virginia, "Captain B. K. Kimberley [who] was an experienced and skillful baseball player . . . took the lead in inaugurating a series of games of baseball"[158] among the troops. Shortly afterward, Kimberley

---

157. Brooklyn *Daily Eagle*, May 19, 1879
158. Nash, Eugene A. *A History of the 44th Regiment: NY Volunteer*

suffered a serious leg injury; despite this (or perhaps because of it), he joined 18th New York Cavalry. After the war he moved to Colorado and became a rancher and state legislator. Brooklyn's 14th NYSM, nicknamed the "Red-Legged Devils," had a rivalry with the 13th NYSM that was expressed on the baseball diamond. In 1863 all-star teams from the two regiments played in Virginia. In 1864 they played another game at Brooklyn's Capitoline Grounds to raise money for the Veteran's Relief Society.

JOSEPH CONSELYEA PINCKNEY was an anti-slavery Whig who became an early member of the New York State Republican Party. An accountant, he was a star baseball player for the Unions of Morrisania. In 1855 William Cauldwell, the publisher of the *New York Sunday Mercury*, and real estate developer and Republican politician David Milliken formed the Union baseball club. In the mid-1850s using the name Union sent an unmistakable political message. A supporter of Abraham Lincoln, Pinckney quit his job when the Civil War broke out and began recruiting volunteers for the 66th New York. While serving with the 66th Pinckney saved a runaway slave from being caught by hiding him in a military field hospital. Fighting at Chickahominy during the Peninsular Campaign, Pinckney contracted a disease that damaged his liver and left him unfit for combat. He refused a medical discharge, serving out the war in command of a supply unit. Given the brevet rank of brigadier-general, he was referred to for the rest of his life as "General Pinckney."

Divorced in 1857, Pinckney was a *bon vivant*, particularly interested in the theater and in actresses. An 1880 story in *The New York Times* notes that General Joseph C. Pinckney was among the society fans, who "studied Mlle. [Sarah] Bernhardt's

---

Infantry in the Civil War, Chicago: R.R. Donnelley and Sons, 1911, p. 166

intonation and gestures from seats in the orchestra and upper rows of boxes" while she played in Halévy's *Froufrou*.[159] He was a joiner. He belonged to the Freemasons and was one of the first members of the Benevolent and Protective Order of Elks, which grew from a New York City club for theater aficionados into a national men's organization. Like the Freemasons and the Elks, baseball clubs of the Amateur Era were tightly knit social and fraternal organizations, not merely sports organizations. Their members were neighbors, close friends, business partners, in-laws, and blood relatives. When Pinckney died in 1881 his will left an Upper East Side brownstone to an infant named Joseph Conselyea, described as the "son of one Annie Gallagher." Gallagher was Pinckney's maid and the boy was his illegitimate son. Pinckney's will appoints David Milliken, the former president of the Unions of Morrisania, as guardian of the boy's finances.[160]

IN 1864 TWO TEAMS from the 47th NYSM, including Mort Rogers of the Resolutes, played in a game at Brooklyn's Union Grounds that was umpired by a soldier who belonged to the Eckfords. The list of New Yorkers and New York units that played baseball in uniform goes on and on, but baseball was also played by soldiers from other states. In his 1899 memoir Captain John G.B. Adams of the 19th Massachusetts tells of a baseball game from 1863. Other accounts verify that the game was played, but we cannot be sure which bat-and-ball game Adams is talking about. You would think that soldiers from eastern Massachusetts in 1860 would be playing the Massachusetts game, but then again, some men of the 19th Massachusetts were from southern Maine, baseball country, and their opponents were from a Michigan unit that was full of transplanted New Yorkers.

159. *The New York Times*, November 11, 1880
160. *The New York Times*, March 19, 1881

It is doubtful that Adams really saw Confederate troops playing baseball, but his story is even more far-fetched if they were playing the Massachusetts game, "just the same as we were."

> While in camp at Falmouth [Virginia] the baseball fever broke out. . . . It started with the men, then the officers began to play, and finally the 19th challenged the 7th Michigan to play for sixty dollars a side. . . . The game was played and witnessed by nearly all of our division, and the 19th won. The $120 was spent for a supper, both clubs being present with our committee as guests. It was a grand time, and all agreed that it was nicer to play *base* than *minie* ball. What were the rebels doing all this time? Just the same as we were. While each army posted a picket along the river they never fired a shot. We would sit on the bank and watch their games, and the distance was so short that we could understand every movement and would applaud good plays.[161]

There are at least two credible examples of the Civil War directly helping or facilitating the spread of baseball to virgin territory. The first involves Frank Jones. Born in Massachusetts in 1832, Jones moved to Brooklyn in the 1850s and joined the Excelsiors. In 1855 he was a young man boarding in the house of a shipping agent named Charles Dougherty. Living next door was newspaper editor Addison Farnsworth, a future colonel who would be badly wounded at the battle of Bull Run. Farnsworth was also a friend of James Creighton's brother John; in 1857 the two men were arrested together on their way to join William Walker, who led an army of amateur imperialists on an invasion of Nicaragua in defiance of federal law. Frank Jones married his landlord's daughter Adelaide and in 1861 joined the 71st NYSM along with his brother-in-law Addison Dougherty.

---

161. Adams, Cap. John G. B. *Reminiscences of the 19*[th] *Massachusetts Regiment*, Boston: Wright and Potter, 1899, pp. 60 ff.

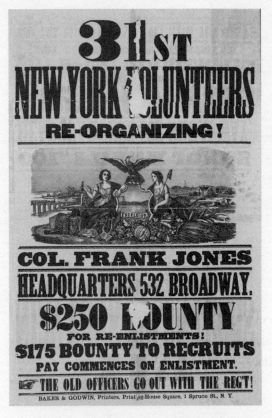

Most Union army units were recruited by popular men from the worlds of politics and firefighting. Successful recruiters would then be put in command. Many of these officers were also prominent baseball men. Colonel Frank Jones of the 31st NY belonged to the famous Excelsiors of Brooklyn and later the Washington Nationals.

The 71st NYSM began in the 1850s as a nativist militia company called the American Guard. It was tied to the Know Nothing Party and excluded anyone not born in the United States. In July 1857 the American Guard and the 7th New York National Guard were deployed during the Dead Rabbit riots in lower Manhattan. Stationed in Washington in 1861, Frank Jones met members of the new National baseball club founded by A.P. Gorman, a rising young Maryland politician and future U.S. senator. (Gorman was also a member of the infamous Mills Commission but to his credit he died before endorsing its findings.) Jones and Gorman arranged a game on July 2 that matched a fusion team made up of Nationals and members of the newly formed Potomac club, against a team of experienced baseball men from the 71st NYSM. The New York side included Alexander G. Babcock of the Atlantics, Theodore Van Cott of the Gothams (son of Gothams cofounder William Van Cott), and members of the Nassau, Social, Quickstep, Manhattan, Champion, and Putnam clubs. Not surprisingly, the New Yorkers won 42–13.

In a rematch five weeks later the Nationals defeated a far weaker 71st NYSM lineup, 28–13. This New York team had no players from the first game and only one recognizable baseball name, Captain David Meschutt of the Atlantics. The likely reason for the turnover is the intervening first Battle of Bull Run, fought on July 21, in which the 71st NYSM was badly beaten up. It lost 10 men killed, 40 wounded, and 12 captured. Both games were played on the White Lot, an open space south of the White House that is now known as the Ellipse. Presidents Abraham Lincoln and Andrew Johnson, a friend of A.P. Gorman, watched baseball there. The Potomacs, Nationals, and African American clubs used the White Lot into the 1870s; baseball and softball were played on the Ellipse as late as the 1980s.

Mustered out of the Army in 1863, Colonel Jones took a job with the federal government and continued his work building the Washington baseball scene. He joined the Nationals and in 1867 was elected president. Like Colonel Fitzgerald in Philadelphia, Jones used his connections in the New York City and Brooklyn baseball worlds to improve his club and to establish the sport in another city. His military and government connections were useful as well. Working with Gorman, Jones recruited players from New York and arranged patronage jobs for them. Two of his recruits had played in the 1861 games with the 71st NYSM, a New Yorker named Gardner and Theodore Van Cott. In 1866 Van Cott was playing for the Nationals and listed as a clerk in the Treasury Department, also the employer of Colonel Jones. Other Nationals, including the great George Wright, were on the books of the Treasury Department. It may be that some actually worked there. Jones continued the Excelsiors' proselytizing work. He arranged the Nationals' 1867 western tour that helped spread baseball to the Midwest and inspired the Cincinnati Red Stockings to create the club that modern Major League Baseball considers its direct ancestor.

ALL BUT ONE of the Brooklyn Excelsiors who served in the Civil War wore blue; first baseman and medical doctor A.T. Pearsall chose gray. (Actually, ex-Excelsior pitcher Charles Etheridge also fought for the Confederacy, but Etheridge was a native Virginian who had gone home before the war started.) Like so many other Excelsiors, Pearsall was a baseball missionary. After the war he became one of the founding fathers of the game in Alabama. Pearsall told two slightly different stories of how, when, and why he ended up in the Confederate Army. What is interesting about them is that neither is true. The first comes from a memoir published in 1899 by a man who served with Pearsall in the 9th (Confederate) Kentucky Cavalry. "Dr. A. T. Pearsall," it says, "was in Europe, completing his medical studies, when the war commenced; and while the guns of Beauregard were thundering away at the walls of Sumter, he was on his way across the Atlantic, to offer his services to the 'Bleeding South,' the land of his nativity."[162] The second version appears in Pearsall's obituary in the *Tioga County Record*, a newspaper in Owego, New York, near Pearsall's childhood home. It says that, "He was graduated in October, 1861, from the College of Physicians and Surgeons in New York. He at once went south and

162. Austin, J.P. *The Blue and the Gray, Sketches of a Portion of the Unwritten History*, Atlanta: Franklin: 1899, p. 63

entered the Confederate army as assistant surgeon. . . ." Pearsall did graduate in the fall of 1861 from Columbia's College of Physicians and Surgeons but he did not immediately join the Confederate army. He never went to medical school in Europe and was not out of the country when the Civil War started. He had joined the Excelsiors around 1859, while in medical school, and continued to play for the club after graduating. Pearsall was an excellent defensive first baseman and almost as good a hitter. When he left New York and headed south in August or September of 1862 the Civil War had been going on for 17 months.

A.T. Pearsall's own accounts do not tell us why he went over to the Confederacy but they do tell us that he did not want to be thought of as a traitor. This is why he led people to believe that he was a genuine native of the South. He was not. Neither of his parents had southern roots; both came from near Binghamton, New York. The Pearsalls returned to Upstate New York when A.T. was between four and six years old. It is clear that something happened late in 1862 that led Pearsall to abandon his medical practice in Brooklyn and join the Confederate army. There is one glaringly obvious suspect. On June 19, 1862 President Abraham Lincoln signed the Territorial Abolition Act, which outlawed slavery in all United States territories outside the control of any state. On July 22 the other shoe dropped. Lincoln read the first draft of the Emancipation Proclamation to his cabinet. From then on, Lincoln was openly committed to abolishing slavery throughout the United States. A significant number of northerners were pro-Union but also pro-slavery; they took this as a betrayal. Up to that time, including in his 1860 presidential campaign, Lincoln's position had been that while he regarded slavery as wrong, he had no definite plan to abolish it. Unlike the Secessionists he had no wish to break up the Union over slavery.

Many northerners were torn between their loyalty to the

New York City photographer and member of the Knickerbocker baseball club Henry Anthony took this picture of Union troops destroying southern railroads. The damage caused by the Civil War to the civilian infrastructure of the Confederate states set back baseball in the South for a generation.

Union and their ideological support of slavery. (I have letters written by an ancestor who was killed in the Civil War; reading them, it is hard to tell which group he hated more, Abolitionists or Confederates.) Slavery had only ended a generation or so earlier in New York and other Union states. In the 19th century Tioga County, where the Pearsalls lived, was an unfriendly place for an Abolitionist. In the late 1840s nearby Binghamton was described as one of the "most pro-slavery villages" in central New York. In 1846 Owego's Presbyterian minister was fired and sent home to Massachusetts after he attempted to lead a prayer for "our brethren in bonds." In 1856 the *Owego Gazette* called Republicans "Negro worshippers." Thirty years later, Binghamton was the site of a revolt by white baseball players against the comparative racial tolerance of the International League, a top minor league. In this time minor baseball leagues were independent, not controlled by Major League Baseball. Nine members of the IL Binghamton Bingoes signed a petition demanding that their two African American teammates be released. This was the beginning of a backlash against integration that ultimately resulted in professional baseball becoming all white by the late 1890s.

IT SEEMS THAT Lincoln's anti-slavery measures of June and July 1862 were the last straw for Pearsall, who one day simply disappeared from the Excelsiors and his successful medical practice. He resurfaced in the Confederate capital of Richmond, Virginia. We know this because he ran into an old friend there. The *New York Clipper* tells the story.

> A BASE BALL PLAYER TURNED REBEL—The Excelsior Base Ball Club of Brooklyn, recently expelled one of its members, A. T. Pearsall, for deserting the flag of the Union, and going over to the rebels. He was a physician, and doing a good business. During the past winter he left, and no one knew where he had gone. Some time since he was heard from in Richmond, Va., as a Brigade Surgeon, on the rebel General Morgan's staff. He had charge of some Union prisoners . . . when he recognized a gentleman of Brooklyn, formerly a member of the Excelsior Club, and entered into conversation. He asked particularly about Leggett, Flanley, Creighton, and Brainard, whom . . . he wished particularly to be remembered to.[163]

Another reason to suspect that Pearsall went over to the Confederacy for political and not personal reasons is that he did not go to Richmond alone. With him was another Brooklyn ballplayer, Alexander Babcock of the Atlantics, who was born in Princeton, New Jersey. He had served with the 71st NYSM and played in the July 1861 game arranged by Frank Jones in Wash-

---

163. *New York Clipper*, July 4, 1863

ington. Late in 1862 Pearsall and Babcock helped found the first baseball club in Richmond, the Pastimes. Alexander Babcock was a brother of William Babcock, a founding member of the Atlantics. Both men were printers and engravers; Alexander helped produce Confederate currency before joining Mosby's Rangers as a captain. Late in the war, Babcock was captured and was being led through Manhattan in chains with other POWs when he spotted someone that he knew from his New York printing days, Horace Greeley, editor of the *New-York Tribune*. "How are you Horace?" he yelled, "What do you think of such treatment of prisoners of war?"[164] His more conventional older brother William Babcock fought for only one side in the war, the Union. After the war ended Alexander Babcock lived for the rest of his life in Richmond. He joined the Freemasons, owned an ice business, and remained an active member of the Pastimes through the late 1860s. In the 1880s he was one of the backers of a railway line that served visitors to the Seven Pines National Cemetery outside Richmond; the men buried there are Union soldiers killed in the Battle of Seven Pines in 1862.

After the war A.T. Pearsall married and settled down in his wife's hometown near Montgomery, Alabama. There he practiced medicine and played for the Pelhams, one of Alabama's earliest baseball clubs. It was named for Captain John Pelham, a Confederate war hero. Divorced in 1878, Pearsall moved back to Owego, where he lived the life of a small-town general practitioner. In the 1880s and 1890s the *Tioga Record* social column noted that he made regular visits by train to New York City but did not say who he was visiting. If he met up with any of his old Excelsiors teammates, none of them reported it; neither did Henry Chadwick, who liked to put news about old amateur

---

164. Connery, William S. *Mosby's Raids in Civil War Northern Virginia*, Charleston: 2013

ballplayers into his *Daily Eagle* column. Then again, the hard feelings from the Civil War had a long life and Pearsall had been drummed out of the club as a traitor. We cannot be sure if any of the old Excelsiors did see him on the sly during his visits, but there is an intriguing item in the 1880 Columbia College of Physicians and Surgeons alumni directory. It lists Pearsall as a consulting doctor with the Delaware, Lackawanna and Western Railroad. One of the railroad's directors was Pearsall's ex-teammate and wealthy cotton dealer Harry Polhemus.

BASEBALL ALSO WENT south in chains. The game was widely played during the war by Union POWs in southern prison camps. Although baseball probably did not spread beyond the camps, within the walls men from New York and other baseball-playing states mixed with men from other places. We know a lot about one of these games, which took place on July 4, 1862 in Salisbury, North Carolina, because a reporter from the Albany *Argus* newspaper was there. We even have a detailed picture, drawn by a prisoner who happened to be a professional artist. In the last years of the war, the population of the Salisbury camp, which had been designed for about 2,500 men, reached four times that. Food rations were cut, conditions had deteriorated and thousands of Union prisoners died of dysentery and pneumonia. The reason for the overcrowding was that prisoner exchanges had stopped. After significant numbers of African Americans began to serve in the Union army in 1863, the Confederates refused to treat them as POWs, either returning them to their former owners, selling them into slavery or forcing them into work gangs. The Union retaliated by cutting off Confederate prisoner exchanges. (Toward the end of the war the Confederates agreed to treat captured African American and white soldiers equally and the exchanges resumed.)

Judging by memoirs of former POWs, however, in 1861 and 1862 Salisbury prison camp was not too unpleasant a place, especially for officers, who seem to have played baseball almost daily. Enlisted men were denied the privilege. In 1862 the Union Prisoners' Association put on the kind of July 4th celebration that the men would have had back home, with one exception— they were forbidden by the camp commander from singing the National Anthem. After prayers and readings of the Declaration of Independence and George Washington's Farewell Address, there was a lunch, followed by a "grand pig race," foot races, a sack race, and a blindfolded wheelbarrow race. At 4 p.m. two teams played a baseball game for a silver medal. The *Argus* lists the players' names and units. There were seven New Yorkers, three players from Maine, two Ohioans, one Minnesotan, one Illinoisan, one from Connecticut, and three unidentified. Eleven of the 15 players whose units are named came from states where baseball was popular before the war.[165]

One of the second basemen was Captain Giles Waldo Shurtleff of Ohio. Natives of Massachusetts, where Giles was born in 1831, the Shurtleffs travelled a route taken by many of the New Yorkers and western New Englanders who settled the upper Midwest, and by primitive forms of baseball. In 1836 the Shurtleffs went by wagon through western Massachusetts to Albany, where they took an Erie Canal boat to Buffalo. They crossed Lake Erie by steamship and took the railroad from Toledo, Ohio, to Adrian, Michigan (the town that Hall of Famer Adrian "Cap" Anson was named after). A much rougher wagon trip brought them to their prairie homestead near Rockford, Illinois, a future baseball hotbed. In 1853 Giles Shurtleff enrolled in Oberlin College in Ohio, a national center of Abolitionist activism. It was

---

165. *The New York Times*, August 8, 1862

also the future alma mater of Fleetwood Walker, who in 1884 became first openly African American player in the major leagues; Fleetwood and his brother Welday were also the last African Americans in the majors until Jackie Robinson took the field with the Brooklyn Dodgers in 1947. After graduating, Giles Shurtleff was hired by Oberlin as a Latin instructor. In 1861 he joined the 7th Ohio Infantry as captain of a company made up of Oberlin students. At the Battle of Cross Lanes in August 1861 he and his men made a stand against a much larger force in order to protect retreating comrades. They were captured and Shurtleff spent 12 months as a prisoner.

In his war reminiscences Shurtleff writes that he played daily baseball games at Salisbury. He recalled one particular game in which his team held a late-inning, one-run lead. "A long fly ball was hit toward the Captain in right field," Shurtleff said, "but in order to catch it and win the game, he was forced to cross the 'deadline,' the demarcation between the prison yard and escape. In that instant he had to decide if he would cross the line, with the very real risk of being shot, or let the ball drop harmlessly to the ground giving advantage to the other team. He opted to make the catch because he was fairly certain the guard on duty that day would not shoot. They won the game."[166] A month after the July 4, 1862 game, Shurtleff was exchanged. He returned to active duty as commander of the 5th U.S. Colored Infantry, a new African American unit, eventually reaching the brevet rank of brigadier-general. After the war he returned to Oberlin College and spent the rest of his life teaching Caesar, Cicero, and Virgil. He was a professor of Latin in the late 1870s and likely taught future African American major league baseball player

166. Shurtleff, G.W. *A Year with the Rebels, from Sketches of War History 1861–1865*, Cincinnati: The Robert Clarke Company, 1896, p. 405

Fleet Walker, who studied Latin at Oberlin in 1879. In 1911 the college commissioned a statue of General Shurtleff that still stands on South Professor Street in Oberlin, Ohio.

The July 4th celebration at Salisbury prison camp ended with a parade led by Grand Marshall Colonel Michael Corcoran, the camp's highest ranking officer. Born in County Sligo in Ireland, Corcoran had emigrated to New York City in the potato famine year of 1849 and joined the 69th NYSM, the Irish Brigade, a unit made up of Irish immigrants. Among them was 1848 revolutionary Thomas Francis Meagher, who was sentenced by the British to exile in remote Tasmania but escaped to New York City. Corcoran was a Tammany Hall politician and a leader of New York's Irish immigrant community. In 1860, then a colonel in command of the 69th, he had refused to march his men in a parade honoring the visiting Prince of Wales (later King Edward VII) as a protest against British complicity in the deadly Irish famine. Corcoran was stripped of his command and was facing a court-martial when the Civil War broke out. When it occurred to the Union Army leadership that the winning side in the Civil War might be the one with the most Irish in it, the charges were dropped and Corcoran was put back in charge of the 69th NYSM. He was taken prisoner at the first Battle of Bull Run and celebrated July 4th in Salisbury. After being exchanged Corcoran raised five entire Irish American regiments that were known collectively as the "Corcoran Legion." He died in 1863 after being thrown from his horse.

FOURTH OF JULY

In 1862 51-year-old Captain Otto Boetticher of the German American 68th NY celebrated the Fourth of July in a Salisbury, North Carolina POW camp. A highlight of the festivities was a baseball game played by prisoners. A professional painter and lithographer who had served in the Prussian Army, Boetticher was known for military subjects; his 1851 work, *Seventh Regiment on Review* (now in the Metropolitan Museum of Art), shows the famous New York City militia unit parading on Washington Square. Boetticher returned to the city after the war, serving as a German consular agent, and died there in 1886. He drew a poignant panorama of the Salisbury prison camp that includes the July 4th baseball game. The drawing served as the basis of a color print published in 1863. Dozens of the participants, the umpire, scorers, and spectators are clearly portraits of individuals. The players on one side are wearing red ribbons pinned to their shirts. The worn basepaths confirm Ohio Captain and second baseman Giles Waldo Shurtleff's memory that baseball games were a regular event in the camp.

Boetticher's drawing conveys prison life with some humor. Pigs are being fed. Oblivious to the baseball game, Confederate prison guards are throwing dice. A prisoner is caught stealing food from the camp kitchen. Behind a low wall in the distant shadows we glimpse a man squatting on a latrine. In 1912 the *Buffalo Enquirer* reported that Albert Spalding had discovered a copy of the Boetticher print and was looking for former Salisbury POWs to help him identify its subjects. "Those who have carefully examined the drawing," wrote the *Enquirer*, "feel convinced" that two of the men in the picture were the famous Generals Phil Kearny and Franz Sigel.[167] Convinced or not, they were wrong; neither one was ever imprisoned at Salisbury (and Kearny would have been conspicuous with his one arm). But the officer with the good seat, the rightmost spectator, looks a lot like Colonel Michael Corcoran, the charismatic Irishman who commanded New York's Fighting 69th. Both the uniform details and the unusual forward sweep of his hair are correct.

---

167. Buffalo *Enquirer*, November 4, 1912, p. 8

ANOTHER WAY TO look at how the Civil War affected the spread of baseball is by the numbers. Club attendance figures from NABBP conventions from 1857 through 1867 show baseball's trajectory toward becoming a national sport. The total number of clubs rose steadily from 14 in 1857 to 23 in 1858 to 60 in 1860; the number of states represented rose from one in 1857, New York, to six plus Washington, DC in 1860. The war years of 1861 through 1864 show a drop in club attendance into the 20s and 30s, although it is hard to say if this reflects a lack of interest in baseball or in wartime conventions. A record 91 clubs attended the baseball convention of 1865, which took place eight months after the end of the Civil War. The following year, so many new clubs applied to join the NABBP that subsidiary state baseball associations were set up so the main convention would not be swamped with delegates. In 1866 a new record 202 clubs sent delegates to the convention and 200 more were represented by delegates from their state association.

To give an idea of baseball's widening geographic reach, among the in-person attendees were 73 clubs from New York State, 48 from Pennsylvania, 26 from New Jersey, 20 from Connecticut, 10 from Washington DC, five from Maryland, and four from Ohio. The following year, delegates were sent by 145 clubs in Illinois, Indiana, Ohio, and Wisconsin. These numbers tell us that the Massachusetts game was still holding out in and around Boston. On a national level, they tell us that baseball enjoyed a burst of popularity as soon as the Civil War ended. Part of the increase in NABBP membership in 1866 and 1867 could have been pent-up demand; that is, clubs were formed in those years that might have been formed earlier if the young men who belonged to them had not been away fighting a war. Finally, they tell us that the greatest proportional postwar increase in the number of baseball clubs happened in western states that contributed large numbers of troops to the Union Army. The numbers suggest that during the war baseball continued to spread in ways that are not easily visible to us.

The state of Illinois contributed 259,000 soldiers to the Union Army, more than any other state except New York, Pennsylvania, and Ohio. According to the website *Protoball. org*, the first baseball club was founded in Illinois in 1856, followed by none in 1857, six in 1858, five in 1859, 13 in 1860, and only eight more through 1864. The number of new Illinois clubs then jumped to 13 in 1865 and peaked at 70 in 1866, before falling to 53 in 1867 and 74 in 1869. Other western states follow a similar pattern. The pattern also holds if we measure interest in baseball another way, by mentions of the game in online newspaper databases. Using *Newspapers. com*, a search of the phrase "base ball" in Illinois newspapers for the years 1866 through 1869 shows 246, 609, 457, and 194 mentions per year. If we use *GenealogyBank.com*, we get 454, 920, 727, and 633 mentions in the same four years. Doing the same searches for other western states that contributed large numbers of troops to the Union Army but had few prewar baseball clubs (Wisconsin, Indiana, Kentucky, Michigan, and Missouri) gives similar results. The number of new clubs founded and the number of mentions of baseball in the state's newspapers rise dramatically in 1866, peak in 1867 or 1868, and then level off or decline. These numbers do not prove that the wartime mixing of servicemen from west and east, particularly New York, drove the spread of baseball. But they are consistent with that scenario.

WHETHER OR NOT the Civil War helped baseball, the reverse is undeniable. Like other young men in the North, amateur baseball players enthusiastically signed up, re-upped, and fought.

So many answered President Lincoln's call for volunteers in 1861 that the Union Army could not take them all. Because of how volunteer regiments were recruited and created, the cultural and social connections among baseball clubs, volunteer fire companies, and citizen militia units were imported to the military. Countless fire companies and militia units enlisted *en masse* and became regimental companies. Members of baseball clubs were already concentrated in particular militias before the war. Regiments such as the First and Second New York Fire Zouaves were recruited from New York and Brooklyn fire companies, whose membership overlapped with that of dozens of baseball clubs. The New York Historical Society has a large collection of Civil War military recruitment posters. A look through them shows how closely intertwined Amateur Era baseball was with other areas of life that today could not be more separate from the bubble that is the world of professional sports.

Remember that the vast majority of soldiers on both sides of the Civil War were volunteers. Imagine that you are a young man in his 20s who is walking the streets of Manhattan. What kind of sales pitch might persuade you to enlist? These posters typically make three kinds of promises. The first is money. "Bounties Paid to Recruits," read a poster for the 66th New York Regiment, "$129 BEFORE Leaving the STATE." Recruits are promised a total of $217 in bonus money, in addition to regular army pay of $13 to $20 per month. The second is safety, in the form of experienced leadership. "The Old Officers to Go Out With the Regiment!" reads a poster for the 31st New York Volunteers. The third is a credible and trustworthy commander, a man with popularity and social capital with whom the rank and file could feel a sense of personal connection and loyalty. (Irish immigrants signed up by the thousands to fight with the ethnic hero Michael Corcoran; among German American troops the popular catchphrase was "I fight mit Sigel" (German-born General Franz Sigel). Many of these commanders were important figures in the worlds of politics, citizen militias, and volunteer firefighting. Some were baseball men. On a recruiting poster for the 66th NY, the name of Colonel Joseph C. Pinckney appears in large type in the second line from the top. Pinckney was a Republican politician, but he was also a well-known star baseball player with the Gothams and the Unions of Morrisania. For the 31st NY, the colonel whose name appears in large black letters on recruitment posters is Frank Jones, member of the Excelsior club of Brooklyn and future officer and backer of the Nationals, Washington's most important early baseball club.

Volunteer fire departments, citizen militias, and other traditional grassroots city institutions were destined to disappear in the postwar years, victims of reform, professionalization, and modernity itself. In 1865 the New York City and Brooklyn volunteer fire departments were eliminated and replaced by professional departments under the direct control of local governments. The same thing happened in Philadelphia and almost every other city. The United States government moved away from reliance on citizen soldiers and toward a professional standing army. The armed forces stopped admitting whole self-constituted militias recruited and outfitted by politicians and community leaders. Baseball itself was on the verge of professionalization.

But during the four years of civil war, amateur baseball went back in time. Games were played for fun, with little media coverage, and without fans or big money. In later wars, professional baseball would be criticized for helping its star players, Babe Ruth among them, evade real military service. It would protect its public image by putting on a show of flag-waving patriotism at all of its games. The Civil War was different. Joe Leggett,

Dr. Joseph B. Jones, Fergy Malone, Tom Pratt, Joe Sprague, Joseph Pinckney, Mort Rogers, Phoney Martin, George Zettlein, Thomas Dakin, and thousands of other amateur baseball players willingly put their health and their lives on the line for their country.

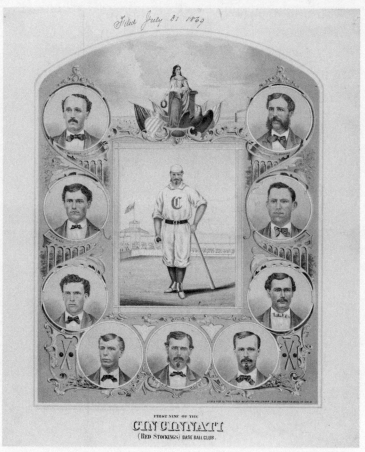

Filed July 31 1869

FIRST NINE OF THE
CINCINNATI
(RED STOCKINGS) BASE BALL CLUB.

With professionalism legalized for the 1869 season, the Cincinnati Red Stockings signed all ten of their players to one-year contracts and published their modest salaries in the newspaper. Star shortstop George Wright was the club's least-underpaid player at $1400.

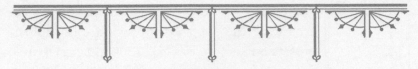

CHAPTER NINE
Traveling Team

Professionalism was strictly forbidden by the [NABBP], which ruled the game from 1857 to 1871. But the rule was largely ignored . . . Harry Wright and his Red Stockings were tired of this hypocrisy. . . . During the winter of 1868-69 the players of the old Red Stockings and the followers of the team held many discussions in which the situation was thoroughly mulled over; and Harry Wright decided that the answer was to form a team which proudly and defiantly proclaimed itself as **professional**.

—Lee Allen, *100 Years of Baseball* (1950)[168]

While not the first "professional team" in organized baseball, the Cincinnati Reds of 1869 were **unique***, because they alone among the many professional teams girding for the diamond wars chose to be an* **all-salaried** *team, using this device to hold each man to his contract for a full season.*

—David Voigt, *American Baseball* (1983)[169]

The Cincinnati Red Stockings of 1869 were baseball's **first openly all-professional team,** with ten **salaried** players.

—Wikipedia.org (12/24/2019)

---

168. Allen, Lee. *100 Years of Baseball*, New York: Bartholomew House, 1950, p. 14
169. Voigt, David. *American Baseball* vol. 1, University Park: Penn St. University Press, 1983, p. 15 ff.

**HIS BOOK ENDS** the way it begins, with a bogus origin story. The game of baseball had the Knickerbockers, the supposed first club. Baseball the professional sport has the 1869 Cincinnati Red Stockings, the supposed original professional baseball club. For more than one hundred years, Major League Baseball honored the Red Stockings club as its forebear by giving Cincinnati a home game on Opening Day. It no longer does this, but last season (2019), every major league player wore a patch commemorating the 150th anniversary of the 1869 Red Stockings.

As the story is usually told, in the 1860s the NABBP, baseball's governing body, publicly maintained its longstanding rule forbidding professionalism, while in private doing nothing to stop more and more clubs from paying their players. The Cincinnati Red Stockings took a noble stand against the NABBP's hypocrisy by proclaiming to the world that they were professional and proud. They published their players' salaries in the paper. Their honesty—along with their success—legitimized compensating players, which clubs had been doing under the table for years, and pulled the curtain down on the Amateur Era. The Red Stockings ushered in a new era of clean, corporate baseball, one that began in 1871 with the first professional baseball league, the National Association, and which continues to the present day.

What really happened was this. After the 1868 season the NABBP changed its rules and legalized professionalism in a limited way. On the surface this was a simple acknowledgement of reality. In the late 1860s the absolute ban on paying players was the deadest of dead letter. Although the vast majority of NABBP member clubs remained faithful to amateurism as they understood it, they did so out of moral conviction, not fear of the NABBP. But many of the top clubs were already being run as professional organizations. The NABBP told its members, in effect, to take sides. Starting with the 1869 season they could compete legally as professionals, paying all of their players, or as amateurs, paying none of them.

The NABBP combined this rules change with another, requiring a player who switched clubs to wait 60 days before appearing in a game for his new club. This is a clue that the key issue was not player compensation, which the NABBP had shown remarkably little interest in policing, but rather the elite clubs' control over the elite players, who had become valuable commodities. In this, nothing in baseball has changed. For most of its 150 years, professional baseball has fought tenaciously for club control over players—in the 1980s, even to the point of repeatedly violating a labor contract and having to pay monetary damages. The issues of player compensation and player movement are linked but Amateur Era baseball made it clear by its actions that it was primarily concerned with the latter. Remember that in 1866, when Colonel Thomas Fitzgerald called on the NABBP to discipline the Philadelphia Athletics for illegally compensating players, all he got was a busy signal.

Of course, in a genuinely amateur sporting universe—like, say, country club tennis or your local bowling league—players are perfectly free to leave one club or team and join another; a question of fairness arises only when the player acts as a "ringer," switching sides for money or another reward. This was strongly suspected to be the case in the 1856 Joseph Pinckney affair, which led to the formation of the NABBP. The roster raiding and the poaching of players, which became routine in the post–Civil War years, was a sign that at the top competitive level, baseball amateurism as we understand it today was already a non-issue. Once again, this did not affect all baseball clubs equally. The interest of a club in controlling its players increases in direct proportion to how much money is at stake. For the Brooklyn Atlantics or the

Cincinnati Red Stockings the stakes were large; for the Clackamas club of Oregon City or the Alerts of Cumberland, Maryland they were nominal. In 1868 the NABBP leadership realized that as long as professionalism was illicit, preventing star players from "revolving," or jumping from one wealthy club to another for higher pay, would be impossible. With professionalism legalized, it would become a simple matter of enforcing a contract. The fact that the NABBP convention of late 1868 addressed these two issues together is telling. Baseball histories tend to follow the NABBP's lead by conflating them. But player control was the real issue in baseball in the 1860s; and it was an issue because amateurism was not. Casting the rules changes of 1868 as an attempt to preserve amateurism or to legitimize professionalism is to buy into what was essentially a public relations fig leaf.

ENTERING THE 1869 season the vast majority of NABBP members who were bona fide amateurs opted to remain in that category. Most of the clubs that were already paying all of their players stepped out of the closet and joined the professional classification. The new rule caused the most disruption for the many clubs in between, those that had both paid and unpaid players in their "first nine." When the Unions of Morrisania and the Buckeyes of Cincinnati—to pick just two examples—chose amateur status, it was reported that they "threw some dozen first-class players out of employment."[170] Other semi-professional clubs, including the Irvingtons of New Jersey, the Lowells of Boston, and the Eckfords of Greenpoint, Brooklyn, ignored the new rule and stuck with the unholy status quo. Ultimately the reform failed; the professionals withdrew from the NABBP and in 1871 the professional National Association, or NA, emerged

---

170. Cincinnati *Enquirer*, April 6,1869, p. 3

from the wreckage. Amateur baseball lived on but its leadership no longer spoke for all of baseball, controlled the baseball rules, or determined national championships.

To no one's surprise the 1869 Cincinnati Red Stockings chose the professional option. They replaced their three amateur starters with hired men. But they were not alone. The New York Mutuals, the Brooklyn Atlantics, the Philadelphia Athletics, the Washington Nationals, and the Troy Haymakers all went professional at the same time. If choosing to play openly as professionals in 1869 made the Red Stockings the "fathers of professional baseball," then these clubs have an equally strong paternity case. In fact you could argue that the Mutuals, Atlantics, and the others have a closer connection to professional baseball than the Red Stockings, because most of them went on to play in the National Association, or NA, the first professional league. The Red Stockings folded before the NA opened for business in 1871. And contrary to what many fans believe, there is no connection between the original Cincinnati Red Stockings and today's major league Cincinnati Reds. This is complicated, but here goes—and believe it or not, this is the short version. The current Reds were formed in 1882 as a member of the American Association, a now-defunct major league; in 1890 they moved to the National League, where they remain today. The history of the first Cincinnati Red Stockings club ends in 1870, but in 1871 Harry Wright took the club's name and several of its players to Boston to join that city's new franchise in the NA, which folded after the 1875 season; in 1876 that club joined the new National League, where it is still playing as the Atlanta Braves. Today's Boston Red Sox—originally also called the Red Stockings—are yet another unrelated organization using that name that was one of the original members of the American League, founded in 1901; it revived the disused name of the old Boston NL club.

The Cincinnati Red Stockings of 1869 were not the first Amateur Era club to pay their players, the first to pay all of their players, or the first to be transparent about paying their players. They were not the first club to legally incorporate. (Many amateur clubs incorporated; the New York City's Eagles, Empires, and Knickerbockers all did so as early as 1860.) Some historians claim that the Red Stockings were the first players to sign a contract or earn a fixed annual salary instead of being paid a share of the gate from each game played. That is not true either. When it comes to professionalism the 1869 Red Stockings have been cast as drivers of history when they were, like most of us, among the driven. Professional baseball had no real founding fathers other than, perhaps, the thousands of anonymous spectators who came out to watch baseball games in Brooklyn in the late 1850s. Baseball as an entertainment business and as a profession became an inevitability when the first fans paid to see a game.

PIONEERS OF PROFESSIONALISM or not, the Cincinnati Red Stockings of 1868–1870 made history in other ways. They helped baseball realize its first and greatest ambition, to become a truly national sport. Until the twilight of the Amateur Era all of the best baseball clubs were located on the east coast. Great dynasties like the Atlantics, Athletics, and Nationals took playing trips to what was then the West to promote the sport of baseball and to charge the natives 25 cents a head to watch their local champions get destroyed by an eastern powerhouse. The Red Stockings, the West's first baseball power, turned the geographical tables. The greatest travelers of the road-tripping late Amateur Era, they made exhausting playing tours to the East, mostly by rail. They also visited the North, South, and far West. These tours lasted from several weeks to more than a month and totaled almost 12,000 miles. The 1869 Red Stockings were the first baseball club to play on both coasts in the same season. They were also the first baseball club to wear the knicker-style uniform, the prototype of every baseball uniform worn today, and they made the bright red stockings that it exposed into a famous trademark. It is a measure of their impact that baseball clubs ever since have imitated the Red Stockings by wearing distinctively colored or patterned socks. Fans today may not realize it, but the White Sox and Red Sox are not the only professional franchises who took their names from the color of their socks. So did the Kansas City Royals (named after the color royal blue), the St. Louis Cardinals (named after the color cardinal red), and many others. The Cincinnati Red Stockings out-traveled their eastern rivals; they also outplayed them, not losing a single ballgame from October 1868 to June 1870, a streak of 84 games.

ALMOST ALL OF the Red Stockings players were mercenaries imported from other cities, but the club's aggressive management was very much a product of its time and place. In the first half of the 19th century Cincinnati was a western, not a midwestern city. The term Midwest had no meaning until the present West was settled, divided into states, and integrated culturally and economically into the United States. This happened slowly. In 1800 the mean population center of the United States was only 18 miles from Baltimore; fifty years later it had only got as far as West Virginia. In the early part of the 19th century Ohio was a small riverboat port on America's western frontier. By the middle of the century, Cincinnati had become the largest American city not located on the eastern seaboard. It was western in spirit, muscular, enterprising, and open to new ideas. It had a relaxed attitude toward vice. Cincinnati was the first American city to professionalize its fire department and to employ steam-driven fire engines; both set national trends. It is where John Roebling, architect of the Brooklyn Bridge, built his first suspension bridge, then the world's longest.

Cincinnati's two 19th-century nicknames tell the story of the city's rise. The sweeter-smelling of the two was the Queen of the West. Her Highness is depicted as a sister of Lady Liberty, flanked by a baseball game, a factory puffing smoke, and garnished with patriotic paraphernalia, at the beginning of this chapter. From the 1830s to the 1860s Cincinnati was the largest U.S. city without a seaport. It was a transportation hub, but of a new kind. Settlers traveling west by road through the Cumberland Gap (some of whom brought with them the game of town ball from Pennsylvania), riverboat traffic on the wide Ohio River, and the canals that linked the Ohio to Lake Erie in the 1830s and 1840s fueled the city's rapid economic growth. Cincinnati's population tripled in 20 years, from 46,000 in 1840 to 161,000 in 1860.

Steam was the transformative technology of the 19th century. It made a massive impact on transportation. Riverboats propelled by steam engines made Cincinnati rich. Old trade patterns were reversed. In the past, lumber, grain, and meat had been floated counterclockwise down the Mississippi on flatboats powered only by the river current, loaded onto ships, and taken by sea from the Gulf of Mexico to eastern port cities and abroad. Thanks to steam power they could be shipped instead to the Northeast by canal or upriver to the Great Lakes and the Erie Canal, or to the middle Atlantic states by connecting to the Baltimore and Ohio Railroad at Wheeling, West Virginia. Cincinnati was where the populous East came to buy food from the agricultural West. It became a center of meatpacking, particularly pork, and industries that used its main by-product, fat. This explains Cincinnati's other nickname, Porkopolis, whose aroma did not dissipate until the 20th century. Procter and Gamble, the iconic packaged goods behemoth that gave America Ivory

Soap, Crest toothpaste, and Pepto-Bismol, was founded there in 1837 by two men, a soap maker and a candlemaker, who made their livings from fat.

Also powered by steam, the railroad put the 19th-century transportation revolution into overdrive. In the 1860s America's railroad lines, most of which were regional and many of which were feeders to riverboat and canal systems, began to coalesce into vast national networks that threatened to make riverboats, canals, and other kinds of transportation obsolete. The original function of the Wells Fargo and American Express companies was to coordinate long distance shipments across different states and railroad systems with their bewildering variety of fares, regulations, taxes, and track gauges. In the 1840s moving cargo by Ohio River steamboat to Pittsburgh, then by canal to Philadelphia and by rail to New York City, took a least three weeks. In the 1850s going by river and canal to Lake Erie, then to New York City via the Erie Canal and the Hudson River took 18 days. However, starting in 1852 the Erie Railroad and its connecting lines could do the job in six to eight days.[171] Unlike riverboats and canals, railroads were independent of the four seasons and largely shrugged off floods, droughts, storms, and ice.

Just as Major League Baseball could not have expanded to the west coast in the 1950s without the new Boeing 707 jet airliner, which made cross-country air travel practical, neither the Red Stockings' tours nor the coming national professional baseball leagues would have been possible without the transcontinental railroad and the vast railroad systems of the 1860s and 1870s. From doubleheaders (a train pulled by two engines) to schedules to making the grade, professional baseball is full of terminology that springs from its long, intimate relationship

171. Rogers, George Taylor. *The Transportation Revolution, 1815–1860*, New York: Rhinehart, 1951, p. 443

with railroad travel. For the Queen of the West the railroad expansion of the late 1860s was an opportunity, but it was also a threat because it devalued waterways and helped cities like Chicago, St. Louis, and Detroit begin to catch up with Cincinnati. Economic competition from these cities was an important reason why Cincinnati's civic leaders wanted to beat them at baseball.

The Red Stockings were not Cincinnati's first baseball club. Baseball was brought to Ohio by two of the usual suspects, New Yorkers and Civil War veterans. An earlier Cincinnati club called the Buckeyes was founded by three men from Rochester, New York. The Buckeyes were renamed after Rochester's Live Oak club, which was among the clubs beaten by James Creighton's Brooklyn Excelsiors on their undefeated 1860 tour. Dr. John Draper, an important man in early Cincinnati baseball and a former member of the Live Oaks of Rochester, served in the Civil War, as did the founding trio from Rochester. (Oddly enough, in 1957 the old NBA Royals also moved from Rochester to Cincinnati.)

By the Red Stockings' own account, the club was born in a Cincinnati law office in July 1866, formed by a group of young lawyers who liked to get up early and play baseball before work. In less than three years, this pickup game grew into the best baseball club in the country. The energy and ambition that drove this transformation had several intriguing sources. One was Harvard College. Harvard's first baseball club was formed by freshmen from New York who belonged to the Class of 1866. At least five of the lawyers who founded the Red Stockings were members of that class or were studying at Harvard during the early and mid-1860s. The best ballplayer in the group was J. William Johnson, who had played for the Harvard '66 club. Playing right field for the Red Stockings in 1868, Johnson won one of nine gold medals awarded by the *New York Clipper* to the best hitters in the country at each position. He would have been part of the all-professional 1869 club but Johnson had no interest in baseball as a career; he turned down sports immortality to practice law.

Another contributor to Cincinnati's rise in baseball was old-fashioned American boosterism. Along with its rivalry with other rising midwestern cities, Cincinnati felt inferior to the East, the birthplace of baseball and the home of its best clubs. Aaron Champion, Alfred Goshorn, George Ellard, and other club backers wanted to use the sport to put Cincinnati on the map. In 1867 the Red Stockings took over the Lincoln Park playing grounds from the Union Cricket Club, which was then employing the versatile New Yorker Harry Wright as a cricket pro. Red Stockings president Aaron Champion built a clubhouse and stands for 4,000 spectators. In 1868 the Red Stockings took their first steps toward filling those stands by assembling a nationally competitive club. They hired away Harry Wright to be team captain, a job that combined that of player–manager with some of the duties of a modern baseball front office. The baseball establishment took notice. NABBP secretary Mort Rogers made the long trip from Boston to umpire the 1868 Opening Day game between the Red Stockings and the Great Western club of Cincinnati. With chutzpah that fellow Ohioan George Steinbrenner would have applauded, in 1869 club president Champion tried to buy all nine of the *Clipper* medal winners and create an instant national all-star team. He only got five but one of them was Harry Wright's brother, the great George Wright.

Nothing succeeds like success—or a baseball club with George Wright playing shortstop. You might want to be sitting down when you read Wright's 1869 batting statistics. In 57 games Wright batted .633 with 49 home runs and 339 runs scored. He never struck out.[172] (The fact that George Wright is classified by the Hall of Fame as an "executive" tells you all you need to know about professional baseball's indifference to the Amateur Era.) Historians and sportswriters tend to paint Champion, Goshorn, et al. wearing halos. In our puritanical American souls, we view success as evidence not only of talent but also of virtue. The lawyers and business executives who paid the bills for the Red Stockings have been lionized. President Aaron B. Champion, to cite one example, has been described as "a man of the highest integrity in character [who] never swerved in his faithfulness to duty and in his devotion to high principle."[173] The Louisville *Courier-Journal* wrote of Champion, "There were few men in Cincinnati engaged in the profession of law who bore a more reputable name and enjoyed a more lucrative practice than the Hon. A.B. Champion [and] no man deserved more fame and fortune than have been honorably attained by this excellent and clean gentleman."[174]

This is exactly what it sounds like—bullshit. The purpose of the false narrative of the Red Stockings as the first professional club was to whitewash professional baseball's origins, as the Knickerbockers story did for amateur baseball, by providing it with respectable founding fathers. Its premise is that the Red Stockings' professionalism was honest and above-board, and that the club was run by ethical business and professional men like club president Aaron Champion, who had wholesome, if not altruistic, motives. However, like Mark Twain's proverbial death, the respectability of the men who ran the Cincinnati Red

172. Thorn, John. *George Wright,* SABR BIOProject SABR.org
173. Ellard, Harry. *Base Ball in Cincinnati: A History.* Cincinnati, Ohio: Subscription Edition, 1907, p. 209
174. Louisville *Courier-Journal* quoted in *Cincinnati, the Queen City,* 1788–1912, vol. 3. (Chicago: S. J. Clarke Publishing Co., 1912), 374

Stockings has been greatly exaggerated. Club president Aaron Champion was a lot of things but a moral example was not one of them. There was a third driving force behind the Amateur Era's greatest 19th-century touring club that Major League Baseball does not celebrate or acknowledge—organized crime and its friend with benefits, politics.

IT IS ONLY human for individuals to squabble over the credit for a group accomplishment. Harry Ellard's 1907 history of baseball in Cincinnati downplays the roles of Red Stockings club officers Aaron Champion and Alfred Goshorn in favor of that of the author's father, George Ellard. But later historians have gone even further with club secretary John P. Joyce. They wrote him out of the story almost entirely. The reason is Joyce's associations outside of baseball, which were always dubious, but which accumulated moral opprobrium over time. As the 19th century gave way to the 20th, Cincinnati's easy, western attitude toward vice was replaced by a more modern midwestern concern for propriety. In 1877 the Cincinnati *Enquirer* had called Joyce "nationally known as the brains of the Cincinnati baseball club in its glorious inaugural season."[175] In the same year the *Chicago Tribune* referred to him as—yes—the "Father of Baseball." To the annoyance of Henry Chadwick, some contemporary sportswriters gave Joyce, not Harry Wright, primary credit for the club's famous professionalism. "[Joyce] saw," one wrote, "that the first club with a nine well organized, systematically disciplined, incessantly practiced, temperate and regular in habits, would sweep the field, and all the players for the season were engaged with the understanding that they had hard work before them."[176]

175. Cincinnati *Enquirer*, June 2, 1877, p. 7
176. Cincinnati *Enquirer*, June 5, 1907

Baseball historians have long assumed that Harry Wright recruited the Red Stockings' stars; after all, he was the prominent baseball veteran with the eastern connections. But it was John P. Joyce who spotted teenage outfielder Cal McVey on an Indianapolis amateur club.[177] Unable to sign star Philadelphia catcher John Radcliffe, Joyce "spent a week quietly watching amateur games on the fences surrounding brickyards in the suburbs of Philadelphia, and from among the players picked out and sent to Cincinnati [22-year-old Doug] Allison. . . ."[178] Finding a first-class prospect like a McVey or an Allison obviously requires more baseball acumen than signing an established star. After the Red Stockings disbanded following the 1870 season, Cincinnatians made several attempts to build a new competitive professional club; each time the man chosen for the job was Joyce. (Joyce also represented the city of Cincinnati at the December 1875 meeting in Louisville where the plot to form the second major professional baseball league, the National League, was furthered.)[179] John P. Joyce did not play baseball for the Red Stockings or, as far as we know, for anyone else; how did he become the club's go-to talent evaluator and Cincinnati's Mr. Baseball? The answer to this question is the dustiest skeleton in baseball's closet—gambling.

JOHN JOYCE WAS a mysterious figure. He still is. Contemporary news stories about the Red Stockings management described him as "John P. Joyce of John P. Joyce and Co.,"[180] but there was no John P. Joyce and Co. Born in Ireland about 1840, Joyce had

177. Cincinnati *Enquirer*, June 5, 1907
178. Champion, Aaron. *The Original Reds*, Saxby's Magazine, August 1887
179. Stern, Joseph S., Jr. "The Team That Couldn't Be Beat: The Red Stockings of 1869." *Cincinnati Historical Society Bulletin* 27 (Spring 1969)
180. Philadelphia *City Item*, June 26, 1869

sailed to America with his father as a young boy, possibly in 1851. The Joyces were Gaelic-speaking famine refugees, likely from a part of Galway and Mayo called Joyce Country; to this day the area is full of people who speak Gaelic as their first language and carry the surname Joyce. As John Joyce told the story, when he arrived at South Street in New York City, he stepped off the boat and was accidentally separated from his father on the crowded dockside. They never saw each other again.[181] Not speaking a word of English, John was placed in an orphanage. Corroborating Joyce's account of his childhood is that, although he was an outspoken atheist and anti-cleric, it was revealed after his death that for years he had quietly visited and donated money to Cincinnati's Catholic St. Joseph's Orphanage;[182] he was also known to speak fluent Gaelic.[183] The rest of Joyce's life story up to 1865, when he appears in Cincinnati working for a Kentucky organization that sold state lottery tickets, is fragmentary. But connecting the dots it seems that Joyce, like other city orphans, worked as a newsboy. Newsboys also sold lottery tickets. This would explain how Joyce met Richard France, the "Lottery King" of Maryland, who became his de facto adoptive father.[184]

In 19th-century America, lotteries and the related numbers rackets were important revenue streams for organized crime. They originated as legal ways to raise money for public projects, especially in the South. Both the University of Virginia and the College of William and Mary were partly paid for by state lotteries. In order to prevent them from becoming a popular form of gambling, the lotteries sold shares in high denominations, five dol-

---

181. Cincinnati *Daily Gazette*, November 22, 1882
182. Cincinnati *Commercial Tribune*, November 24, 1882; and Cincinnati *Enquirer*, January 5, 1874, p. 8
183. Cincinnati *Daily Star*, February 28, 1877
184. Cincinnati *Daily Gazette*, November 22, 1882

lars and up, that were beyond what ordinary people could afford. Men like Richard France exploited the state lotteries in two ways. The first was to buy all of the tickets in a particular lottery from the issuing state agency at a negotiated discount and then handle the public sale and drawing, saving administrative expenses for the government. They then retailed shares in individual tickets at affordable prices. They added to their profits by selling policy, a betting game based on drawn lottery ticket numbers that is similar to the racket known as "numbers," and by forging and selling duplicate tickets. Policy was the crack cocaine of gambling, cheap and marketed to the poor and hopeless. It was particularly popular in poor African American communities. A series of scandals led most states to outlaw lotteries in the pre–Civil War years. But criminal organizations imported lottery tickets from Cuba and other countries, and bribed legislators in Louisiana, Kentucky, and other states to keep their state lotteries going. They sold these tickets illegally throughout the country, which required paying local politicians and police to turn a blind eye.

The adult John Joyce worked for a man named William "Policy Bill" Smith, who with his partner William France, one of Richard France's sons, operated in Cincinnati from a base across the Ohio River in organized crime–friendly northern Kentucky. They belonged to a pyramid of overlapping companies owned by bookmakers, crooked politicians, and horseracing figures. At the top of the pyramid were two men: Benjamin Wood, the brother of New York City mayor Fernando Wood, and John Morrissey.[185] Until they split over southern secession in 1861, Fernando Wood was the political sponsor of Excelsiors pitcher James Creighton's older brother John Creighton. A bookmaker, boxer, and Tammany Hall politico, Morrissey built the Saratoga,

185. Buel, Clarence C., *The Louisiana Lottery*, The Century Magazine, New York: Nov. 1891–April 1892, pp. 618 ff.

New York, horseracing track and controlled one of the country's best baseball clubs, the Unions of Lansingburgh, also known as the Troy Haymakers. John Joyce may have played baseball at some point in his life—we simply don't know—but it would not be surprising if he acquired his baseball expertise and connections working in a gambling operation. Bookmakers often understand sports in a more profound and comprehensive way than sportswriters, executives, fans, or even players. With the large sums of money they have at stake, they have to.

There is no denying the importance of John Joyce's role in the story of the Cincinnati Red Stockings. According to sportswriter Henry Millar, who traveled with the club during their famous undefeated streak of 1868–1870, it was Bill Smith, not the Harvard lawyers, who suggested founding the Red Stockings.[186] Smith invested money in the club, but he may have been too disreputable to serve as an officer. Joyce, his employee, was well placed to represent his interests; Joyce was a political ally and close friend of club president and Democratic politician Aaron Champion, so close that Champion's political enemies tried to smear him by hinting in print that the two men were lovers.[187] Joyce moved in with Champion and his family when Joyce's health failed in the later years of his life. Their relationship was based on something deeper than friendship: mutual self-interest. Aaron Champion used the popularity of the Red Stockings to further his political ambitions and John P. Joyce helped him in order to protect his illegal gambling business. Politics took precedence over sport. Baseball historians have struggled to understand why, immediately after the end of the Red Stockings' undefeated streak—and before the end of the baseball season—

186. Ball, David. Et al. *Base Ball Pioneers 1850–1870*, Jefferson, N.C.: McFarland and Co. 2012, p. 157
187. Cincinnati *Commercial Tribune*, September 19, 1870, p. 4

Joyce and Champion resigned from the Red Stockings on the same day. (The club played on but disbanded shortly after the end of the 1870 season.) The reason for the joint resignation was the urgency of their primary project, getting Champion elected as Prosecuting Attorney for Hamilton County, where Cincinnati is located. This gave off a foul odor at the time. In September 1870 the Cincinnati *Commercial Tribune* wrote, in its foggiest, most lawsuit-resistant prose:

> It is understood that Mr. John P. Joyce, formerly Secretary of the Red Stocking Club, is among the most active workers for Mr. Champion's election. . . . There is a tradition, however, that Mr. Joyce was once engaged in assisting people to make fortunes through the agency of those blessed institutions which are legalized in Kentucky, but not in Ohio; and a rumor runs that he has the management of several policy offices in the city of Cincinnati, of which, accurately speaking, there are forty-two, though it would be difficult to find a policeman who would swear to the existence of one. These policy offices do business illegally, and it would not be pleasant to have a prosecutor for the county who would look too closely after them. . . . There are those uncharitable enough . . . to suspect that Mr. Joyce knows the value of a friend at court, and that it offers some explanation of his extraordinary enthusiasm for Mr. Champion.[188]

As it happened, Aaron Champion did not lose the 1870 election because of his association with gambling. The Fifteenth Amendment to the Constitution, which gave African American men the right to vote early in 1870, shook up the political balance of power across the country. Democrats were in a panic because African American voters were expected to vote overwhelmingly for the party of Abraham Lincoln and U.S. Grant.

---

188. Cincinnati *Commercial Tribune*, September 19, 1870

Of course, they did. In Philadelphia, African American civil rights leader and baseball man Octavius Catto was assassinated on Election Day 1871 by thugs sent into the streets by the city's Democratic Party machine to suppress African American turnout. In Cincinnati Joyce and Champion were shrewd enough to court African American votes through African American surrogates but the political headwinds were too strong. Republicans swept every race in Hamilton County. Despite the "desperate effort [of] corrupt rings and other disreputable parties," as the *Daily Gazette* put it, Champion lost his race by 513 votes, which was actually the best performance of any Democrat.[189] Turning to Plan B, John Joyce got himself appointed as Secretary of the Police Commission. His first act was to take charge of the hiring process for the Cincinnati police force, which was being reformed and enlarged—in order to fight corruption and vice.[190]

No one notices the beginning of a winning streak. The Red Stockings' historic undefeated streak began late in the 1868 season, when they were still a semi-professional mix of local amateurs and hired pros. The paid imports were pitcher Harry Wright, catcher Doug Allison, second baseman Asa Brainard, third baseman Fred Waterman, and left fielder John Hatfield. The native Cincinnatians were first baseman Charlie Gould, shortstop Con Howe, center fielder Rufus King, and right fielder J. William Johnson. In September 1868 the Red Stockings made their first baseball tour of the East, visiting Washington, Baltimore, Philadelphia, Brooklyn, and Upstate New York. They went an impressive 36–7, splitting two games with the Unions of Morrisania and the Nationals, and losing twice to the Athletics. Their final loss of the season came on October 1 against the Atlantics in

189. Cincinnati *Daily Gazette*, October 13, 1870
190. Cincinnati *Enquirer*, April 22, 1873

Brooklyn. Cincinnati's 29–28 close win over the Mutuals the next day marks the beginning of the famous undefeated streak. The Red Stockings won the last eight games of the 1868 season.

The Red Stockings were led on the field by Harry Wright, the English-born convert from cricket who invented the job of baseball manager. Beside playing centerfield and pitching, Wright was a teacher and a brilliant tactician who was said to have invented coaching signs. He exercised an understated authority. When he felt that a player wasn't hustling, the soft-spoken Wright took him aside and told him "you want a little ginger." Harry Wright was on the cutting edge of the science of physical training. In preparation for the long baseball road trips that the club was planning, he put the Red Stockings through intense workouts. He also made sure that he would have youth on his side. Stamina was especially important in the days before gloves, facemasks, elbow guards, the 25-man roster, modern pharmaceuticals, and Tommy John surgery. In 1869 Harry Wright managed a 10-man roster that included three 21-year-olds, two 22-year-olds, a 23-year-old, and a 19-year-old. 27-year-old pitcher Asa Brainard was the oldest man on the club except for Wright himself, who was 34. Harry Wright occasionally relieved Brainard; other than that, the Red Stockings' lineup was virtually the same, day in and day out, for months on end.

Harry Wright was cricket's last and greatest gift to baseball. While baseball was spending two decades working to sell itself to America's EUB as a respectable amateur sport, Wright stood with one foot in baseball and the other in a foreign sport, cricket, that had arrived in America having already integrated professionalism. Harry Wright, his father, and his brothers were universally respected in the American sports world despite being professionals. Baseball-playing Americans—even believers in orthodox amateurism—understood that cricket and baseball were cultures apart in this and in other ways. It is revealing that none of the controversies about hired men or player jumping in the late 1860s touched them. They did not belong to the EUB and had no need for baseball as a vehicle for social ambition. They simply wanted to win.

Born into cricket, Harry Wright worked in that sport while he waited for America to accept that baseball could be a legitimate career and that professionalism was not inherently incompatible with integrity. It is not a coincidence that Wright's full career conversion from cricket to baseball came at the end of the Amateur Era, when baseball and the public were ready to embrace professionalism. American attitudes on this point had been slow to change. In an 1839 New York City directory, Harry and George Wright's father, Sam, who came to America because he was hired as a professional athlete, is listed as a "toolmaker." The 1855 New York State Census is the first official document that we know of that gives his occupation as cricket player. Even in 1869, when the Red Stockings openly and legally paid their players, some newspapers continued to write that Harry Wright's profession was jeweler. It was not until 1870 that his real business, "baseball," was acknowledged in the U.S. Census.

THE WRIGHT BROTHERS

When they were young, Harry Wright and his brother George played both cricket and baseball at a high level. The problem was that in the 1850s cricket offered the possibility of a career and baseball did not.

Wright's father, Samuel Wright, was an English cricket professional. His mother was Ann Tone, a niece of Wolfe Tone, hero of the failed 1798 Irish Rebellion that sent Thomas Fitzgerald's parents to New York City as refugees. In the late 1830s when Harry was four or five, the Wrights moved to New York, where Sam worked as a professional for the St.

George Cricket Club and where George was born. After he married in 1858 and had a family to support, Harry Wright also played and taught cricket professionally. He played baseball with the New York Knickerbockers on the side. When the Civil War caused the Knickerbockers to stop playing, Harry and his brother George begin to appear in box scores playing for the Gothams.

Harry Wright was 31 years old going into the 1866 season. He was a good athlete, but George was 12 years younger and even more talented. Harry played centerfield and shortstop, and did a little pitching, but George played catcher, the position where base-ball clubs of the early 1860s put their best athletes. In 1866 the Union Cricket Club of Cincinnati hired Harry Wright as a cricket pro. In September of that year, his wife Mary died at 31 in a typhoid fever epidemic;[191] two years later Harry married Cincinnati native Caroline Mulford. The couple had five children. By this time, Wright had been hired by the Cincinnati Red Stockings, who went 84–0 from October 1868 to June 1870. George played shortstop and was the club's best hitter.

The Cincinnati Red Stockings club folded after the 1870 season in a dispute among its backers over money. After a group of Boston businessmen made him a financial of-fer that he could not refuse, Harry took his younger brother and the club's famous red stockings to Boston to play in the new National Association. In the five years of the NA's existence Harry Wright won four pennants; the 1875 club went an amazing 71–8. (Albert Spalding pitched in 72 of the club's games.) In 1876 Wright continued to manage the Boston Red Stockings in the newly formed National League, where he won two more pennants. He went to Philadelphia in 1884 to join Al Reach's Phillies, then called the Quakers, and managed them through 1893. His second wife Caroline died in 1892. After retiring from managing, Wright was made chief of National League umpires despite (in all seriousness) being functionally blind. He died in 1895 in his 60s but not before mar-rying a third time, to the evident embarrassment of his friends and family. Newspapers ignored the marriage or reported it without mentioning the new Mrs. Wright's name. She was 45-year-old Isabella Fraser, a Bronx schoolteacher and the younger sister of his first wife, Mary.[192] Harry Wright's grave in Philadelphia's West Laurel Hill Cemetery is topped by a bronze statue of Wright on a stone base inscribed, "The Father of Baseball."

---

191. Hamilton County, Ohio Death Record, September 30, 1866
192. U.S. Census 1920, ED 440 Bronx, NY, Sheet 12; and NYS Census 1855, 19th Ward, 3rd Distr. NYC

In November 1868 the NABBP legalized professionalism for the 1869 season. As we know, players on the top clubs were already being paid and the years 1865–1868 had seen a free-for-all of player jumping and roster raiding, both the result of clubs bidding against each other for players' services. After having lost Joe Sprague, Tom Devyr, Ed Duffy, and Al Reach to other clubs, the disgusted Greenpoint Eckfords ran a sarcastic newspaper ad reading: "*Baseball Players Furnished.*-- Any club desiring to have a champion nine this season, and who are in want of some good players to fill their nine, may call on the Eckford Baseball Club, as they still have some very desirable players yet ... N.B.--No club need apply unless they are willing to pay the highest market price."[193] The 1869 Cincinnati Red Stockings added shortstop George Wright, second baseman Charlie Sweasy, left fielder Andy Leonard, and right fielder Cal McVey—all pros. Asa Brainard, the man who had replaced James Creighton on the 1862 Excelsiors, moved to the mound (actually behind the pitcher's line—the first pitching mounds appeared in the 1880s). The only Cincinnatian on the club was first baseman Gould, but he, too, was a professional.

The club published its players' yearly salaries in the *New York Clipper*, but this was no protest against hypocrisy. Once the NABBP dropped its rule against professionalism, the Red Stockings no longer had any reason to pretend that they did not pay their players. The club's pay scale ranged from George Wright's $1,400 and Harry Wright's $1,200 to the $800 made by Sweasy, Gould, Allison, Leonard, and McVey and $600 for

---

193. Philadelphia *City Item*, June 23, 1866

sub Dick Hurley. These salaries are surprisingly low, roughly only three or four times what a common laborer would earn. Baseball players did work less than ordinary workers, who put in six-day, 60-hour weeks, and baseball was only played seven or so months out of the year. On the other hand, in the 1860s all baseball players were everyday players; the only Red Stocking who was substituted for with any frequency was fastball pitcher Asa Brainard; Harry Wright would come in to baffle hitters with his slow stuff and Brainard would move to a position in the field. Dick Hurley's main job was to be ready if flying moon men kidnapped George Wright. However, despite both the rules changes of 1869 and the Red Stockings' transparency, baseball's amateur ethic retained a certain moral momentum. When the Red Stockings visited Washington to play the Nationals, the Washington *Evening Star* listed the Cincinnati players' ages, weights, heights, and—either for appearance's sake or out of habit—their bogus occupations.[194] But in June 1869 not even little boys believed that George Wright was an engraver, that Cal McVey made pianos, or that Charlie Sweasy was a hat finisher.

THE CINCINNATI RED STOCKINGS were built to travel. Multicity baseball tours were an idea that dated back to the Excelsiors' 1860 trips to Upstate New York, Philadelphia, and Baltimore. During the Civil War years clubs regularly traveled between the east coast cities. As railroads expanded, longer tours became possible. In 1840, when adult New Yorkers were starting to form the first baseball clubs that we know much about, New York State had a total of 453 miles of railroad lines. In 1850 that number had risen to 1,409 and in 1860—the year of baseball's first multicity tour—to 2,682. There was similar growth in Pennsylvania

---

194. Washington, DC *Evening Star*, June 25, 1869, p. 1

and Virginia. Railroad growth in the booming upper Midwest was even more dramatic. In the two decades between 1840 and 1860, Indiana went from 20 miles of railroad tracks to 2,163; Illinois from 26 to 2,799; and Ohio from 39 to 2,946. Not long after settlers, war, and trade brought baseball to these states, the established eastern clubs came calling. They took the train. An extension of the old custom of sporting clubs, militias, and fire-houses exchanging visits and hospitality, the original purpose of these trips was to spread the game. In the post–Civil War years, they became more about profit, but they continued to popular-ize baseball. The tours also pointed the way, with a big bright arrow, to baseball's future as a national entertainment business. Essentially, this is what a modern professional sports league is: a series of road trips organized and structured to produce a cred-ible champion. Even when they are both playing at home, we still call the two sides in every baseball game from Little League to the major leagues the "home team" and the "visitors."

THE NATIONALS OF Washington DC, child of the Brooklyn Ex-celsiors and grandchild of the New York Knickerbockers, had made baseball's first journey to the West in July 1867. Henry Chadwick also made the trip, which covered 3,000 miles, mostly by rail. Loaded with eastern stars like George Wright, Asa Brain-ard, and Frank Norton, the Nats obliterated opponents in Ohio, Kentucky, Indiana, and Missouri, winning by crazy scores like 106–21 and 113–26. In Cincinnati they beat up on the new Red Stockings, 53–10. It was the Red Stockings' only loss of the season and it taught them a needed lesson: They needed George Wright. The Nationals' final destination was a multi-team tournament in Chicago that included that city's two top clubs, the Excelsiors and the Atlantics, both of which were named after famous Brook-lyn clubs. But the Nationals shocked everyone by losing the first game of the tournament to the Forest City Club of Rockford, Illinois, population 10,000—a club of nobodies from nowhere. After the Nationals went on to rout Chicago's finest, 49–9 and 78–17, howls went up from angry Chicago fans, who accused the Nationals of dumping the Rockford game in order to manipulate the betting odds in the later games. It is possible that they were right, but there is a better explanation. Among the Rockford nobodies were two 17-year-old future somebodies: second baseman Ross Barnes and pitcher Albert Spalding, both of whom would go on to dominate professional baseball in the 1870s.

This episode shows that baseball amateurism had developed a serious perception problem in the late 1860s. While the Nationals and other clubs publicly refused to accept money from gate receipts, baseball fans had to pay to see their games, usually 25 cents, and they knew that some of the players were being compensated in one way or another. If you stretch the definition of the word compensation to include sinecures and no-show jobs, every member of the 1867 Nationals was paid. The Nationals' travel expenses may have been covered by a combination of local hospitality, wealthy backers, and membership dues, but other clubs' tours were funded in part by gate receipts and gambling.

Because it was a threat to the sport's credibility and its public image, gambling lurked in the shadows in baseball clubhouses, hotel bars, and railroad cars. Henry Chadwick tried his best to keep it there. "We are not sorry," he wrote after an 1868 Athletics upset of the Brooklyn Atlantics, "that some of the gamblers who follow in the wake of the Atlantic club and bet on their skill and good fortune, lost heavily on Monday last. They have brought disrepute upon a noble pastime . . . and they ought to be served by the police like pickpockets, seized and marched off the grounds. . . ."[195] It is highly likely that players and club backers routinely bet on

---

195. Brooklyn *Daily Eagle*, September 11, 1868, p. 2

games and that baseball tour costs were defrayed in this way. In June 1868 the Findlay, Ohio, *Jeffersonian* wrote that on the Philadelphia Athletics' visit to Cincinnati, where they swept the Buckeyes and the Red Stockings, the Philadelphians drew "one half of the gate money, their share in the two games amounting to six or seven hundred dollars." The paper also reported, "It is said that the Athletics 'played off' in their game with the Buckeyes and that some of them had 'money that said,' during the day, that they could double or even treble the score of the Red Stockings."[196] The opportunities and incentives for corruption were obvious and explain why fans and bettors were quick to be suspicious of an upset or a bad defensive inning. When the undefeated 1870 Red Stockings lost their first game of the season in June, club president Aaron Champion felt it necessary to publish an open letter defending his players' honesty.

IN 1868 THE Philadelphia Athletics and the Brooklyn Atlantics made crisscrossing western tours. The Atlantics' odd, lone 19–15 loss to the Niagaras in Buffalo raised eyebrows. The Athletics beat the Niagaras, 34–14, but then suffered an equally fishy defeat at the hands of Rochester, 26–20. In 1905 outfielder John C. Chapman described life on the road with the Atlantics in 1868 in a revealing interview that gives us a window on what both baseball tours and train travel were like in the late 1860s. It is equally revealing about baseball's close relationship with gambling, which seems to have helped pay for these baseball tours. (Chapman must have made a strong impression on his hosts; six of the cities the Atlantics visited later hired him to organize or manage their first professional clubs.) The Brooklyn club played at Albany, Troy, Utica, Syracuse, Rochester, Buffalo, Cleveland, Toledo, Detroit, Chicago, Rockford, Freeport,

196. Findlay (Oh.) *Jeffersonian* June 12, 1868, p. 2

Springfield, St. Louis, Indianapolis, Louisville, and Cincinnati, winning all but one game. After playing the Central City Club at Syracuse, the Atlantics took the westbound train for Buffalo, having reserved the last car for themselves and their entourage. As Chapman tells the story,

> The total number in the party as far as Buffalo was over fifty. When the train was about thirty miles out of Syracuse, the conductor rushed into the players' car saying: "Boys, I might have to call on you for help as there are four big toughs coming through the train insulting the passengers and my helpers." He left and returning in a few seconds said: "Here they come, boys, watch out." In the first seats of the car were several of the friends of the Atlantics who were considered very clever with their "dukes" in those days. Among them were John J. Dwyer, Mike Henry and another good fellow called "Honest Crowd" Smith, a retired butcher. Smith was the first man tackled by the largest of the toughs and "Honest" landed on the loafer good and hard, knocked him down and jumped on him, while Henry and Dwyer worked on two of the others until they were almost helpless. The intruders saw that they had struck a large sized snag and tried to make their escape through the car to the rear guard of the Atlantics and received another sound thrashing. When finally, the conductor told the boys that the toughs had received punishment enough the train was stopped and the intruders kicked off the car, much to the delight of the passengers and trainmen who congratulated the Brooklyn boys on their good work. The four bullies pulled themselves together and took to the woods in very bad condition.[197]

We can identify two of the "friends of the Atlantics" in Chapman's story. John J. Dwyer was a boxer who later became U.S.

---

197. Brooklyn *Daily Eagle*, March 26, 1905, p. 13

heavyweight champion. In 1880 he killed a man with a pool cue in a bar fight, but was not charged because his brother was a Brooklyn assemblyman. Mike Henry was a gambler, book-maker, impresario, and owner of a tavern at 69 Fulton Street in downtown Brooklyn that served as the Atlantics' headquarters and clubhouse. He was described by the Brooklyn *Daily Eagle* as the man who "looked after the gate" for the Atlantics' players.[198] Henry made unpleasant enemies; he was the victim of several knife attacks and a shooting in the 1870s and 1880s. In the late 1870s he partnered with Chapman and the less than reputable Atlantics club officer Alexander R. Samuels to promote Madame Anderson, a professional "pedestrienne," or speed walker. Female pedestrianism, in which attractive athletes competed in short, tight-fitting outfits before all-male audiences, was a kind of softcore porn show in sport's clothing. Mike Henry's last job was groundskeeper at Washington Park, where the club that would later be called the Brooklyn Dodgers played their home games from 1883 through 1891. The Atlantics took a cut of gate receipts on the trip, as they did at home, and "Honest Crowd" Smith was apparently a reliable man to give the job of counting ticket revenues and calculating players' shares. This Jack Chapman anecdote leaves little doubt about the intimate connection between Amateur Era baseball and gambling, with all of its shady associations. Why were the touring Atlantics accompanied by gamblers, bookies, and criminals? It is hard to believe that the answer has nothing to do with crime, money, and gambling.

THE 1869 AND 1870 Red Stockings made their national tour in segments. The first, from May 15 through July 1, was a long circle through Upstate New York, Massachusetts, Brooklyn,

---

198. Brooklyn *Daily Eagle*, May 10, 1889

New Jersey, Philadelphia, Baltimore, Washington, and West Virginia. They won all 21 games fairly easily, including beating the Atlantics, 32–10, and the Athletics, 27–18. The closest full-length contest was a 4–2 thriller against the New York Mutuals at Brooklyn's Union Grounds. The shocking stat from this game is the barehanded Red Stockings' zero wild pitches and passed balls. After a short trip to Illinois, where they swept the Rockford Forest Citys, 53–32 and 28–7, the Red Stockings played at home through September 9. Their record on that date was 43–0. With each victory reported around the country by newspaper and telegraph, the streak became a growing national sensation. In mid-September the Red Stockings went to St. Louis and then took the train to San Francisco, a city founded by New Yorkers during the Gold Rush and therefore the center of baseball on the West Coast. They beat the Eagles, the best club in California and a satellite of sorts of the old New York City Eagles, 35–4 and 68–4. These were not the most lopsided scores of the trip.

Back home in August, the Red Stockings beat the Southern club of New Orleans, 35–3, inspiring a *tour de force* of excuse making by the New Orleans *Bulletin*.[199] In an article unsubtly headlined, "PROFESSIONAL BASE-BALLERS," the paper pointed out that Cincinnati had put in three long hours beating up on the amateur Southerns' pitching. "All the other clubs which have played the 'Red Stockings'" it boasted, "were beaten inside of two hours, and in some cases inside of one hour." The *Bulletin* added that the Southerns had been exhausted from their long train trip, that the game time temperature was "102 in the shade," that their starting catcher had been hurt, that the Red Stockings were well-paid mercenaries in splendid physical condition, and finally that the other guys were bigger—shortstop George

---

199. New Orleans *Bulletin*, September 6, 1869

Wright outweighing his Southern counterpart, 165 pounds to 110. When the 1869 season ended in Cincinnati on November 8, the Red Stockings' streak stood at 65–0.

A GLIMPSE OF STOCKING

In the late 1860s well-dressed women wore wide, bell-shaped skirts that brushed the ground. They wore a lot of clothing underneath, including stockings—wool, silk, or cotton, depending on economics and the weather—but unlike today, in those days stockings were not normally on public display. We tend to exaggerate the modesty of our Victorian ancestors; a glimpse of stocking was probably not as shocking as Americans today think. Showing more lower leg, however, had erotic impact, judging by photographs of mid-19th-century prostitutes, who often pose lifting a skirt to the knee and staring insolently at the camera. Male calves also had appeal. The Red Stockings wore knicker pants that stopped at the knee; below that the players wore tight red wool stockings. Familiar today, this was an entirely new style of uniform when the Red Stockings adopted it in 1867. In 1869 the San Francisco *Chronicle* wrote, "It is easy to see why they adopted the Red Stocking style of dress which shows their calves in all their magnitude and rotundity. Every one of them has a large and well-turned leg and every one of them knows how to use it."

Celebrity, of course, can have more sexual power than the human body or even sex itself. In the middle of their sensational undefeated 1869 season the Cincinnati Red Stockings came to Philadelphia, where a newspaper described what happened after the Red Stockings defeated the local Athletics, 21–4.

The evening came, and the ball players sought their couches at a respectable hour and arose yesterday morning refreshed, reinvigorated and with clear heads. How far they had succeeded in winning the especial admiration of some of Philadelphia's fair daughters may be determined from a slight circumstance. During Sunday night the rain had fallen pretty freely, and thus an excuse was afforded several of the Philadelphia darlings for raising their skirts, just to keep them from trailing on the wet sidewalk in front of the hotel at which the Cincinnati folks were staying, and to show just enough of pretty ankles, enclosed in red stockings, which, despite the intense heat of the day, the proprietors of the aforesaid pretty ankles had procured and donned to assure the visitors that they had influential "friends at court" . . . the fine-looking young men composing the Cincinnati nine had gained, beyond a doubt, the favor of the ladies.[200]

THE CLOSEST THE Red Stockings came to losing in 1869 was an August 26 game with John Morrissey's Troy Haymakers. Played in Cincinnati, the game began amicably. A crowd of 10,000 warmly applauded the Troy players and cheered a superb catch by Haymakers outfielder, future Cuban professional baseball pioneer, and Fordham College graduate, Esteban Bellan. But as umpire John Brockaway of Cincinnati's Great Western club made one close call after another against the visitors, Troy president James McKeon, who fans and some reporters mistook for John Morrissey, repeatedly ran out onto the field and complained. Finally, with the score 17–17 in the fifth, he took his players off the field. The umpire forfeited the game to Cincinnati. Modern historians often say that the forfeit was a trick by Morrissey to avoid losing a wager, but this is dubious. There were rumors that Morrissey had money on the Red Stockings; others said that he had bet on Troy. In any case, Morrissey was not at the game or in Cincinnati.

As winter 1870 turned to spring, the improbable winning streak refused to die. In April the Red Stockings made a kind of spring training trip to New Orleans, which had a lively baseball scene, and obliterated the Pelicans, the Atlantics of New Orleans, and the diminutive but well-rested Southern club by scores of 51–1, 39–6, and 80–6. New Orleans salvaged a bit of dignity when the Lone Stars and the Robert E. Lees each held the Red

---

200. New York *Herald*, June 22, 1869, p. 1

Stockings to under 30 runs. Cincinnati made another eastern trip in June, arriving at Brooklyn's Capitoline Grounds on June 14 to face the Atlantics. In 1870 this matchup was as big a draw as there was. It attracted a massive crowd, estimated at between 9,000 and 20,000 people. They each paid 50 cents; in 1870 the Red Stockings had begun exploiting the streak by doubling the normal ticket price. This Atlantic club was past its prime, but it still possessed the swagger of the greatest dynasty of the Amateur Era. It was also the last club to have defeated the Red Stockings—twenty months earlier.

After nine innings the score was tied at five. No one had expected this and there was uncertainty about the protocol for extra innings. The umpire conferred with club officials to discuss whether to continue the game, to call it a tie, or to continue it the following morning. The Red Stockings wanted to keep playing. The Atlantics did not. Huge pregame underdogs, the Atlantics regarded not losing as glory enough. The massive amount of money that had been bet on the game may also have been a factor. As Atlantics left fielder Jack Chapman remembered, while spectators milled about the field, the Atlantics ducked into their clubhouse for a rest and a rubdown. The Brooklyn fans screamed for the game to continue. Pitching for Cincinnati that day was Brooklyn native Asa Brainard. Descriptions of the delivery he used to achieve his overpowering, moving fastball are markedly similar to descriptions of James Creighton. "In delivering the ball," wrote Harry Ellard, "he would cross his legs, placing the left toe behind his right foot and then take a step forwards."[201]

Like all other pitchers of the day, Brainard carried a brutal workload. For comparison's sake, consider that in the pitching-dominated 1960s, a durable starter might have thrown

201. Ellard, Harry. *Base Ball in Cincinnati: A History.* Cincinnati, Ohio: Subscription Edition, 1907, p. 159

15 or 20 complete games; in 2014 the Los Angeles Dodgers' Clayton Kershaw led the major leagues with six. Asa Brainard must have thrown at least 70 or 75 complete games during his team's 84-plus-game winning streak. Yet he somehow acquired a reputation for being unreliable. There are many anecdotes about the Red Stockings' exasperation with Brainard's drinking, poor work habits, and supposed hypochondria about his pitching arm. Harry Wright said that Brainard "complained of imaginary ailments." Managers have been saying the same thing about pitchers for a century and a half. Wright liked to remind Brainard that if he did not pitch, he would not be paid.

ASA BRAINARD WAS born in Albany, New York, and moved to Brooklyn as a boy. Although he went by Asa as an adult, there is confusion about the spelling of his full first name, which is sometimes written as "Asel" and other times as "Asahel." Censuses spell it both ways. Asel is a rare name outside of Scandinavia, while Asahel is an equally obscure biblical name. The biblical Asahel was a nephew of King David; the Book of Samuel describes him as "swift of foot, like a gazelle in the open field," but has nothing on his arm strength. Incidentally, the common story that the baseball term "ace," meaning star pitcher, comes from Brainard's first name is false. Like other early baseball terminology, it comes from card playing. Aside from the fact that he came from a family that today would be classified as upper middle class, Asa Brainard's life story is more typical of a modern professional baseball player than of a player from the Amateur Era. In 1859 he was promoted from the Stars to the Excelsiors, where he played through the 1866 season. During that time, Brainard had no profession outside of baseball and held either seasonal or no-show jobs. He did not serve in the Civil War.

Restless during the wartime Brooklyn baseball lull of 1861—and possibly hard up for cash—Brainard played some cricket and, together with James Creighton, made an abortive attempt to jump from the Excelsiors to the more active Atlantics. Brainard replaced Creighton as the Excelsiors' pitcher after Creighton's death in October 1862. In 1867 Brainard was hired away by the Nationals and the following year by the Cincinnati Red Stockings. Asa Brainard chased women and, apparently, vice versa. Nicknamed "The Count" for his sharp dressing style, he cut a dashing figure with his manly mutton-chop sideburns. He was married in Cincinnati, but abandoned his wife and young son when he left town in 1871. Like many professional baseball players, Brainard excelled at billiards and anything else that required good eye-to-hand coordination. After retiring from baseball he exploited his celebrity to promote billiard halls. Brainard also managed an archery range in Port Richmond on Staten Island. In 1882, in an incident that gives off a strong odor of alcohol, he was shot through the hand by an arrow. The hard-living Brainard contracted tuberculosis and in 1886 or 1887 moved to Denver for the supposed health benefits of dry mountain air. When he died there in late December 1888, the New York *Herald* called him "the well-known and popular superintendent of the Markham Hotel billiard room." He was 47.

BACK IN BROOKLYN'S Capitoline Grounds on June 14, 1870, umpire Charlie Mills ordered the Atlantics back out onto the field. The game resumed and the crowd fell silent as Cincinnati scored two runs in the top of the 11th. In the bottom of the inning, however, the Atlantics mounted the most celebrated baseball comeback of the 19th century. Third baseman Charlie Smith singled and first baseman Joe Start drove him in with a booming triple over Cal McVey's head in right. With one out, catcher Bob

Ferguson drove in the tying run and little center fielder George Hall won the game with a savage line drive that handcuffed Red Stockings first baseman Charlie Gould. According to the *Daily Eagle*, "Hats, coats, sticks and crutches even, darkened the air, thrown up by the enthusiastic attendants on the ball field. The crowd broke from their confines, and rushed upon the Atlantic players, whom they elevated upon their shoulders and carried to the clubhouse."[202] The fans at the Capitoline Grounds were not the only ones celebrating; all over Brooklyn people had gathered at newspaper offices and other places where they could follow the play by play via telegraph. "The scene at Mike Henry's place," reported the *Eagle*, "was similar to that of an election night at the victorious party's headquarters." As Jack Chapman later recalled, "Brooklyn was one continuous scene of hilarity that night, Atlantic Avenue, from the ferry up, being ablaze with bonfires."

The fans celebrating the Atlantics' 1870 victory over the Red Stockings did not know it, but they had witnessed the last important contest of the Amateur Era. The game's more sophisticated spectators, however, could see that baseball was on the cusp of fundamental change. This change was not about professionalism as such. Everyone knew that the Cincinnati players were paid a salary and that the Atlantics were paid with a share of the gate (for this one game, $364 each). The coming change was cultural. Paid or not, nearly all of the Atlantics' players were locals who had come up through the club's network of junior clubs. The same was true of many other Amateur Era organizations. After 1870, top-rank baseball clubs would no longer belong to their communities in the way that the Atlantics and Eckfords belonged to Brooklyn or the Athletics belonged to Philadelphia. The best clubs and

---

202. Brooklyn *Daily Eagle*, December 30, 1894, p. 4

their players were now commodities. On the same page as its coverage of the June 14 game, the Brooklyn *Daily Eagle* ran the following editorial.

There are incidents about the grand victory of our local batters which make it historical. The result was opposed to the expectation of everyone.... The triumph marks the first break in the line of battle hitherto waged by the ball organization of any one city against the organization which chooses to call itself Cincinnati's, but which, in membership, as in repute, belongs to the four quarters of the country.... It was the greatest game that was ever played between the greatest clubs that ever played, and ... this Red Stockings club was not formed as our Ball Clubs have been, by young men who loved the game for itself and played for pleasure and exercise. They are literally nothing but a picked nine of professional players, the best that could be hired from all parts of the country, and the purpose of their organization is to make money by ball playing....[203]

Starting with the arrival of the National Association, baseball's first professional league, in 1871, and continuing to the present day, all of the top baseball clubs would be "nothing but picked nines," playing for the highest bidder. The Red Stockings themselves split up after the 1870 season, with George Wright, Harry Wright, Gould, and McVey following the money to Boston; and Waterman, Allison, Leonard, Brainard, and Sweasy going to play for the Washington DC Olympics. The Brooklyn Atlantics did not join the National Association in 1871 and lost nearly all of their stars to clubs that did. The Mutuals took Pearce, Charlie Smith, Joe Start, and Bob Ferguson. Lipman Pike went to Troy; George Zettlein went to Chicago; and George Hall, the hero of June 14, joined the Red Stockings contingent in Washington.

203. Brooklyn *Daily Eagle*, June 15, 1870, p. 2

The Atlantics' victory over the Red Stockings was not, as it is usually portrayed, the final death throe of pure amateurism, fighting Camelot-like against money in baseball. The founding of the professional National Association in 1871 marked the beginning of today's vast professional baseball monopoly, but it in no way meant the end of amateur baseball, which lost control of the sport at the uppermost competitive levels, but which continued to thrive and expand. Today amateur baseball dwarfs its professional cousin as a participatory sport. Every year almost 16 million Americans over six years old play Little League baseball, high school baseball, college baseball, or in one of thousands of independent amateur baseball leagues. Softball, which is a kind of baseball—and which in many ways is closer than the modern game to 19th-century baseball—is played by an estimated 40 million men, women, and children. By comparison, in 2017 there were fewer than 10,000 players employed by minor and major league baseball, combined. These figures only include the United States.

THE ATLANTICS' VICTORY over the Red Stockings was, however, an ending in other ways. It was the last important victory of baseball's first great dynasty, the Brooklyn Atlantics, and it marked the beginning of the end of Brooklyn as the center of the baseball universe. The city of Brooklyn would continue to supply talent to professional baseball for the rest of the 19th century, but it would be home to fewer and fewer important clubs. Brooklyn's Atlantics joined the National Association in 1872, its second year of existence, and played three more seasons. The Eckfords of Greenpoint played only one season in the NA; and the Brooklyn-based New York Mutuals played in the National Association for all five seasons of its existence. But New York City and Brooklyn were almost completely shut out of the Chicago-based National

League, which began in 1876, especially in its early years. The Mutuals joined the NL in 1876 but were expelled after one season. The next New York or Brooklyn club to play in the NL was the New York Giants in 1883. Brooklyn returned to the majors in 1884, when the Dodgers joined the short-lived and generally forgotten American Association. (In 1890 the Dodgers transferred to the NL, where they remain.)

The Cincinnati Red Stockings' primary contributions to history are who they were and what they did, not how they were paid. They played 84 consecutive games without a single defeat over two seasons, while traveling almost continually. The Cincinnati Red Stockings were the first great western club and the first club to play in California and in the deep South in the same season. The Cincinnati Red Stockings' tours were a preview of coming attractions for the first national baseball leagues.

The Amateur Era ended because fans and their money raised the stakes. The officers of most of the top baseball clubs and the leadership of the NABBP were simply not up to the job of managing a national entertainment business. In the case of the Brooklyn Atlantics and many other clubs, there was no management; Atlantics players Bob Ferguson and Jack Chapman scheduled games, made travel arrangements, and handled club finances. Only a small minority of member clubs took the NABBP's offer to be classified as professional for the 1869 season. Part of the reason for the low number was dissatisfaction with the NABBP itself, which had proven itself unable to clean up the ongoing championship criteria, roster raiding, and other messes.

The Red Stockings continued to sell tickets and to dominate baseball after June 14, but when the 1870 season ended they disbanded in jealousy and petty disputes over money. Failed district attorney candidate Aaron Champion put Cincinnati's Union Grounds up for sale and sold its wooden stands for scrap.

When the cheering died down and the fans went home, the reality remained that the 1870 Red Stockings had barely broke even financially. They are called the first professional baseball club, the first openly professional club, or the first all-salaried club. They were none of these things. Cincinnati was not the first club to put their players under contract or to do so openly; New York's Mutuals did both in 1869.[204] And it was not the first club to operate as a corporation. (The Red Stockings sold stock when they ran out of funds to pay player salaries; that may have been a first.) If the Red Stockings were first in anything important, it was in completely discarding any pretense that baseball players had personal ties to the communities where their fans lived. We fans still want to believe that the sports franchises that we watch and support belong to us. They do, but only in one narrow sense. We pay for them.

---

204. Philadelphia *City Item*, July 24, 1869

AFTERWORD

HISTORIES OF BASEBALL typically begin with the year 1900 or another arbitrary date. Sometimes they go all the way back to the founding of the first major league, the National League, in 1876. (Today, there seems to be a consensus that the professional National Association does not deserve to be classified as a major league.) They also tend to drive by the Amateur Era or skip it entirely, as if the baseball played before today's professional leagues and their predecessors was somehow not baseball. Most modern sports begin as casual folk games, played in an unorganized way for fun, and evolve over time into sports with sophisticated rules, a high degree of organization, clear championship criteria, media coverage, and fans. Not all sports, however, become professional. By the late Amateur Era—from the mid-1850s to 1870—baseball had traveled virtually the entire evolutionary distance from game to sport. You could quibble about the NABBP's weak structure, erratic leadership, and primitive championship criteria, but in every other respect, the baseball of 1870 was a fully realized modern sport. It had also transcended its New York origins to become truly national. Professional baseball sometimes behaves as if it owns baseball history, but the truth is that however it improved the product that it has been selling for 150 years, it did not invent it. The sport of baseball was built by several thousand part-time athletes, the vast majority of whom did not play the game for a living.

Ultimately, the rise of professional baseball meant that the highest level of baseball competition in the United States would be controlled by a legal monopoly that would then sell it as an entertainment commodity. This is a long distance from the original goals of the movement that gave us amateur baseball, which were to inspire ordinary adult Americans to exercise and create a participant sport that would serve as an instrument of national unification. This movement succeeded spectacularly on both counts. If Henry Chadwick, Dr. Joseph Jones, Thomas Fitzgerald, and the other prime movers of amateur baseball could travel in a time machine to pay us a visit today, they might be taken aback at the wealth and power of the Major Leagues, but they would be utterly delighted to see baseball, softball, and the many other sports that followed it played in all 50 states by professionals and amateurs young and old, male and female. Albert Spalding in particular would feel vindicated by baseball's slow but steady international expansion and the existence of thriving baseball scenes in Australia, the Dominican Republic, Japan, and many other countries. (He believed that baseball would conquer the world, but expected it to take decades, not centuries.) Thanks to the heavy lifting of baseball's amateur forefathers, today Americans do not have to be convinced of the value or respectability of adult sports.

While many early baseball figures were avowed racists and would be disturbed to see whites, African Americans, Asians, and Latinos playing together, Thomas Fitzgerald is not the only amateur baseball man who would view modern baseball's racial and ethnic diversity as progress. Fitzgerald, Dr. Joseph Jones, and others would dream of seeing women play baseball alongside men. Henry Chadwick would feel fatherly pride in the baseball analytics revolution, which continues to fulfill his purpose in creating baseball statistics—to make the sport a serious adult endeavor that is self-perfecting through the rational and accurate measurement of player and team performance. This is the true meaning of his favorite phrase, "scientific and manly." He would enjoy watching baseball on a television, computer, or phone, and poring over the wealth of statistical and other information available literally at our fingertips. He would love Statcast, WAR, and extreme defensive shifting. (He would be less enamored of high-tech sign-stealing and gambling disguised as fantasy baseball.) Chadwick would also be relieved to see the underworld focusing its efforts on corrupting sports with point spreads and underpaid players, not his beloved baseball. The visionaries of Amateur Era baseball marketed the game to the emerging urban bourgeoisie as a means to an end, to make baseball a durable, honest, and respectable national institution—not as an end in itself. The fact that they succeeded in this as well has made the social and racial exclusion practiced by the early amateur baseball clubs unnecessary and obsolete.

There is something else that these early baseball men would have to tell us. Before the sport conquered New York City, Boston, Philadelphia, and other eastern cities in the years before the Civil War, young American men belonged to fire companies and militias. These same young men took up baseball, but the clubs that appeared at the end of that period grew out of and ultimately replaced the fire and militia companies. When the Civil War came, hundreds of militia companies enlisted intact in volunteer army regiments. In keeping with the egalitarian and democratic culture that produced them, they elected their own officers, something that is unthinkable today. Made up of friends and neighbors, volunteer fire companies were multipurpose community organizations that gave convivial chowder suppers, raised money for charity, and made road trips to other neighborhoods and other cities; these trips included competitions of firefighting skills, such as team water pumping contests. Neighborhoods took pride in their fire companies, which were supported by youths who "ran with the machine," cheering their heroes on, clearing the streets, and carrying firefighting equipment, and sometimes sabotaging or assaulting rival companies racing to the same fire. Volunteer firefighting was an incipient form of athletic competition.

BOTH OF THESE civic institutions were characterized not by bureaucracy, professionalism, and enforced order and discipline, as they are in our world, but rather were decentralized, voluntary, and neighborhood-based. Like the early baseball clubs, they derived their power from the bottom up, from their individual members and communities. In the 1840s and 1850s, however, the egalitarianism and freedom of the old city life began to be viewed as disorderly and un-modern. Change was gradual because there was always resistance to community disempowerment and its replacement by top-down authority. But after the Civil War, both the civilian militias and volunteer fire companies were taken away from their members, professionalized and reorganized as agencies of the state.

Like almost all reform movements, the amateur baseball movement contained both utopian and reactionary ideas. It looked forward in some things, backward in others. The purpose of the amateur baseball movement was not only to build a better, healthier future and a more unified nation, but also to preserve the physicality and fraternity of traditional city culture, a culture that was endangered by the Industrial Revolution and the emergence of the modern middle class. When we build a green baseball diamond in the sprawling modern city or play baseball or softball in the park, we are celebrating and honoring that culture. We are reviving the ancient joy in youth, physical exercise, and companionship that enriched urban life and that the sport of baseball was created to save.

ACKNOWLEDGMENTS

THIS BOOK WOULD not exist without the love and support of my family. To my wife Lisa, who has made me the envy of every married man I know; to my wonderful grown children Wesley and Susannah, and to my brother Craig: Thank you for reading endless drafts and, worse, listening to me talk about 19th-century baseball. To my father, the Marine fighter pilot and patriarch of our clan, and to my kind and wise late mother, who inspired those around her to be and do their best: Thank you.

A *gratias ago* to Jack Lynch and to Yale College, for exposing me to serious scholarship and for discouraging me from a career in academia. To the DBL, my Brooklyn pickup game for 38 years: Thanks for teaching me things about early baseball that I otherwise could not have learned without a time machine. Thanks also to my SABR brothers and sisters, including the dynamic 19th Century Committee under chairman Peter Mancuso. To outstanding researchers Bob Tholkes and Richard Hershberger: Thank you for generously sharing your clipping files of undigitized mid-19th-century newspapers. Thanks, Jeff Richman and the Green-Wood Cemetery Historic Fund, for allowing me to include previously published material on James Creighton. Thanks also to Larry McCray and the contributors to Protoball.org.

Thanks to those who made this book happen, including known typophile, book designer, and professional non-Irishman Jerry Kelly; and the excellent people at David R. Godine, Publisher, especially David Allender, Joshua Bodwell, and Ally Findley. I am especially grateful to David R. Godine himself, who is God's gift to writers.

To the great John Thorn: Thanks for being the great John Thorn. In our thing, John is a seemingly inexhaustible font of wisdom, erudition, and inspiration. We do not know how he does it, but we are immensely grateful that he does.

THOMAS W. GILBERT

BIBLIOGRAPHY

BOOKS

Adams, Peter. *The Bowery Boys: Street Corner Radicals and the Politics of Rebellion.* Westport, Connecticut: Praeger, 2005.

Adelman, Melvin L. *A Sporting Time: New York City and the Rise of Modern Athletics, 1820–1870.* Urbana, Illinois: University of Illinois Press, 1990.

Anbinder, Tyler. *Nativism and Slavery: The Northern Know Nothings and the Politics of the 1850s.* New York City, New York: Oxford University Press, 1992.

Anbinder, Tyler. *Five Points.* New York City, New York: Free Press, 2001.

Asbury, Herbert. *Ye Olde Fire Laddies.* New York City, New York: Alfred A. Knopf, 1930.

Barth, Gunther. *City People: The Rise of Modern City Culture in 19th century America.* New York City, New York: Oxford University Press, 1980.

Bayor, Ronald H. and Meagher, Timothy J., Editors. *The New York Irish.* Baltimore, Maryland: Johns Hopkins University Press, 1996.

Beckert, Sven. *The Monied Metropolis: New York City and the Consolidation of the American Bourgeoisie, 1850-1896.* New York City, New York: Cambridge University Press, 2001.

Bergmann, Hans. *God in the Street: New York Writing from the Penny Press to Melville.* Philadelphia, Pennsylvania: Temple University Press, 1995.

Blanchard, John Adams. *The Harvard Book of Harvard Athletics, 1952-1922.* Boston, Massachusetts: Harvard Varsity Club, 1923.

Block, David. *Baseball Before We Knew It: A Search for the Roots of the Game.* Lincoln, Nebraska: University of Nebraska Press, 2005.

Blumin, Stuart M. *The Emergence of the Middle Class: Social Experience in the American City, 1760–1900.* New York City, New York: Cambridge University Press, 1989.

Chadwick, Sir Edwin. *The Health of Nations*. London, U.K.: Longmans, 1887.

Chadwick, Henry. *The Game of Base Ball*. Reprint Edition. Columbia, South Carolina: Camden House, 1983.

Cohen, Patricia Cline, Gilfoyle, Timothy J. and Horwitz, Helen Lefkowitz. *The Flash Press: Sporting Male Weeklies in 1840s New York*. Chicago, Illinois: University of Chicago Press, 2008.

Costello, Augustine E. *Our Firemen: A History of the New York Fire Departments Volunteer and Paid*. New York City, New York: Published by the Author, 1887.

Dattel, Gene. *Cotton and Race in the Making of America: The Human Costs of Economic Power*. Chicago, Illinois: Ivan R. Dee, 2009.

Devyr, Thomas A. *The Odd Book of the 19th Century, Or "Chivalry" in Modern Days*. Greenpoint, New York: Published by the Author, 1882.

Dickens, Charles. *American Notes for General Circulation*. New York City, New York: Harper Brothers, 1842.

Dreifort, John E. *Baseball History from Outside the Lines*. Lincoln, Nebraska: University of Nebraska Press, 2001.

Eaton, Dorman B. *The "Spoils" System and Civil Service Reform in the Custom House and Post Office at New York*. New York City, New York: G. P. Putnam's Sons, 1881.

Ellard, Harry. *Base Ball in Cincinnati: A History*. Cincinnati, Ohio: Subscription Edition, 1907.

Fishman, Robert. *Bourgeois Utopias: The Rise and Fall of Suburbia*. New York City, New York: Basic Books, 1987.

Foster, George G., Edited and with an Introduction by Stuart M. Blumin. *New York by Gas-Light and Other Urban Sketches*. Berkeley, California: University of California Press, 1990.

Foster, George G. *New York in Slices*. New York City, New York: W. F. Burgess, 1849.

Geisst, Charles R. *Wall Street: A History*. New York City, New York: Oxford University Press, 1997.

Gienapp, William E. *The Origins of the Republican Party, 1852–1856*.

New York City, New York: Oxford University Press, 1987.

Gilbert, Thomas W. *Playing First: Early Baseball Lives at Brooklyn's Green-Wood Cemetery*. Brooklyn, New York: Green-Wood Cemetery, 2015.

Gilbert, Thomas W. *Baseball and the Color Line*. New York City, New York; Franklin Watts, 1995.

Goldstein, Warren. *Playing For Keeps: A History of Early Baseball*. Ithaca, New York: Cornell University Press, 1989.

Gorn, Elliot J. *The Manly Art: Bare-Knuckle Prize Fighting in America*. Ithaca, New York: Cornell University Press, 1986.

Gray, Barry. *Matrimonial Infelicities*. Cambridge, Massachusetts: H. O. Houghton, 1865.

Gutman, Allen et al. *Essays on Sports History and Sports Mythology*. College Station, Texas: Texas A&M Press, 1990.

Headley, John Tyler. *The Great Riots of New York, 1712–1873*. New York: Thunder's Mouth Press, 2004.

Henderson, Mary C. *The City and the Theatre*. New York City, New York: Backstage Books. 2004.

Henshaw, Robert E., Editor. *Environmental History of the Hudson River*. Albany, New York: State University of New York Press, 2011.

Higham, John. *Strangers in the Land: Patterns of Nativism, 1860–1925*. New Brunswick, New Jersey: Rutgers University Press, 1955.

Hoffman, Dean A. *Harness Racing in New York State*. Charleston, South Carolina: The History Press, 2012.

Humber, William. *Diamonds of the North: A Concise History of Baseball in Canada*. New York City, New York: Oxford University Press, 1995.

Huntzicker, William E. *The Popular Press, 1833-1865*. Westport, Connecticut: Greenwood Press, 1999.

Jensen, Don, Editor. BASE BALL, New Research on the Early Game, Volume 10. Jefferson, North Carolina: McFarland & Company, 2018.

Knox, Thomas W. *Underground, or Life Below the Surface*. Hartford, Connecticut: J. B. Burr, 1874.

Lancaster, Clay. *Old Brooklyn Heights: New York's First Suburb*. New York City, New York: Dover, 1979.

Leavitt, Judith Walzer and Numbers, Ronald L., Editors. *Sickness and Health in America: Readings in the History of Medicine and Public Health*. Madison, Wisconsin, University of Wisconsin Press, 1978.

Lovett, James D'Wolfe. *Old Boston Boys and the Games They Played*. Boston, Massachusetts: Privately Printed, 1906.

Lowry, Thomas P. *Tarnished Eagles: The Courts-Martial of Fifty Union Colonels and Lieutenant Colonels*. Mechanicsburg, Pennsylvania: Stackpole Books, 1997.

Martin, Albro. *Railroads Triumphant: The Growth, Rejection and Rebirth of a Vital American Force*. New York City, New York: Oxford University Press, 1992.

McCaughey, Robert A. *Stand Columbia*. New York City, New York: Columbia University Press, 2003.

McIlwraith, Thomas F. and Muller, Edward K., Editors. *North America: The Historical Geography of a Changing Continent*. Lanham, Maryland: Rowman and Littlefield, 2001.

Melville, Tom. *The Tented Field: A History of Cricket in America*. Bowling Green, Ohio: Bowling Green University Popular Press, 1998.

Metcalfe, Alan. *Canada Learns to Play: The Emergence of Organized Sport, 1807–1914*. Toronto, Canada: McClelland and Stewart, 1987.

Morford, Henry. *Sprees and Splashes: Droll Recollections of Town and Country*. New York City, New York: Carleton, 1863.

Morris, Peter et al. Editors. *Baseball Founders*. Jefferson, North Carolina: McFarland & Company, 2013.

Morris, Peter et al. Editors. *Baseball Pioneers, 1850–1870*. Jefferson, North Carolina: McFarland & Company, 2012.

Morrone, Francis. *An Architectural Guidebook to Brooklyn*. Salt Lake City, Utah: Gibbs-Smith, 2001.

Nucciarone, Monica. *Alexander Cartwright: The Life Behind the Baseball Legend*. Lincoln, Nebraska: University of Nebraska Press, 2009.

Orem, Preston D. *Baseball (1845–1881) From the Newspaper Accounts*. Altadena, California: Published by the Author, 1961.

Patell, Cyrus R. K. and Waterman, Bryan. *The Cambridge Companion to the Literature of New York*, New York City, New York: Cambridge University Press, 2010.

Peverelly, Charles A. *The Book of American Pastimes*. New York City, New York: Published by the Author, 1866.

Phalen, William J. *The Consequences of Cotton in Antebellum America*. Jefferson, North Carolina: McFarland & Company, 2014.

Puleo, Stephen. *A City So Grand: The Rise of an American Metropolis, Boston 1850–1900*. Boston, Massachusetts: Beacon Press, 2010.

Rock, Howard B. *The New York City Artisan 1789–1825*. Albany, New York: State University of New York Press, 1989.

Rock, Howard B. *Haven of Liberty: New York Jews in the New World, 1654–1865*. New York City, New York: New York University Press, 2012.

Rorabaugh, W. J. *The Craft Apprentice: From Franklin to the Machine Age in America*. New York City, New York: Oxford University Press, 1986.

Rosenberg, Charles E. *The Cholera Years*. Chicago, Illinois: University of Chicago Press, 1962.

Seymour, Harold. *Baseball: The People's Game*. New York City, New York: Oxford University Press, 1990.

Scherzer, Kenneth A. *The Unbounded Community: Neighborhood Life and Social Structure in New York City, 1830–1875*. Durham, North Carolina: Duke University Press, 1992.

Schiff, Andrew. *"The Father of Baseball": A Biography of Henry Chadwick*. Jefferson, North Carolina: McFarland & Company, 2008.

Schudson, Michael. *Discovering the News: A Social History of American Newspapers*. New York City, New York: Basic Books, 1978.

Shiffert, John. *Base Ball in Philadelphia: A History of the Early Game, 1831–1900*. Jefferson, North Carolina: McFarland & Company, 2006.

Sisson, Richard et al. Editors. *The American Midwest: An Interpretative Encyclopedia*. Bloomington, Indiana: University of Indiana Press, 2007.

Spalding, Albert G. *Baseball: America's National Game 1839–1915*. New York City, New York: American Sports, 1911.

Stilgoe, John R. *Borderland: Origins of the American Suburb, 1829–1939*. New Haven, Connecticut: Yale University Press, 1988.

Stilgoe, John R. *Common Landscape of America, 1580–1845*. New Haven, Connecticut: Yale University Press, 1982.

Stott, Richard. *Jolly Fellows: Male Milieus in Nineteenth-Century America*. Baltimore, Maryland: Johns Hopkins University Press, 2009.

Swanson, Ryan A. *When Baseball Went White: Reconstruction, Reconciliation and Dreams of a National Pastime*. Lincoln, Nebraska: University of Nebraska Press, 2014.

Tangires, Helen. *Public Markets and Civic Culture in 19th century America*. Baltimore, Maryland: Johns Hopkins Press, 2003.

Tayor, George Rogers and Neu, Irene D. *The American Railroad Network 1861–1890*. Urbana, Illinois: University of Illinois Press, 1956.

Thorn, John. *Baseball in the Garden of Eden: The Secret History of the Early Game*. New York City, New York: Simon and Schuster, 2011.

Thorn, John, Editor. BASE BALL, New Research on the Early Game, Volumes 1–9. Jefferson, North Carolina: McFarland & Company, 2007-2017.

Trollope, Frances. *Domestic Manners of the Americans*. London, U.K.: Whitaker, Treacher, 1832.

Tygiel, Jules. *Past Time: Baseball as History*. New York City, New York: Oxford University Press, 2000.

Ultan, Lloyd. *The Northern Borough: A History of the Bronx*. Bronx, New York: The Bronx County Historical Society, 2005.

Weigley, Russell F., Editor. *Philadelphia: A 300-Year History*. New York City, New York: W. W. Norton, 1982.

Wilentz, Sean. *Chants Democratic: New York City and the Rise of the American Working Class, 1788–1850*. New York City, New York: Oxford University Press, 1984.

Willis, Nathaniel P. *American Scenery*. London, U.K.: George Virtue, 1840.

Wilson, David A. *United Irishmen, United States: Immigrant Radicals in the Early Republic*. Ithaca, New York: Cornell University Press, 1998.

Wright, Marshall D. *The National Association of Base Ball Players, 1857–1870*. Jefferson, North Carolina: McFarland & Company, 2000.

Young, Terence and Riley, Robert, Editors. *Theme Park Landscapes: Antecedents and Variations*. Washington, D.C.: Dumbarton Oaks, 2002.

Zahler, Helene Sara. *Eastern Workingmen and National Land Policy*. New York City, New York: Greenwood Press, 1941.

DIGITALIZED DATABASES/WEBSITES

Newspapers.com

Genealogy.com

Hudson River Valley Heritage - news.hrvh.org

MLB Memory Lab - mlb.mlb.com/memorylab/spread_of_baseball/earliest_clubs.jsp#

California Digital Newspaper Collection - cdnc.ucr.edu/cgi-bin/cdnc

National Park Service Soldiers and Sailors Civil War Database - nps.gov/civilwar/soldiers-and-sailors-database.htm

Fulton History - fultonhistory.com/fulton.html

Illinois Digital Newspaper Collections - idnc.library.illinois.edu

NYS Historic Newspapers - nyshistoricnewspapers.org

John Thorn's Our Game Blog - ourgame.mlblogs.com

Protoball - protoball.org/chronologies

New York Genealogical and Biographical Society - newyorkfamilyhistory.org

Family Search - familysearch.org

Italian Genealogical Group - italiangen.org

OldNYC - oldnyc.org

Ancestry.com

New York Historical Society - nyhistory.org

New York Public Library - nypl.org

Library of Congress - loc.gov

University of Michigan Digital Collections -
quod.lib.umich.edu/lib/colllist

American Antiquarian Society - americanantiquarian.org

Hathi Trust Digital Library - hathitrust.org

Google Books - books.google.com

Jstor - jstor.org

Stevens Digital Collections - librarycollections.stevens.edu

INDEX

1st Pennsylvania National Guard, 232

2nd U.S. Dragoons, 75

5th U.S. Colored Infantry, 304

6th New York, 205, 207; See also Wilson's Zouaves

7th Michigan, 294

7th New York State Militia (AKA 7th NY National Guard, Seventh Regiment), 68, 126, 285, 295, 306

7th Ohio, 304

13th NYSM, 287-289, 291-292

14th NYSM, 292

15th Amendment to the Constitution, 263

18th New York Cavalry, 292

19th Massachusetts, 293-294

31st New York, 295, 309-310

44th New York, 291

47th NYSM, 293

66th New York, 292, 309-310

68th New York, 280, 306

69th NYSM, 305-306

71st NYSM (AKA American Guard), 294-296, 300

90th New York, 289-291

A Glance at New York, by Benjamin Baker, 11, 129

A History of New York, by Washington Irving, 141

Abolitionism, 28, 40, 107, 131, 133-134, 136, 148, 200, 202, 206, 248, 265, 276, 287, 298-299, 303

Abortion, 102

Achilles, 48

Adams, Daniel "Doc", 8, 64-65, 70, 142-143, 146, 156, 229

Adams, John G. B., 293-294

Admission charges, 9, 11, 16, 19, 83, 87, 113-114, 151, 164, 173, 180, 233, 258, 260, 263, 341, 345

African American baseball, 12, 29, 53, 65, 114, 197-199, 260-262, 264-267, 296, 300, 304, 354

Alden, Joseph, 233-234

Alert clubs, 138, 261, 264, 316

Allison, Doug, 326, 331, 335, 349

Amateurism, 9, 17-19, 34, 62, 70, 79, 84, 158, 163, 193, 251-257, 314-316, 332-333, 335-336, 338, 350

American Eclipse vs. *Henry* (1823 horse race), 88-89

America's Cup, 88

America's National Game, by Albert Spalding, 28, 65-66, 282-283

American Express Company, 321

American Football, 15, 114, 174, 208, 276

American Notes for General Circulation, by Charles Dickens, 124, 186

American Pastimes, by Charles Peverelly, 64, 232

American Revolution, 20, 33, 67, 90-91, 97, 124-125, 136-137

Americus Engine Company #6, 138, 216

Amherst College, 278

Amtrak, 91

Amusement parks, 89, 109, 112

Analytics, 31, 354

Anderson, Madame, 341; See also Pedestrianism

Anthony Street (AKA Worth Street), 186-188, 190, 200; See also Five Points, Slumming

Anthony, Henry T., 227, 299

Anthony, Susan B., 276

Anti-rent War, 133

Anti-Semitism, lack of, 254

Apprenticeship, 245-247

Asahel, 346

Astor Theatre riot, 11, 125-127, 189, 224; See also Riots

Astor, John Jacob, 94

Athleisure, 15

Athletic club, 18, 60, 111, 135, 224-225, 227, 232, 235-239, 241-242, 247, 251-254, 256-261, 265-266, 272, 278, 285, 315, 317-318, 331, 338-339, 342-343, 348

Atlantic Hose Company #14, 216

Atlantic club, 12, 18, 55-56, 59, 111, 138, 160-162, 165, 167, 169-180, 196-197, 210-212, 217, 227-228, 235, 239-242, 252, 257-260, 278, 284-285, 287-289, 296, 300-301, 315, 317-318, 320, 331, 337-342, 345, 347-351

Atlantics vs. Excelsiors, 171, 173-179

Aurora, 131

Babcock, Alexander, 300-301

Babcock, Orville, 205

Babcock, William, 227, 301

Baltimore and Ohio Railroad, 320

Banquets, 45, 48, 59, 63, 76, 138, 156, 193-194, 257; See also Post-game meals, Chowders

Barnes, Ross, 338

Barnum, P. T., 95-96

Barre, William, 259, 291

Baseball club names, 50, 135-142, 232, 319

Baseball Conventions (New York game), 48-49, 62, 64, 119, 128, 157, 214, 221, 235-236, 262-263, 265-266, 275, 278, 283, 307, 316

Baseball Conventions (Massachusetts game), 268-269

Baseball cards, 208, 215, 270, 275

Baseball in the Garden of Eden, by

John Thorn, 9, 45, 53

Baseball Tours, 11, 12, 24, 28, 52, 84, 112, 172, 181, 196, 220, 278, 297, 318, 321-322, 325, 331-332, 336-342, 344-345, 351

Battle of Cedar Creek, 291

Battle of Cross Lanes, 304

Battles of Bull Run, 285, 294, 296, 305

Battle of Seven Pines, 301

Battle of Santa Rosa, Nicaragua, 203

Battle of Santa Rosa, Florida, 205

Bayard, William, 91, 94

Beaver trade, 121, 128

Bedford (now Bedford-Stuyvesant), 174, 180, 259

Beecher, Henry Ward, 148, 206

Belding, Henry, 219

Bell's Life in London, 37

Bell, William H., 62, 263, 265

Bellan, Esteban, 12, 274, 344

Benefit games, 84, 196, 199

Bentham, Jeremy, 143

Berkenstock, Nate, 238-239

Bernhardt, Sarah, 292

Binghamton, NY, 298-300

Bingo club, 300

Bisons club, 197-199

Blackface entertainment, 105-107, 109, 129, 266

Block, David, 9, 23

Bloomingdale, NY, 82

Boeing 707 airplane, 321

Boetticher, Otto, 280, 306

Bookmakers, 64, 111, 165, 168, 328-329, 338, 341

Boothenian Dramatic Society, 238

Boston Common, 269, 271, 275-276

Botts, Alexander, 88

Botts, John Minor, 282, 285

Boughton, Frederick K., 176, 179

Bowdoin club, 273

Bowery, The, 63, 84, 127-131, 205

Bowery B'hoys, 11, 58, 68, 127-133, 135, 200, 216

Boxing, 16, 37, 58, 109-110, 117-118, 132, 146-148, 158, 160, 224, 328, 340

Brady, Mathew, 227

Brainard, Asa, 159, 170, 217, 273, 331-332, 335-336, 345-347, 349

Brainard, Harrison, 159

Braves club, 317

Broadway Tabernacle, 200

Broderick, Dave, 130

Brooklyn *Daily Eagle*, 38, 44, 143, 159, 160, 162, 167, 175, 185, 197, 204, 207, 212, 215, 287, 289-291, 341, 348, 349

Brooklyn Heights, 147, 155, 160, 191

Brooklyn Yacht Club, 173

Brooklyn-New York City rivalry, 31, 75, 162-165, 167, 169-170, 180, 181, 182

Brooklynese, 62

Brown University, 278

Brown, Harvey, 205-206

Buchannan, James, 203

Buckeye club, 257, 316, 322, 339

Building Societies, 153; See also Suburbanization

Bulkeley, Morgan, 287

Bullshit, 17, 21-22, 324

Buntline, Ned, 126-127; See also Judson, Edward

Burr, Aaron, 91-92, 94, 265

Burr, John Pierre, 265

Burr, Raymond, 265

Bush, Archie, 278

Butcher Boys, 57; See also Nativism, Short Boys

Butchers, 55-59, 97, 340; See also Food markets

California Gold Rush, 27, 32, 50, 129-130, 228, 342

Camac's Woods, 239, 258

Camden and Amboy Railroad, 11, 67, 90-91, 223-224, 228, 234

Cammeyer, William, 180

Canada, 4, 11, 20, 120, 222, 269

Canals, 32, 82, 85, 90, 120, 172, 202, 220-221, 235, 303, 320-321; See also Erie Canal

Capitoline Grounds, 180, 258-259, 292, 345, 347-348

Carroll Park, 137, 148, 156, 162, 173, 288

Cartes de visite, 208, 215

Cartwright, Alexander, 21, 27-29, 44, 46-47, 50, 65, 76, 229

Cartwright, Benjamin, 76

Catholicism, 54, 71, 98, 103-104, 123, 130, 188, 224, 245, 248-249, 274, 327

Catto, Octavius, 12, 261, 264-265, 267, 331

Cauldwell, William, 38, 144, 292

Central High School of Philadelphia, 224, 232, 239

Central Pacific Railroad, 220

Central Park, 84, 89, 94, 107-109, 112, 164, 174

Chadwick, Andrew, 133

Chadwick, Edwin, 93, 143

Chadwick, Henry, 21-23, 26-28, 36-39, 48, 88, 93, 113, 133-134, 143, 165, 168, 170, 175-177, 180-182, 185, 207, 210, 217, 240, 246, 255, 259-260, 282, 285, 291, 301, 325, 337-338, 354-355

Chadwick, James, 133

Champion, Aaron, 323-325, 329-330, 339, 351

Chapman, John C. "Jack", 184, 197-199, 212, 217, 339-341, 345, 348, 351

Charleston, SC, 68, 73, 85, 221

Charter Oak club, 287-289

Chartism, 133

Chatham Square, 50, 62, 82

Cholera, 9, 11, 92, 143-145, 160, 172, 245

Chowder recipe, 60-61

Chowders, 49, 58-60, 73, 78, 128, 134, 355;
See also Banquets, Post-game meals
City Hall Park, 57, 82, 127, 134, 204
City Item, 243, 247-248, 252, 254,
261, 267, 277
Civil War, American, 14-16, 18-19, 21,
30, 33, 40, 46, 60-61, 66, 69, 73,
75, 84, 107, 122-123, 137-140, 161,
170, 173, 178, 188-189, 193, 196,
202-204, 222-224, 228, 232, 259,
261-262, 274, 278-279, 281-282,
284-287, 290-292, 294, 297-299,
302, 305, 307-310, 315, 322, 328,
334, 336-337, 346, 355-356
Clancy, John, 71
Class of 1866 club, 12, 277, 279, 322;
See also Harvard University
Cleopatra's Needle, 108
Clinton, DeWitt, 235
Cobble Hill, 155, 185, 191
College of Physicians and Surgeons,
50, 142, 148, 156, 158, 297-298,
302; See also Columbia University
Colonnade Hotel, 96, 99-101, 104-
106, 108, 113; See also McCarty's
Hotel, Pavilion
Color Line, 29, 65, 198, 262, 265
Columbia University, 50, 57, 66, 90,
136, 142, 156, 224, 233, 274, 298, 302
Colyer, William, 243, 246, 250
Commerford, Charles, 134
Commerford, John, 134
Commission Merchants, 69, 234
Commuting, Origins of, 152;
See also Suburbanization
Constitution Engine Company #7, 237
Corcoran, Michael, 280, 305-306, 309
Corlear's Hook, 61
Cotton, 32, 68-70, 221, 259, 302, 343
Creighton, James Jr., 9, 53, 122, 132,
137, 158-159, 170-175, 182-196, 199,
207-216, 226-227, 254-256, 273, 288,
294, 300, 322, 328, 335, 345, 347

Creighton, James Sr., 185, 188-191,
194, 207
Creighton, John, 189, 194, 199-207,
294, 328
Cricket, 7, 15, 19, 25, 31-32, 36-38, 66-
67, 74-75, 79, 82-84, 87-88, 96, 104,
107-109, 112-114, 117-118, 122-125,
128, 135, 161, 165, 177-178, 187, 193-
194, 196, 210, 212, 214-215, 224,
228, 232, 239, 256, 261, 271-272,
281, 323, 332-334, 347
Croton water system, 92
Crotona Park, 154
Cuba, 12, 32, 202, 274, 328, 344
Cuban Giants club, 114, 198
Cubs club, 20, 28
Cummings, Candy, 207
Curry, Duncan, 69, 229
Curve ball, 184, 207-209, 211
Customs House, 69, 195-196, 201,
203, 255
Cyclone club, 228

Dakin, Thomas, 164, 169, 235, 311
David, King, 346
Davis, James Whyte, 65, 70, 75-76,
156-157, 164, 193, 262-263, 265
DeBost, Charles, 75
Demilt, Samuel, 146
Demilt, William, 146
Dead Rabbits Riot, 188, 204; See also
Five Points, Riots
Dead Rabbits gang, 205
Delaware and Raritan Canal, 221
Delaware, Lackawanna and Western
Railroad, 302
Delmonico's Restaurant, 78
Democratic Vistas, by Walt Whitman, 132
Designated Hitter, 63
Devyr, Thomas A. Jr., 133, 246-247, 335
Devyr, Thomas A. Sr., 133, 246-247, 276
Dickens, Charles, 16, 124, 186, 193

Dispensary System, 145-146, 148, 160

Dixie, 107

Dixwell's Private Latin School, 275-276

Dockney, Patsy, 253-254, 257, 260

Dodge, Daniel Albert, 156

Dodgers club, 32, 114, 135, 155, 181, 288, 304, 341, 346, 351

Dodgers-Giants rivalry, 181

Doesticks, P.B., Q.K. Philander, 139-140; See also Thomson, Mortimer

Donaldson, Josh, 74

Doonesbury, 88

Dorr Rebellion, 123,131

Doubleday, Abner, 17, 20-23, 27-28, 30-31, 46-48, 65, 118, 151, 229, 287

Douglass, Frederick Sr., 200-201, 261

Douglass, Frederick Jr., 261

Downton Abbey, 124

Draft Riots of 1863, 58, 206

Draper, John, 322

Drew, Louisa Lane (AKA Mrs. John Drew), 237, 248

Drummond, Alex, 69

Dulles, Foster Rhea, 117

Dupin, Auguste, 102

Dwyer, John J., 340

Eager, William B., 142, 146

Eagle club of New York, 25, 34, 36, 38, 43-45, 48-49, 51, 55, 63-64, 68, 72, 74, 77, 112, 114, 134, 161-162, 170, 180, 217, 228, 240, 286, 318, 342

Eagle club of San Francisco, 228, 342

Ebbets, Charles H., 288

Ebbets, Ebenezer, 288

Eckford club of Brooklyn, 55-56, 61-62, 88, 133, 137, 160, 165, 169-170, 197, 222, 228, 237-238, 241, 243, 246, 254, 263, 265, 287, 293, 316, 335, 348, 350

Eckford, Henry, 61, 137

Elks, Benevolent Protective Order of, 293

Ellard, George, 323, 325

Ellard, Harry, 325, 345

Elle, 24

Ellipse, 296

Elysian Fields, 9, 36, 38, 45, 50, 53, 59, 64, 67, 73, 80, 87-91, 94-115, 154, 161-162, 164, 173, 189, 196, 221, 239, 285-286

Emancipation Proclamation, 290, 298

Emerging Urban Bourgeoisie, 34, 35, 37, 39-40, 52, 54-56, 58, 68, 70, 77, 79, 95, 107-108, 110, 112-113, 117, 123, 154, 156, 161, 170, 177, 192, 218, 224, 232-234, 236, 259, 262, 265, 272, 285, 332-333, 355

Emmett, Dan, 106-107; See also Blackface entertainment

Empire baseball club, 45, 64, 68, 112, 114, 136, 160, 162, 170, 228, 240, 271, 286, 318

Empire political club, 53, 126, 130, 189, 200, 203

Engravers, 227, 273, 301, 336

Epidemic disease, 11, 92-93, 143-145, 160, 245, 334

Equity club, 91, 227, 234-235, 252-253, 256

Erie Canal, 32, 82, 120, 172, 219-221, 235, 303, 320-321; See also Canals

Esculapian club, 148-149, 287-288

Etheridge, Charles, 297

Evacuation Day, 124

Evans, George Henry, 134

Excelsior club, 11-12, 42, 52, 55, 69, 74, 77, 113, 137, 139, 149, 155-160, 162, 164-165, 170-180, 184-185, 192-194, 196, 207, 211-217, 221, 224, 226-228, 239, 252-253, 255-256, 258-259, 264, 273, 277-278, 282, 285, 288-289, 291, 294-295, 297-298, 300-302, 310, 322, 328, 335-337, 346-347

Excelsior, by Henry Wadsworth

Longfellow, 139

Fairmount Park, 84
Fans, 7, 10, 16-18, 39, 41, 46-47, 54-55,
    81, 111, 113-114, 164, 167, 173-174,
    176-178, 180-181, 198-199, 233-234,
    258-259, 285, 310, 317-319, 329,
    338-339, 344-345, 348, 351-353
Farnsworth, Addison, 202-203, 294
Fashion Course series, 75, 164-167,
    169-170, 173, 180, 262
Fathers of Baseball, 9, 27, 29-30, 38-
    39, 48, 65, 159, 229, 297, 317-318,
    324-325, 334, 354
Feminism, 36, 40, 88, 148, 159, 276-277
Fenian Brotherhood, 79, 133
Fenwick, Millicent, 88
Feral pigs, 92
Ferguson, Robert, 197, 229, 348-
    349, 351
Ferries, 11, 45, 67, 82, 86-87, 90,
    93-94, 97-98, 104, 115, 147-148, 151-
    152, 155, 162, 220, 223-224, 276,
    289, 348
Fijux, Francis, 77-78
Filibusters, 202-203, 207
Fire Zouaves, 309
Firemen's Memorial, 216
Fitzgerald, Catherine, 245
Fitzgerald, Edmund Sr.,244
Fitzgerald, Edmund Jr., 245,250
Fitzgerald, Ellen, 244-245, 250-251
Fitzgerald, Garrit, 245
Fitzgerald, Riter, 238
Fitzgerald, Thomas, 60, 221, 235-257,
    261, 266-267, 277, 296, 315, 333, 354
Five Points, 71, 186-188, 190, 204; See
    also Anthony Street; Slumming
Flagg, George, 277
Flanley, George, 159, 170, 177, 185,
    192, 197, 212, 255, 273, 278, 300
Flash, Grandmaster, 154

Flying moon men, 35, 336
Folie Beaujon, 95
Food Markets, 55-59, 97, 129, 254, 258;
    See also Butchers, Washington Market
Fordham University, 12, 274, 344
Forest City club, 28, 338, 342
Forrest, Edwin, 125-126
Foster, George G., 57, 247-248, 250
Fourth Ward of NYC, 243, 245, 250-251
Fox Hill, 36, 96, 104, 107, 114
France, Richard, 327-328
France, William, 328
Franklin Square, 243
Fraser, Isabella, 334
Fraser, Mary, 83
Freemasonry, 27, 51, 293, 301
Fuller, Willliam, 146-147
Furey, Robert, 259, 291

Gambling, 9, 16, 29, 35, 39, 45-46,
    52, 58-59, 64, 66, 101, 111, 113, 117,
    130, 161, 163, 167-168, 173, 177, 240,
    252, 258-259, 326-330, 338-339,
    341, 355
Game vs. Sport, 7, 15-19, 23, 25-26,
    30, 32-33, 36, 40, 44-46, 55, 79, 82,
    85, 118, 147, 159, 307, 353-354
Game-fixing scandal of 1865, 246
Gangs of New York, by Herbert As-
    bury, 58
Gangs of New York, by Martin
    Scorsese, 58
Garrison, William Lloyd, 200-201
Gaskill, Charles, 239
Gaskill, Edwin, 239
Geraldines, 242, 249
Giants club, 114, 181, 263, 351
Gibbons v. Ogden, 90
Glaeser, Edward, 121
Godey's Ladies Book, 60, 248
Gorman, A.P., 295-296
Goshorn, Alfred, 323-325

Gotham Inn, 63, 127

Gotham club, 25, 36, 43-45, 48-51, 55, 59, 62-65, 68, 72, 74-77, 97, 112-114, 134, 141, 145, 154, 160-162, 170, 180, 217, 222, 224, 228, 240, 257, 271, 286, 296, 310, 334

Gould, Charlie, 331, 335, 348-349

Govern, Stanislaus Kostka, 114

Graham's Magazine, 248

Grand Trunk Railway, 269

Grant, Frank, 198-199

Grant, Ulysses, 285, 330

Gray, Barry, 78

Great Eastern, 137; See also Shipbuilding

Great Fire of 1835, 68

Great Western Railroad, 222

Greeley, Horace, 117, 131, 204, 301

Green-Wood cemetery, 39, 58, 185, 199, 213, 215-216, 263, 357

Greenberg, Hank, 154

Greenpoint, 56, 61-62, 88, 162, 222, 237, 241, 243, 246, 265, 316, 335, 350

Greenwich Village, 82, 187

Grenelle, William, 69

Griswold, Merrit, 228

Griswold, Rufus, 250

Guild, Benjamin Franklin, 268, 271

Gymnastics, 9, 104, 117-118, 146-148, 158-159, 224

Hague Street, 243-244, 246, 250

Hale, Sarah Josepha, 60

Hall of Fame, Cooperstown, NY, 17, 21, 26, 39, 46-47, 84, 151, 154, 169, 184, 207, 303, 324

Hall, George B., 202

Hall, George, 348-349

Halleck, Fitz-Greene, 79

Hamilton College, 278

Hamilton Village, 152, 234

Hamilton, Alexander, 67, 91, 94, 136

Harlem, 82-83, 85, 109, 152-154, 187, 222

Harness Racing, 85, 89, 96

Harrison Literary Institute, 232

Harvard University, 12, 142, 273-275, 277-279, 322, 329

Haverford College, 125

Hawley, Madame Beaujeu, 148

Haydn and Handel Society of Philadelphia, 238

Hayhurst, Hicks, 238-239, 252, 265

Henderson, Robert, 9, 46

Henry, Mike, 340-341, 348

Hershberger, Richard, 225, 357

Hip-hop, 154

Hired men (AKA baseball mercenaries), 84, 197, 252-253, 255-257, 260-261, 317, 319, 331, 333

Hoboken Land and Improvement Company, 87, 108

Hoboken, NJ, 9, 11, 26, 30, 45, 50, 53, 55, 60, 66-67, 74, 80, 82-83, 86-88, 90-91, 93-95, 97-99, 101, 103-104, 108, 112-115, 140, 151, 162, 164, 196, 224, 253, 286

Holder, John, 158, 165, 167-168, 193

Homestead Act, 134

Hosack, David, 94

Houston Colt 45s club, 284

Howard, Harry, 130, 216

Hyer, Tom, 132

Immigration, 15, 53-54, 58, 98, 103-104, 106-107, 114, 116, 120-121, 130, 131, 185, 187-188, 190, 200-201, 205, 243, 244, 246, 285, 288, 305, 309

Incorporation of baseball clubs, 318, 352

Inguinal Hernia, 213

Institute for Colored Youth, 261-262

Insurance, 34, 69, 156, 192

Interclub play, 29, 31, 46, 63-65, 113-114, 138, 162-163, 169, 224, 268, 282, 287

Irish Famine, 103-104, 186, 305, 327
Irish Republicanism, 244
Irving, Washington, 60, 126, 139, 141

Jackson, Andrew, 89
Jardin de Tivoli, 85; See also Tivoli, Pleasure Gardens
Johnson, Andrew, 296
Johnson, J. William, 322, 331
Johnston, Frances Upton, 146
Jolly Young Bachelors Club, 77; See also Excelsior club
Jones, Frank, 216, 282, 294-295, 297, 300, 310
Jones, Joseph B., 42, 147-149, 156-160, 171, 181, 194, 213-214, 217, 239, 253, 259, 277, 288, 354
Journalism, 9, 16, 19, 35-38, 40-41, 48, 51-52, 73, 101, 111, 117, 122-123, 130, 132, 134, 137, 161, 177, 182, 185, 202, 207, 217, 247-248, 250, 284-286, 342
Joyce, John P., 325-331
Judaism, 72, 110, 121, 254, 259
Judson, Edward, 126; See also Buntline, Ned
Junior clubs, 158-159, 170, 192, 194, 232, 243, 257, 259, 275, 288, 348

Kelly, Frank, 264
Kennedy, John F., 251
Kent, David, 185
Kershaw, Clayton, 346
Kimberley, Benjamin K., 291-292
King's Highway, 221
King, Charles, 90
Kissam, Samuel, 156, 289
Knickerbocker club, 11, 22, 25, 27-28, 30-31, 34, 36, 42-51, 53-56, 58-59, 62-79, 82-84, 87, 91, 96, 101, 105, 112-114, 118, 123, 141-143, 146-147, 151, 156-157, 161-164, 170, 180, 193, 215, 217, 220,
227-228, 240, 262-263, 265, 271, 289, 299, 318, 324, 334, 337
Knickerbocker, Diedrich, 141
Knickers, 66, 71, 141
Knickers, lack of, 71
Know-Nothings, 104, 126

L'Ouverture club, 264
Labor Union movement, 131, 133-134
Ladd, William F., 123
Land Reform movement, 133-134
Latinos, 274, 354
Launch angle, 74
Lawrence, James, 136-137
Leisure, 81, 85-86, 89, 94, 100, 110, 282
Leonard, Andy, 335, 349
Les Quatres, 86, 118
Liberty Bell, 235, 260
Liberty Poles, 124
Liberty club, 136, 157, 221
Lichtenstein, Seaman, 59, 97
Light at Last, by Thomas Fitzgerald, 248
Lillywhite, John, 210
Lincoln, Abraham, 60, 107, 204, 248, 264, 290, 292, 296, 298, 300, 309, 330
Liquor Laws, 190
Live Oak clubs, 136, 322
Longfellow, Henry Wadsworth, 139
Lotteries, 327-328
Lovett, James D'Wolfe, 271-273
Lowell club, 273-275, 277, 316
Lowell, John, 227, 273-274
Loyalism, 20
Lyon, Mary, 277

Macready, William, 125-126
Maddux, Greg, 161
Madison Square, 51, 82
Magnolia clubs, 53-54, 59, 71, 136, 189
Maifest, 104, 109

Malone, Fergy, 239, 311

Marketing, 22, 31-32, 39-40, 44, 46, 65, 71, 72, 79, 177, 209, 218, 355

Martin, Al "Phoney", 154, 311

Marx, Karl, 131

Massachusetts Game, 118, 234, 267-269, 271-272, 277, 293-294, 307

Massapoag club, 268

Masten, Myron, 168-169

Mathewson, Christy, 46

McBride, Dick, 239, 253, 257

McCarty's Hotel, 96, 105-107; See also Colonnade Hotel, Pavilion

McCarty, Michael, 96, 101, 104-106

McClure, James, 278

McLaughlen, Napoleon Bonaparte, 75

McLaughlin, Hugh, 259

McMahon, William, 175, 229

McVey, Cal, 326, 335-336, 347, 349

Meagher, Thomas Francis, 305

Medicine, 18, 34, 50-51, 62, 93-95, 142-146, 148-149, 156, 158-159, 191, 209, 224, 288, 300-302; See also Physicians, Public health reform

Melville, Herman, 126

Mercantile club, 120, 234

Merchants Exchange, 189,192

Meschutt, David, 296

Methodism, 133, 185, 187

Mets club, 21, 48, 164, 181, 209, 234

Mets-Yankees rivalry, 181, 234

Miasma theory, 93, 144

Michigan Central Railroad, 228

Militias, 49, 58, 60, 68, 109, 123, 127-129, 138-140, 157, 188, 199-200, 202-203, 205, 207, 224, 232, 234, 237, 239, 285-290, 295, 306, 309-310, 337, 355-356; See also Target companies

Millar, Henry, 329

Miller, Elizabeth Fitzhugh, 277

Miller, Gerrit, 274-277

Miller, John, 50, 146

Milliken, David, 136, 153, 292-293

Mills, A.G., 21

Mills, Charlie, 347

Minerva club, 227, 232

Montagne Russe, 95

Montgomery, James, 147

Moore, Cecil B., 233

Moore, DeWitt Clinton, 235, 238, 252, 258, 266

Morgan, Joseph S., 289

Morrisania, 12, 38, 64, 136, 144, 153-155, 160, 212, 222, 241, 274, 292-293, 310, 316, 331

Morrissey, John, 58, 328, 344

Morse, Samuel, 227

Mosby's Rangers, 284, 301

Mose the Fireman, 129; See also *A Glance at New York*

Moses, Robert, 109

Mott, Valentine, 144, 147

Moyamensing, 264

Mount Holyoke College, 277

Mudie, F. W., 239

Muscular Christianity, 148

Mutual club, 112-113, 133, 138, 246, 252, 257, 272, 285-286, 317, 332, 342, 349-352

NYU School of Medicine, 144

National Association of Base Ball Players, 12, 19, 28, 38, 43, 56, 64-65, 79, 107, 153, 157, 182, 214, 235-237, 252, 255, 260, 262-263, 265, 267-268, 272, 275, 278, 283-284, 307, 313-317, 323, 334-335, 349-351, 353

National club, 12, 18, 215-216, 241, 295-297, 310, 317-318, 331, 337-338, 347

National Reform Movement, 133-134

National Trades' Union, 134

National game, idea of, 7, 15, 18-19, 21, 25, 28, 32-33, 36, 39-40, 48, 52, 55, 62, 64-66, 79, 84, 90, 91, 107, 118, 122-123, 125, 127, 130-131, 139, 142, 147, 157, 159, 171-172, 177, 179, 181, 215, 218, 220, 222, 224-226, 272, 281-287, 307, 318, 353-355
Native Americans, 97-99
Nativism, 11, 54, 57, 63, 89, 103-105, 116, 126-128, 130-131, 136, 140, 188-189, 200, 224, 287, 295
Nestor of Pylos, King, 48
New Amsterdam, 68, 121
New Orleans, 11, 32, 68, 78, 85, 108, 136, 202, 221-222, 228, 230-231, 284, 342, 344
New York Clipper, 73, 83-84, 107, 114, 161-162, 171, 177, 210, 221, 234-235, 237-238, 241-242, 252, 259, 268, 271, 300, 322-323, 335
New York harbor, 104, 119, 126, 137
New York Nine club, 30
New York *Sun*, 35
New York *Sunday Mercury*, 38, 144-145, 264, 283, 292
New York Yacht Club, 67, 88, 107
New York and Harlem Railroad, 83, 153-154, 222
New York Cricket Club, 37, 112
New York in Slices, by George G. Foster, 57
New York Stock Exchange, 262, 289
Newhart, Bob, 30
Niagara club, 137-138, 158-159, 185, 192-194, 288-289, 339
Nicaragua, 32, 123, 202-205, 207, 294
Nicholas Nickleby, by Charles Dickens, 193
Northern Liberties, 119
Northern Light, 202
Nostrand, James Van, 192

O'Brien, Matty, 167-168
O'Brien, Pete, 209-211
O'Sullivan, John L., 122
Oak Street, 244-245, 250
Oberlin College, 303-305
Oceana Hose Company #36, 76-77, 262
Olbermann, Keith, 216
Olmsted, Frederick Law, 108-109
Olympic club of Philadelphia, 138, 224-227, 232, 267
Olympic club of Washington, DC, 349
Olympic Games, 138
Olympic club, 138, 224-227, 232, 267, 288, 349
Omoo, by Herman Melville, 126
Onassis, Jacqueline Kennedy, 239
Oneida football club, 276
Opiate drugs, 100,101
Order of United Americans, 126
Organized crime, 325, 327-328
Origin stories, 7, 9, 17, 20-22, 25, 27-29, 31-32, 43-44, 46-47, 49-50, 65, 79, 118, 151, 226, 314, 324
Otterson, Andrew, 288
Ottignon, Charles, 147-148
Owego, NY, 297, 299, 301

Pabor, Charlie, 154
Paine, Thomas, 133
Panic of 1857, 189
Pari-mutuel betting, 130
Park Slope, 155
Parkes, James Creighton, 207-209
Parkes, Mary Creighton, 207
Passed balls, 168, 342
Pastime club of Brooklyn, 259, 289, 291
Patchen, Samuel, 288-289
Pavilion, 100; See also Colonnade Hotel, McCarty's Hotel
Pearce, Dickey, 168, 196-197, 349
Pearsall, A.T., 158, 170, 213, 273, 282,

288, 297-302

Pearsall, Thomas, 206

Pedestrianism, 58, 341

Pelham, John, 301

Penn Tiger club, 227, 233

Penn Township, 233

Pennsylvania Railroad, 90, 96, 107, 223, 234

Penny journalism, 35, 52

Penobscot tribe, 97-100, 154

Peterboro, NY, 276-277

Peverelly, Charles, 64, 73-74, 225-226, 232

Phelps, George, 235

Phenom, 193

Philadelphia Riots of 1844, 224, 261

Phillies club, 84, 233, 257, 334; See also Quaker club

Phillips Academy Andover, 278

Phillips Exeter Academy, 277

Photography, 184, 227

Physical education, 36, 41, 93, 117, 142-148, 159, 274, 277, 354

Physicians, 34, 50, 62, 94, 117, 142-148, 156, 158-159, 191, 209, 288, 297-298, 302

Pidgeon, Frank, 56, 62, 88, 133, 168-169

Piermont, NY, 219

Pike, Lipman, 253-254, 257, 260, 349

Pinckney, Joseph, 63-64, 136, 154, 166, 292-293, 310-311, 315

Pioneer club, 136, 222

Pitch counts, 167, 213

Pittsfield, MA, 234, 269

Pleasure gardens, 85-87, 95-96, 100, 108-110, 112, 127, 224

Pleasure railway, 89, 95

Poe, Edgar Allan, 79, 102, 250

Polhemus, Harry, 69, 185, 259, 302

Policy Racket, 328, 330

Poole, William "Bill the Butcher", 58, 130

Porter's Spirit of the Times, 37, 48-49, 63-64, 73-74

Portland, ME, 135, 269, 271, 273

Porter and cider vaults, 186

Post-game meals, 45, 59, 77, 138, 156, 241; See also Banquets, Chowders

Potomac club, 296

Pratt, Tom, 239, 311

Printers, 38, 51, 137, 227, 234, 242-243, 245-247, 249-250, 301

Prisoners of War, 280, 300-306; See also Salisbury, NC

Pro-slavery northerners, 107, 131, 298-299

Procter and Gamble Company, 320

Professionalism, 15, 17-18, 31, 39, 45-46, 59, 138, 140, 180-181, 253-255, 263, 310, 312-316, 318-319, 324-325, 332-333, 335, 348, 356

Prospect Park, 84, 112, 291

Prostitution, 36, 103, 110, 187-188, 244, 247, 343

Protoball.org, 219, 308, 357

Public health reform, 40, 51, 93-94, 133, 142-147, 156, 159-160, 277

Putnam club, 160, 162, 165, 169-170, 174, 228, 235, 296

Pythian club, 260-262, 264-268

Quaker club, 334; See also Phillies club

Quakers (Society of Friends), 50-51, 145-146, 261, 265

Quevedo, Frank, 291

Racial integration, 28-29, 46, 107, 197-199, 266, 300

Racial segregation, See Color Line

Racism, 41, 53, 58, 71, 107, 109, 128, 131, 140, 198, 200, 263-264, 266, 354

Radcliffe, John, 326

Railroad expansion, 11, 33-34, 67, 83, 90, 120, 172, 202, 220, 222, 321-322, 336-338

Ramirez, Manny, 154

Ray's Pizza, 71-72
Reach, Al, 8, 241, 253-256, 260, 334-335
Reach, Benjamin, 256
Recreation Park, 233
Red Hook, 173
Red House, 83, 85-86, 109-110, 161;
    See also Pleasure gardens
Red Rover Engine Company #34, 58, 130
Red Sox club, 234, 317, 319
Red Stockings club of Cincinnati, 12,
    18, 28, 84, 165, 220, 273, 279, 284,
    297, 312-314, 316-319, 321-326,
    329-337, 339, 341-352
Red Stockings club of Boston, 28,
    273, 317, 334; See also Braves club
Reds club, 317
Reefer, 228
Republican Party, 88, 136, 153-154,
    188, 190, 203, 248, 263, 287, 292,
    310, 331
Restaurants, 77-78, 96, 99, 109, 155
Revolving, 197, 255-257, 316, 333,
    335, 347
Rhoticity line, 234
Richmond, VA, 85, 160, 228, 283,
    300-301
Riots, 11, 58, 104-105, 109, 125-127, 188-
    189, 204, 206, 216, 224, 261, 295
Riter, Sarah Levering, 248
Rivalries, 29, 49, 55, 63, 77, 88, 113-
    114, 125-126, 163, 170, 180-181, 211,
    264, 274, 277, 285, 292, 319, 323
Riverboats, 319-321
Robinson, Jackie, 8, 198, 304
Rochester, NY, 11, 52, 172, 221, 291,
    322, 339
Rogers, Mary, 101-102
Rogers, Mortimer, 270, 275, 293,
    311, 323
Rounders, 19, 21-26, 151
Rua, Rafael De la, 274
Ruth, Babe, 46, 74, 183, 310

Rynders, Isaiah, 54, 126-127, 130, 189,
    200-204

Sabbath breaking, 98
Salisbury, NC, 280, 302-306
Salmagundi, 141
Samuels, Alexander R., 259, 341
San Francisco Examiner, 50-51
Sanchez, Gary, 168
Saratoga, NY, 328
Saturnalia, 100
Savage, John, 79
Savannah, GA, 68, 221-222, 230-231
Schmidt, Mike, 260
Scorecards, 270, 275
Scorsese, Martin, 58
Scott, Sir Walter, 139
Scott, Winfield, 127
Secession of New York City, 71, 123, 204
Sensenderfer, John "Count", 232
Sex, non-connubial, 98, 109-110, 206, 343
Shaurman, Nelson, 287-291
Shearith Israel, 121
Shipbuilding, 55-56, 61-62, 88, 133,
    137, 269
Short Boys, 104; See also Nativism
Shurtleff, Giles, 303-306
Sigel, Franz, 306, 310
Sinatra, Frank, 181
Sinn, William E., 262-263
Slavery, 21, 69, 107, 131, 136, 173,
    201-202, 244, 246, 276, 290, 292,
    298-300, 302
Slote, Alonzo, 76
Slote, Daniel, 76
Slumming, 98-100, 186; See also
    Five Points
Smith College, 277
Smith, Bill, 328-329
Smith, Charlie, 347, 349
Smith, Sydney, 141

Soaking, 44,272

Social exclusion, 12, 34, 51, 60, 76, 79, 198, 251, 262, 289, 295, 355

Socialism, 133

Society for American Baseball Research, 47, 263

Sockalexis, Lou, 98

Socks, 319; See also Stockings

Song of Myself, by Walt Whitman, 248

Sons of Liberty, 58, 124

Sons of Temperance, 204

Spalding, Albert, 20-28, 32, 65-66, 229, 282, 306, 334, 338, 354

Spartan Band, 130

Spectators, 9, 16, 83, 96, 111-114, 117, 137, 154, 160-162, 164, 166, 168, 173-174, 177-180, 258, 277, 306, 318, 323, 345, 348

Spink, Alfred, 212

Sprague, Joe, 287-288, 311, 335

Spring Garden, 119, 152

Sri Lanka, 24, 28

St. George cricket club, 82-83, 107, 113-114, 239

St. Patrick's Day, 188

Stanford, Leland, 220

Stanton, Elizabeth Cady, 276-277

Start, Joe, 9, 196, 347, 349

Steam power, 35, 67, 83, 90, 93, 95, 152, 220, 223, 319-321

Steers, George, 88, 133, 137

Steinbrenner, George, 323

Stengel, Casey, 48

Stereotypes, racial and ethnic, 107, 110, 128

Steuben, Baron von, 91

Stevens, Edwin A. Sr., 67, 87-88, 90

Stevens, Edwin A. Jr., 94

Stevens, John C., 67, 88-91, 112, 123, 132

Stevens, Colonel John, 11, 67, 86-87, 89-91, 93-96, 112-113

Stevens, Richard F., 66-67, 75, 91, 95, 122, 226-227, 234

Stevens, Robert L., 67, 90-91, 234

Stockings, 319, 343-344; See also Socks

Stoops, 92

Strangulated Intestine, 212-213

Streetcar suburbs, 32, 152,234

Strike zone, 25, 29, 167-168, 183, 212

Subterranean, 130-131, 134-135, 250

Suburbanization, 32,42,152-155, 190, 222, 234, 267, 269

Suicide, 100-102

Sutherland, J. B., 228

Suydam, John, 77, 113, 192

Sweasy, Charlie, 335-336, 349

Sybil's Cave, 95, 101, 106

Talcott, Edward, 263

Tammany Hall, 54, 130-131, 189, 200-201, 203-205, 207, 216, 250, 305, 328

Tap dancing, 186

Target companies, 109, 128, 138-140, 202; See also Militias

Taylor, George Rogers, 247

Telegraph, 33, 172, 255, 259, 342,3 48

Temperance movement, 40, 133, 190, 204, 278

Territorial Abolition Act, 298

Texas, 123, 136, 197, 202

Thanksgiving, 60, 81, 284

The Innocents Abroad, by Mark Twain, 76

The Legend of Sleepy Hollow, by Washington Irving, 141

The Murders in the Rue Morgue, by Edgar Allan Poe, 102

The Mystery of Marie Roget, by Edgar Allan Poe, 102

The Song of Hiawatha, by Henry Wadsworth Longfellow, 118, 139

The Spirit of the Times, 37-38, 109,

161, 166-167

The Table, 78

The Virginia Minstrels, 106; See also Blackface entertainment

Theosophy, 28

Thompson, Charlotte, 238

Thomson, Mortimer, 92, 140; See also Doesticks, P.B., Q.K. Philander

Thorn, John, 3-4, 10, 45, 47, 53-54, 357

Thorn, Richard, 59, 168

Three-card Monte, 167

Tiffany, Louis, 83

Tilton, Theodore, 206

Tivoli, 85; See also *Jardin de Tivoli*

Topeka, KS, 206-207

Town ball, 67, 81, 91, 118, 138, 223-228, 232, 237-238, 261, 267-268, 272, 320

Traffic, 162, 167

Tri-Mountain club, 222, 268-269, 271, 273, 275

Trollope, Anthony, 96

Trollope, Frances, 16, 96, 99, 124

Troy, NY, 53, 172, 194, 274, 278, 317, 329, 339, 344, 349

Turnvereins, 104

Turtle soup, 60, 86

Twain, Mark, 76, 220, 324

Tweed, Boss, 216

Twin-screw propeller, 90

Typee, by Herman Melville, 126

Typhoid fever, 92, 144, 334

Union Grounds, 12, 113, 180, 182, 293, 342, 351

Union club of Morrisania, 12, 38, 64, 135-136, 144, 153-154, 160, 212, 214, 226, 241-242, 274, 292-293, 310, 316, 329, 331

Updike, John, 152

Van Cott, Theodore, 296

Van Cott, Thomas G., 63, 65, 167-168, 229

Van Cott, William, 64, 296

Vanderbilt, Amy, 56

Vanderbilt, Cornelius, 202, 204, 223

Vanderbilt, Joe, 56

Vaux, Calvert, 108-109

Vauxhall Gardens, 85; See also Pleasure gardens

Vernou, Charles, 239

Vinaigrettes, 92

Virgin Islands, 114

Voigt, David, 66, 313

Volunteer firefighting, 12, 27, 46, 49, 58, 60, 68, 76-77, 127-130, 138, 140, 147, 157-158, 161, 164, 199-200, 205, 216, 224, 237, 262, 289-290, 295, 309-310, 319, 337, 355-356

Voorhis, Thomas G., 182

Wadsworth, Lewis, 75, 229

Walker, Moses Fleetwood, 304-305

Walker, Welday, 304

Walker, William, 32, 123, 202-204, 294

Walsh, Mike, 54, 71, 123, 127, 130-134, 250

War of 1812, 25, 61, 125, 127, 137, 142, 205

Ward, Samuel, 98

Washington club, 43-44, 50, 59, 62, 76, 136, 141, 224

Washington Market, 57-59, 97, 129, 254

Washington Park, 341

Washington Square, 82, 306

Water Witch Hose Company #8, 289

Waverley, by Sir Walter Scott, 139

Wells Fargo Company, 321

Wenman, James, 68-69, 108

Wenman, Uzziah, 68

Wesley, John, 133

Wesleyan University, 278

Wheat Hill, 173, 180

Wheaton, William, 50-51

Whig Party, 58, 126, 201, 292

Whirligig, 95, 98
White Lot, The, 296
Whiting, John C., 159, 288-289
Whitman, Walt, 123, 128, 131-132, 134, 143, 233, 247-248, 287
Wiedersheim, Theodore, 232
Wilkes' Spirit of the Times, 38, 130, 233, 236, 250, 285-286
Wilkes, George, 34, 38, 73, 130-132, 134, 202, 250, 285
Wilkins, Isaac, 239
Willard, Emma, 277
Williams College, 278
Williams, Charles, 106-107
Williams, Ted, 74, 152
Williamsburg, 56, 61, 173, 180, 237, 246
Willis, Nathaniel Parker, 60, 99-100, 154
Wills, Garry, 216
Wilson's Zouaves, 205, 207; See also 6th New York
Wilson, William, 132, 202-207
Winona club, 233, 235, 239
Wolfe, Thomas, 159
Wood, Benjamin, 328
Wood, Fernando, 71, 123, 189, 201-204, 328
Woodhull, Caleb, 126-127
Woodhull, William, 76
Woodward, John, 289
World Trade Center, 57
World War II, 286
Wright, Frank, 277
Wright, George, 8, 122, 154, 297, 312, 323-324, 333-337, 349
Wright, Harry, 28, 75, 83-84, 113, 122, 128, 165, 168, 229, 233, 240, 270, 278, 313, 317, 323-326, 331-336, 346, 349
Wright, Sam, 83, 333
Wyckoff, Van Brunt, 156, 215

Yale University, 274, 278, 357
Yellow fever, 91-92, 94, 144

Yorkville, 82-83, 152, 222
Youghal, Ireland, 132
Young America movement, 122-123, 135-136
Young Men's Christian Association, 148

Zettlein, George, 311, 349

THOMAS W. GILBERT is the author of many baseball books, including *Baseball and the Color Line, Roberto Clemente,* and *Playing First.* From his Greenpoint, Brooklyn stoop he can throw a baseball to the former site of the Manor House tavern, where members of the Eckford Baseball Club enjoyed a post-game drink or two in the 1850s.

TYPESET IN MILLER, MYRIAD, AND SCOTCH TYPES

DESIGN AND TYPOGRAPHY BY

JERRY KELLY